For J. D. Salinger

Baby, It's Cold Inside

BY

S. J. PERELMAN

THE LYONS PRESS

Contents

Contents

Baby, It's Cold Inside

Anna Trivia Pluralized

God only knows how they achieved it, but there it was, set down in the middle of modern-day Dublin—a replica of lower Weybosset Street in Providence, Rhode Island, in the year 1913. The same dingy red-brick façades blackened by rain, the trolleys clanging and shrieking protest as they rounded the intersections, even a couple of those Dickensian factory hands gobbling their noontime pork pies in the doorways. It was a restoration so scrupulous as to make Williamsburg and Old Sturbridge Village shoddy by comparison, and the illusion such that I automatically sought for the favorite memory of my boyhood, the window display of a dry-cleaning establishment named Lewando's, where a stuffed cat, clad in an apron, was pinning up six baby chicks she had just laundered in a washtub. But the downpour was furious by now, the plane journey from London had taken longer than I'd foreseen, and I needed a wash and a brushup before starting my weekend sojourn. The outer door of D'Arcy's Hotel, unfortunately, ambuscaded a precipitous step and a half downward, so that I pitched across the small lobby and fetched up with a crash against the reception desk, nearly concussing the clerk.

"Alannah, don't give it a thought," he said, dismissing my apology. "They fly in here all hours of the day and night." He was the Hibernian stereotype of that vanished era—Barry Fitzgerald to the life. "You'll be the American gentleman who phoned from the airport?"

"Yes, the Shelbourne and the Gresham said they were full up."

"It's the bloodstock sales," he explained. "The county folk replenishing their stables—the town's bursting at the seams. Here's your key and a message from Mr. Donahoe. You're to join him at the Red Bank bar in D'Olier Street on the double."

Unpacking my bag in a bedroom redolent of hair oil and generations of commercial travelers, it occurred to me to wonder how my friend knew I was staying here before I did, but in a small place like Dublin, clearly, there were no secrets for anyone so ubiquitous. Columnist, drama critic, and book reviewer, Donahoe was the tireless encyclopedist of the Celtic Revival, brimming with anecdotes of O'Casey, the Yeatses, Gogarty, and the notables of the Abbey. All these, he had revealed on a previous visit, were warp and woof of a volume of reminiscences he had been compiling for years, and when, an hour later, our reunion in the Red Bank had been duly solemnized with malt, I asked if it was progressing well.

He beamed at me over the empurpled squash that served him for a nose. "Famously, my boy," he said. "The printer's devil was just around to the office with the galleys." I sensed that not a word was on paper. "Ah, 'twill be the grand memoir of our times, in my humble opinion, and there's one portion in particular—" He checked himself, looked around, and lowered his voice. "Give us your oath, now," he said. "You're not writing a book about Joyce, are you?"

"Honor bright," I said. "Why?"

"Because I've unearthed a simply tremendous story about him that's never been told," he said. "It's the crowning chapter of my work—the keynote, no less—and I'm pauperized if you blab a word of it."

Donahoe's informant, it emerged after a preliminary flourish, was a certain Mulcahy, who regularly took his evening glass at a pub in Chapelizod. He had in due course formed a nodding acquaintance with another student of Guinness there, an altogether prosaic old codger in moleskins he judged to be a corporation workman. One day the latter failed to materialize, and when he turned up the following evening, garbed in decent black, Mulcahy inquired solicitously whether anything was amiss.

"Nosey Flynn," the other imparted glumly. "We laid the poor devil to rest yesterday, God save his soul."

"Nosey Flynn?" asked Mulcahy, recognizing a recurrent character in *Ulysses*. "Was he a chum of yours?"

All of that crowd were his butties, the old man replied—Bantam Lyons, Pisser Burke, Corny Kelleher, and Joe Hynes.

Dazzled by the rich literary ore he had stumbled on, Mulcahy began wielding his pick. "Did you ever know old John Joyce, by any chance?" he asked, with a pretense of casualness.

"Aye, indeed." An affectionate sigh. "A hell of a fella with a jar or a stave. Talk your blessed arm off."

"Had a son named Stanislaus, didn't he?"

"Yes, and a studious nipper he was."

Mulcahy pressed on. "And wasn't there a younger lad, now? The one who went to the Jesuit college at Clongowes?"

The man reflected deeply. "Faith, you're dead right," he said at last. "A ne'er-do-well called Jim. He ran that Volta Theatre in Mary Street for a bit. I often wondered what became of him."

A look of positive ecstasy overspread Donahoe's face as he delivered the payoff. "That's the tribute we pay our laureates in this benighted country!" He hooted, and then paused abruptly. "Remember, you promised not to breathe a syllable—"

"*Verbum sap*," I assured him. "My lips are sealed."

The obligation to keep them that way was tested in short order. Toward nightfall I found myself at the *vernissage*, off Grafton Street, of a group of Dublin's avant-garde painters. The gallery boiled with leaders of the social and artistic set, whose names, if household words in Ireland, regrettably meant less than nothing to me. Attaching myself to a raven-haired amazon in jodhpurs with a dimple bewitching enough to coax one into treason, I managed to woo her interest by glib reference to exploits in the hunting field with John Huston. Our colloquy, which might well have flamed into ungovernable passion, was short-lived. A bearded party flaunting a watered-silk waistcoat and a pompadour like a Rambouillet sheep's flung himself between us and shouldered me into a corner. "I'm Shameless McGonigle, the poet," he said. "We shared the podium at Western Reserve University in your country. How is dear Dr. Heublein?"

My protestation that the only Heublein I knew of was a distiller fell on deaf ears.

"A lovely person, and how he worships *you*. Look here," he said in an undertone, "I understand you're combing the town for fresh material on Joyce. I've a simon-pure nugget I was expanding into book form, but, as a mutual pal of Heublein's, I wouldn't be unreasonable. What figure did you have in mind?"

"Only what might appeal to pornographers," I said. "I'm here to work up an album of saucy French photos entitled *Gingersnaps*. The Joyce rumor is hogwash."

He winked conspiratorially. "Oho, Mr. Slyboots," he said. "Ach, I don't blame you for being careful—Dublin's a whispering gallery. But I'll just convey the flavor so you can decide. I was nursing my pint one day in a shebeen in Chapelizod . . ."

Except for the inevitable *broderie irlandaise*, of course, it was the very yarn Donahoe had spun, and, once embarked, McGonigle catapulted to the end, binding me by Masonic vows not to divulge it to chick or child.

When I returned to the hotel to change for dinner, I stopped by at the desk to procure some extra hangers. The clerk observed me scanning the names of several new arrivals in the guestbook—compatriots of mine, he pointed out helpfully, from Iowa and Arkansas. Doubtless shopping for pedigreed horseflesh, I hazarded.

"Pedagogued would be closer to it," he said. "The scholars and savants come through here in droves. Professor Krumholz there mentioned he was an authority on the Irish novel. He's over to pick up any trifles fornenst one of our major writers."

"And do you have any?"

"I have that," he said cunningly. "But I'm not shelling it out to every Tom, Dick, and Harry. Now, if a well-to-do gentleman like yourself—"

"Never mind the hangers," I interrupted, wheeling toward the stairs. "I can use the hooks in the shower curtain." Midway through my ablutions, however, an elderly parlormaid in a headband patterned after Marie of Rumania's bustled in with an armful of rusty wire. So coquettish was her smile that I instinctively drew my bathrobe tighter around me.

"Good evening, Your Worship," she purred. "Was it you pumping the lad in the reception about the pagan who wrote that filthy book?"

I told her she was confusing me with Professor Krumholz, or possibly Dr. Heublein.

Her eye roved to my portable typewriter. "No, you're the one, Lord love you, and praise the Heavenly Father we met, for our bloody fortune's made if you write it down just as I tell it. Oh, wait till my old bucko comes home tonight, spent from digging up half of Ballsbridge, and hears the glorious news! We'll be riding around in a coach, eating off of damask—"

"Madam," I said. "I have made it a principle heretofore never to brutalize a woman older than myself. You force me into a painful position, but in a moment, when this door closes on your foot, you will be in a much worse one." I closed the door on her foot. "Go peddle your vapors elsewhere."

In the ensuing twenty-four hours I balked three further attempts to relate the story—one by a cabby en route to a friend's in

Glasnevin, another by a haberdasher dangling it to bait the purchase of a poplin scarf, and last by a chef at Jury's, who, in his haste to season my meal with local color, carbonized the steak to charcoal. With each repetition, though, I was assailed by increasing doubts. If all those who claimed to have witnessed the incident were to be credited, they would overflow the Seventy-first Regiment Armory, let alone a neighborhood snug. The more puzzling question was the objective. There was, obviously, a prodigious traffic in Joycean apocrypha; I knew the pushers, so to speak, but who were the users? The answer to the riddle revealed itself unexpectedly on the eve of my departure.

I was catching a nap at D'Arcy's before dinner, sunk in a dream wherein my raven-haired goddess of the art show and I were marooned on the Great Barrier Reef. Our plight was hopeless; although breadfruit was plentiful and we had just disinterred a chestful of doubloons, we were far off the steamer lanes and I faced the prospect of becoming her squaw man if I yielded to the importunate Fiona. Suddenly the murmur of voices—rising, it almost seemed, from within the room itself—galvanized me awake. My first surmise, that it issued from the corridor or the adjoining chamber, collapsed on investigation. Then, as the sound continued unabated, I tracked it to the half-open door of the armoire. Sure enough, the backing was a mere sheet of plywood sealing a former doorway, and, as I applied my ear to it, I caught unmistakable midwestern accents.

"Oh, Vernon, isn't it scrumptious?" some woman was exulting. "Those faculty wives will be livid! I shouldn't wonder if you're made head of the department when your book comes out."

"Yes, it's a very important find, indubitably"—a smug voice endeavoring to contain its owner's jubilation. I envisioned a thin little radish swollen with self-importance, a tyrant in the classroom. "It throws Joyce's youth into a wholly new perspective, crystallizing in a phrase, as it does, the denigration of his coevals." I longed for a sword cane to ram through the plywood and spit him like a shish kebab. "You realize, Chlorine, that my discovery of this material threatens to render Harry Levin and Herbert Gorman obsolete. It may, in fact, force Richard Ellmann to hand back his National Book Award."

She cooed dutifully, teacups rattled, and after a pause I detected a note of uncertainty in her voice. "The hundred dollars you gave that man in the saloon," she said. "How can you be sure he won't sell this to some other biographer?"

"No fear of that, baby." Her husband sniggered fatly. "I'll get him to sign a formal release before we leave. Besides, we can always charge it off to the foundation as research, along with those tweeds you bought."

I boarded an Aer Lingus flight to Shannon that night, transferring to the onward jet service to New York. Seated next to me was a sprightly oldster in a brand-new suit set off by an opulent watch chain. In no time his tongue was wagging; he was off to visit his niece in Providence, of all places, and insisted on standing me a drink to celebrate some recent and lucrative transaction. "A wonderful bit of property, son," he confided gleefully. "I keep selling it over and over, and I'm not done yet. The silly bosthoons snap it up like nougat."

"Well, watch yourself in Providence, Mister," I said. "They're a sharp lot there. They'll take you to the cleaners—a place called Lewando's, as I recall."

"A-ah, trust me to handle 'em," he said. "All I need is a small pub somewhere and a handful of Ph.D.s."

"You don't say," I said. "Tell me, who takes care of the store in Chapelizod while you're gone?"

He gave me a long, penetrating look. "Bedad," he said, "I'm thinking you're a pretty sharp lot yourself."

"No," I said. "Only a mark that got away."

Heads I Trim, Frails You Lose

A French engineer has designed an automatic machine to cut every customer's hair according to his own recorded pattern. Patent 3,241,562 granted this week to Jean Gronier of Versailles shows a man seated in an armchair, with clippers and combs held by overhead apparatus. . . . A trimming comb, the patent explains, makes a forward raking movement through the hair; but in the case of hair that is "cut short in a stubble and brushed straight up from the forehead" the comb is of no use and is held out of the way. The client is expected to keep "feelers" in contact with his scalp and to refrain from substantial movements of his head.—The Times

SCENE: *The kitchen of a small dwelling in southwestern France. As the curtain rises, Aristide Perdant, the proprietor of the local bicycle shop, is disclosed at center bowed under an Auto-Coiffeur, a sinister webwork of feelers, clippers, combs, and scissors that brings to mind one of Max Ernst's collages. While the mechanism partially obscures Aristide's face, enough is visible below to explain whence derives the family name of Perdant, or "loser"; this is a man clearly predestined for insolvency and a pair of antlers. At the moment, a photograph of Claudia Cardinale, in Paris-Match, silhouetted against the sunset engages him so completely that he is*

18

insensible to the phone ringing at his elbow. Disentangling himself finally with an effort, he answers.

ARISTIDE: Hello? . . . Who? . . . Speak up—why are you whispering? . . . No, this isn't Mme. Perdant, it's her husband . . . Oh, M. Trompemari, the butcher—yes, yes, of course. Well, give me the message and I'll tell her when she returns. . . . You're saving an order of veal chops, the kind she dotes on. Yes, I will. (*Hangs up with a snort*) What an ass he is, this *charcutier!* Are his veal chops so momentous, then, as to merit a telephone call? One would think he had an ulterior motive, perish the thought. As all the world knows, there is no woman in all Périgord more devoted to her mate than my little Olympe. Her divine form is easily superior to this Claudia Cardinale's, succulent albeit the latter is. (*He resumes his inspection of the, as it were, Roman beauties. The phone rings again.*) Botheration—this place is becoming as frenzied as the Bourse. . . . Hello? . . . Our what? . . . Our *nettoyeur de voisinage* (neighborhood dry cleaner)? . . . Yes, M. Libidineux? . . . But that's preposterous, my dear fellow. How could Madame have asked you to clean a shag rug we do not own? Palpably your records are *sens dessus dessous* (topsy-turvy). . . . No, it's quite all right. (*Disconnects*) Curious person, that—I dislike his oily tongue. And also his business methods, come to think of it. Why does he always pick up and deliver after I've gone to work? A suspicion is beginning to gnaw at me that this M. Libidineux is not altogether sincere. However, let us return to our muttons. (*As applied to Miss Cardinale, the term is a desecration, but Perdant is too benighted to know which end is up. As he reopens the journal, the phone again peals.*) Nom de Dieu, the clamor here is insupportable. . . . Hello? . . . Hello! . . . Who is that on the line? . . . Don't pretend, whoever you are—I can hear you breathing. (*Enraged*) So you won't talk? Very well, then, go soak your head! (*Slams up receiver*)

A VOICE: And keep your own still, idiot. How do you expect these feelers to function if you thresh around like a trout?

ARISTIDE (*dumfounded*): Who's that?

VOICE: Your Auto-Coiffeur, of course. Who'd you think it was— the Angel Gabriel?

ARISTIDE: B-but I don't understand. Nobody ever told me there was a vocal attachment on the machine.

AUTO-COIFFEUR: Look, Charlie, all this gizmo up here does the work of a human being, *n'est-ce pas?* And if they omitted the power of speech, particularly a barber's, the customer'd hardly know he was getting a haircut, would he?

ARISTIDE: Say, that figures. My, but science is a wonderful thing.

AUTO-COIFFEUR: Nicely put—you have quite a gift of gab your-self. All right, let's proceed with the trim. By the way, getting a trifle thin on top, aren't you?

ARISTIDE: If you look real close, there's some fuzz growing back. Olympe massages it every week with a preparation we get from the apothecary.

AUTO-COIFFEUR: Who, the Corsican? Good-looking fellow with dimples?

ARISTIDE: I never noticed any dimp— Why do you ask?

AUTO-COIFFEUR: Oh, nothing—nothing at all. Nice weather we're having.

ARISTIDE: Yes, but the farmers could use some rain.

AUTO-COIFFEUR: Bother the farmers. What about us mechanical barbers? I don't see anyone losing any sleep over *our* problems.

ARISTIDE (*nodding*): Nor us bicycle people's. Believe you me, I've got my own share of troubles.

AUTO-COIFFEUR: Oh, come on, now. You've a nice business, a shapely little wife who waits on you hand and foot. What more could a man want in his declining years?

ARISTIDE (*bristling*): I beg your pardon. I happen to be only forty-four.

20

AUTO-COIFFEUR: *Sans blague?* I would have put you at twice that age. I mean to say, you have a certain mellowness—a spongy quality—

ARISTIDE: Well, I suppose my outlook *is* more mature than most. Nevertheless, there's but twelve years' difference between me and Olympe.

AUTO-COIFFEUR: Ah, a May-and-December union. Those can be idyllic, without doubt, though naturally one hears of exceptions, like that affair in Singerie-sur-Marne.

ARISTIDE: What happened there?

AUTO-COIFFEUR: You missed the account in the *Éclaireur du Sud?* An elderly espoused—by a bizarre coincidence, a motorcycle dealer—came home one rainy afternoon on an impulse. Surprising the local butcher hidden in a closet, he pierced the jackanapes through the pancreas with his wife's *épingle à chapeau* (hatpin) and secured his instant demise.

ARISTIDE: Surely the jury took an enlightened view?

AUTO-COIFFEUR: *Ça va sans dire.* Unfortunately, two minutes after acquittal the defendant dropped dead of hypertension in the dock. . . . Good grief, man, control that twitch of yours, I pray you. You seem horribly upset.

ARISTIDE: No, no, it's—er—the hair sifting down my neck. (*Footsteps off*) Listen, you better clam up—here comes Olympe. It wouldn't be seemly if she caught me talking to a machine.

AUTO-COIFFEUR: Okey-doke, but bear in mind—don't let her bamboozle you.

(*Olympe enters, a market basket over her arm. She is a toothsome package reminiscent of Renée Adorée in* The Big Parade, *with a blouse that persists in slipping off one shoulder. Her lips are perhaps a trifle too sensual for real beauty.*)

OLYMPE (*with a start*): Oh! You're back from the shop already?

ARISTIDE: The pipes burst in the fish market next door, so I decided to have a haircut meanwhile. Why, am I in your way?

OLYMPE: Don't be absurd! It's only that I like to know where you are at all times. I worry about you, *chéri.*

ARISTIDE: And I likewise. Where have you been the last hour, for example? Out shopping?

OLYMPE: Yes, I went to the baker for *croissants,* and the grocer's, and I bought the loveliest material for curtains—

ARISTIDE: A pity you didn't stop at the butcher's. It would have saved his phoning you just now with some hogwash (*lavure d'écuelles*) about veal chops.

OLYMPE (*angrily*): Look you, pantaloon—do you suggest there are Chinese doings (*chinoiseries*) between me and Télémaque?

ARISTIDE: Télémaque, is it? Since when do you call him by his first name?

OLYMPE: Since we were schoolmates, if you must know. He used to twist my pigtails.

ARISTIDE: And the dry cleaner, and the sneak who refused his identity? Were they also schoolmates?

OLYMPE: Hie yourself to an asylum, my old. That robot has affected your brain.

ARISTIDE: On the contrary, it's brought me to my senses! At last I comprehend everything—your feigned solicitude, the delicacies you force on me—laden, I daresay, with arsenic—

OLYMPE: You monster! So that's what you really think of my cooking?

ARISTIDE: A laughingstock throughout the whole of Périgord, am I? Ah, but the worm is about to turn, Madame! (*Thrusting away the Auto-Coiffeur, he whips a pistol from the drawer.*) I'll avenge my honor, never fear!

AUTO-COIFFEUR: Attaboy—give 'em hell!

(*As Olympe, transfixed, gapes at the machine and Aristide yanks open the door, a dignified individual in a bowler and cutaway, clasping a briefcase, appears on the threshold.*)

Frails You Lose

MAN: Good day, all. Is this the residence of Aristide Perdant, the bicycle dealer?

ARISTIDE: It is. What do you want?

MAN: A brief colloquy on a matter of the highest importance. That is Mme. Perdant, I take it. (*Smacks his lips*) Delectable.

ARISTIDE: Who asked for your opinion?

MAN: I offer it gratuitously. One needn't be a connoisseur of china to appreciate a striking dish. No wonder you walk around with a weapon.

ARISTIDE: Monsieur, my patience is ebbing fast. State your business.

MAN: Ah, forgive me. (*Extends card*) I am Hippolyte LaFleur, managing director of the Fabrique Générale des Associés de la Quincaillerie, S.A., at Lyon. Did you by any chance purchase one of our appliances within the past eight months—a secondhand model J-188 home barber?

OLYMPE: Behold it there, showing its fangs. (*Tearfully*) Oh, M. LaFleur, he's never been the same since it came into the house!

LAFLEUR (*resisting an impulse to pat her consolingly*): Poor little thing. . . . Anyhow, thank heaven we've succeeded in tracking it down at last. *Mes amis,* you see before you a stupefying instance of vengeance gone mad.

ARISTIDE: I confess to be at sixes and sevens. Are you moved to explain?

LAFLEUR: Attend. A worker in our employ, deranged by what he conceived to be unjust treatment, implanted in this unit an odious device—a tape recorder casting foul aspersions and calumnies on the user's spouse. The resultant wave of murder, divorce, and domestic tension has well-nigh ruined us. . . . Excuse me, Mme. Perdant, but your blouse is slipping off your shoulder.

ARISTIDE: She'll fix it. You stick with your story.

LAFLEUR: I wasn't sure she could reach. In any case, such was the havoc wrought by the instrument that we posted a goodly reward for its return, and you, M. Perdant, fulfill the conditions. (*Opening briefcase*) Here is our check for a hundred thousand new francs, and now my two burly assistants, who have just entered behind me, will insure that it afflicts society no more. (*His aides unplug the Auto-Coiffeur, stifling its imprecations, and carry it off.*)

ARISTIDE: Think of it, honey! A hundred thousand new francs—it's fabulous!

OLYMPE: A miracle. If only we could somehow recompense the architect of our good fortune. Perhaps, ascetic though he seems, we might persuade him to sup with us.

LAFLEUR: I'd be enraptured. You're sure you have enough in the larder?

OLYMPE: Well, not quite, but Aristide can run down to the grocer's. Take my basket, dear.

LAFLEUR: Yes, and walk—don't run. It's bad for the ticker.

ARISTIDE: O.K. I'll be back in a jiffy, folks.

LAFLEUR: No hurry. (*Aristide exits.*) You know, Madame, as an engineer I've always been struck by the anatomical resemblance of Frenchwomen to Italians. Has anybody ever mistaken you for, let us say, Claudia Cardinale?

CURTAIN

The Rape of the Drape

Riven by ambulance sirens, quaking to the apocalyptic thunder of its subway, Greenwich Avenue baked and bubbled in midsummer delirium as I slogged westward on it yesterday afternoon. Past rookeries of the deviant I went, scorning what treasures of papier-mâché, past yarn shops wan with bankruptcy and vintners that wooed the palate with cut-rate muscatel, and came at last to my destination—the Bon Ton Shoe Repair, Hat Blocking Our Specialty, Crucifixion Our Portion. An expression of the most acute anguish lit up Mr. Benuzzi's troglodyte face as I requested the straw I had left to be cleaned five months before. "I pay my landlord *blood* money for this space!" Benuzzi wailed. "What you think I'm running here—a vacation spot for old hats?" He brushed aside my defense that I had been cast away on Juan Fernández and, burrowing among his shelves, produced first a rough coconut beehive too freakish for even a vaudeville agent and then a varnished boater of the type worn by eighteenth-century press gangs. When my own panama came to light, it had inexplicably become a full size larger. It showed a tendency, I observed with dismay, to slip down over my ears.

"Somebody must of shrunk your head while you were in Africa," Benuzzi remarked. "The pygmies are always doing that, what I hear."

"Africa?" I said, startled. "How'd you know I was there?"

"From this," he said, extending a strip of faded newsprint. "It was folded around inside the sweatband." The man was right; it was an extract from the Mombasa *Times* of January 1954, with which I had evidently taken up the slack in the crown before boarding a dhow to Zanzibar. I paid Benuzzi a fee sufficient to rent a floor at the Manhattan Storage & Warehouse, crushed the hat into some semblance of panache, and retired to a nearby snug to inspect the cutting more closely. Headlined "67 Years' Wear from Jacket," it concerned a piece of apparel quite as extraordinary as my panama:

> From New Year 1887 to New Year 1954 [it read], a Norfolk jacket has been worn constantly and is still going strong. Its knickerbocker and waistcoat companions are also in good order, but are used only occasionally. The suit was new when 21-year-old Cyril Watson, on his appointment as land agent for the Fitzgeralds at Limerick, received it as a present from his parents, Canon and Mrs. Shepley Watson of Bootle Rectory, South Cumberland. His mother wove the material on her spinning wheel from the wool of Herdwicks, hardy mountain sheep that roam Lakeland's fells, and produced a fine heather mixture in herringbone pattern. Returning to his native Cumberland in 1894, when made land agent for Mr. Harris of Brackenburgh Tower, Penrith, young Watson went to a house at Greysouthen, near Cockermouth. Still using the Norfolk jacket almost daily, he rose to be a sporting and public figure, becoming chairman of Cockermouth magistrates and chairman of Cockermouth rural council. Now aged 88, Mr. Cyril Watson continues to live at Greysouthen, where he has been followed on the rural council by his son Mr. George Watson, who also succeeds his father as wearer of the Norfolk jacket—summer and winter.

of the Drape

What earthly significance, I wondered, studying it in perplexity, had this fragment had for me to warrant its preservation? It must have stirred some recollection, some now forgotten incident. And then, in a slow dissolve, it emerged. Of course—my own Norfolk, that grand old garment I had acquired way back in 1932, still impregnable to moth, mildew, and age, hanging in my closet at this moment awaiting our first autumn ramble together. What service it had given me over a lifetime—and also what gray hairs, I thought, remembering the predicament it got me into in southern California. I signaled the barman for a refill and began reconstructing the details.

At the time I bought the jacket, in a Madison Avenue clothier's that dealt in such survivals, my aged salesman had difficulty in containing his emotion. "The last of the Mohicans," he said, baptizing its sleeve with a tear. "This and Bernard Shaw's—they're the only ones left. Well, wear it in good health," he encouraged, with the direct implication that I was courting a visit from the Grim Reaper. I didn't care; I loved every feature of the coat—its four-button front, the great patch pockets, commodious enough for a copy of *The Compleat Angler* (not to mention some bread and cheese), the box pleats in whose recesses I could stow anything from a snuffbox to a flask of poteen, and the bellows back that allowed full play to my powerful shoulders. As for the brown herringbone material, it had never been closer to Lakeland's fells than Nashua, New Hampshire, but it gave me a *frisson* to stroke it. That rich, oily tweed, evocative of peat fires, haggis, and gamekeepers dallying with titled ladies—you know what I mean, man?

It obviously produced the same effect on Waldo Hogan three years later in Hollywood when, emerging from lunch at Al Levy's Tavern, I ran into him. He stood there frozen in the middle of Vine Street, his pale Malemute eyes pinned on my jacket and his nostrils dilated. Like myself, he was a transplant—a journalist I'd

known around Jack & Charlie's in New York, and a man possessed
of a burning yearning to walk with the mighty. Hogan's knowledge
of the *Social Register* was Koranic—he could tell at a glance
whether Joe Blow had prepped at Choate or St. Paul's, he was able
to recite Laddie Sanford's every polo score and the name of every
skipper in the Bermuda Race since its inception, and he knew all
the arcana of bobsledding, cotillions, and similar *goyim nachis*. Not
only an expert on modes and manners was he but an oracle on
men's fashions, and my jacket was a challenge to his authority. He
wasted no time on salutations. "Where'd you get that Norfolk?"
he asked fiercely, and, when I told him, snorted in disbelief. "Impossible. Brooks hasn't carried that model in years."

"It'll cost you five bucks to look at the label," I said, stung to
equal childishness.

"You sewed it in yourself."

"Oh, come on," I said. "Enough of this hair pulling. What's
Mrs. Harrison Williams up to these days?"

He responded in some detail, but it was plain his attention was
still riveted on my jacket. "Look," he said finally. "There's a
Guinea tailor down on Figueroa, a real whiz from the old country,
I'd like to have copy that thing. How's to borrow it for a week or
so?"

Your average person would have recoiled at such brass, but it so
happened that the fellow's presumption amused me. I mean, it was
like asking for the crown of Edward the Confessor to duplicate. So,
good-natured fool that I was, I assented, and the next day his Filipino boy came around to pick it up from my Filipino boy. (Everybody had a Filipino boy in those days, along with a peripatetic
masseuse and a Capehart that chewed up a dozen records in sequence and spat them through a little door.)

Well, not a word did I hear out of him till six weeks later when I
stopped in for a New Year's drink with some people in Beverly.
Despite the poinsettias in bloom and a temperature like the inte-

rior of a steam laundry, the house bulged with British character actors in bulky tweeds and ascots, singing rounds and swilling Tom-and-Jerries. And there in the middle was Ward McAllister redivivus, Waldo Hogan himself, flaunting his version of my Norfolk. It was tailored in some sort of thick blanket material woven of caterpillars—light blue with a green plaid overlay—and, what with all the pleats and gussets, the effect was dizzying. He was busy snowing a Wampas baby star as I approached—one of those cracker-bottomed little predators with a tight platinum bob. "I usually get my lounge suits from Kilgour & French, in London," he was saying. "For breeches, of course, there's nobody like Tautz, in Stratton Street. Now, shooting clothes like these—" He broke off at my greeting and gave me a restrained nod. "Oh, hello there. Long time no see."

"Donkey's years," I said, falling in with the idiom. "Listen, sport, when are you returning that—ahem—pattern I loaned you?"

"What! Hasn't Lascivio brought it back?" he drawled. "I told the creature weeks ago. I'll see you get it first thing in the morning."

"Please do," I said. "I have to wear it to a balloon ascension in Boyle Heights Sunday. All the right people will be there, you know."

Needless to say, his houseboy didn't show, that day or any other, and I became increasingly restive. For all I knew, Hogan was subcontracting the Norfolk all over the place, renting it out to Pasadena's *jeunesse dorée* and spawning a host of tawdry imitations like his own. I called him at Fox, where he was writing a western for Sol Wurtzel, but he was always in conference, at the barbershop, or en route to Musso-Frank's for lunch. After a week of his consistently ignoring my messages, I ultimately tracked him down, and even then he rebuked me for interrupting a call from T. Suffern Tailer. The note of evasiveness in his voice made it imperative to talk cold turkey.

"Quit stalling, Hogan," I said roughly. "Pony up that jacket toot sweet or, by the eternal, I'll have a bench warrant out for you in twenty-four hours." I wasn't sure what the phrase meant, but it had the snap and crackle of the dialogue Cagney was using at the moment, and, to my relief, it worked. He broke down and confessed that among some castoffs he had donated to his Filipino, the latter had unwittingly included my Norfolk. As if to compound the indignity, though, the boy had gone and sold it to a thrift shop in Glendale, the name of which he couldn't remember. I was speechless.

"I feel as bad as you do, believe me," Hogan babbled, "but there's still one ray of hope. Lascivio says he could spot the store if you drove him out there. I'll gladly pay for the gas."

The seismograph at Fordham must have recorded my response, but once I subsided I realized that time was of the essence. Springing into my Auburn, I collected the youth and drove down Los Feliz Boulevard, annihilating chickens left and right. Far from exhibiting any guilt for his blunder, Lascivio chattered away like a jackdaw; here was a street where a voluptuous waitress dwelt, there a complaisant nurse. Our quest eventually led us to a stall run by an evil-eyed crone out of Toulouse-Lautrec, all *maquillage* and amber beads. She had reason to recall the jacket, she said, chuckling, for only yesterday a scout from Western Costume had paid her a nice little profit for it. Their period clothes, and particularly a rarity like my Norfolk, fetched handsome rentals from the studios. She offered me their address if I wanted to press the search. I didn't need it. I knew it was a one-way street.

At ten the following morning I sat in the office of a self-important young squirt on South Canon Drive recounting my plight. Mr. Grubchick, a recent graduate from law school, was the nephew of my agent, recommended by him as a judicial mind second only to Cardozo. He toyed portentously with the key of his legal fraternity as I concluded, his brow furrowed into wide-wale corduroy. "This is a most unusual case, in my experience," he pronounced. "Did you obtain an instrument from said Hogan enjoining him to restore said garment under pain of express penalties?"

"For God's sake, Counselor," I protested. "I'd known the man for years—"

"In barrooms," he said. "Well, my friend, we have two alternatives—either to demand reimbursement in cash or to take him into Small Claims Court, where, I must warn you, you run the risk of being judged a crackpot."

"I *am* a crackpot!" I burst out. "I don't want cash—I want my Norfolk back!"

"Fat chance," he said coldly. "The only time you'll ever see it again will be on the screen, with somebody like C. Aubrey Smith inside it."

I stared at him. "That's it—that's it!" I exclaimed, borne to my feet in a wave of jubilation. "Grubchick, you've hit on the solution. Your uncle was right!"

By the time his jaw had sagged back into place I was across the city in my office at Paramount, performing deep surgery on the script I was involved with. Out of the scene at Shepheard's Hotel in Cairo went the gossipy spinster with a heart of gold, and in her stead appeared a renowned Egyptologist, a bespectacled English don clad in a quaint, outmoded style of jacket. It took a week's supplication to convince my producer that I could handle the part, to say nothing of a special dispensation from the Screen Actors' Guild, but the wardrobe problem was nonexistent—incredibly, Western Costume just happened to have the very outfit. The five speeches required of me were shot eleven times, consuming a whole day and most of the director's restraint; he succumbed to such outbursts throughout that ice had to be applied to his head to avert a syncope. Contrariwise, I was as fresh as a daisy when we broke. I left the set whistling like a meadow lark, and forty minutes later, in full makeup, waved farewell to Los Angeles from the eastbound Chief. Next time you're near a file of the *Hollywood Reporter* for 1935, look up the review of *Beauty from Djibouti*—the subhead marked *Amateur's Nightmare.* Well, sticks and stones may break my bones, but names, et cetera. I've still got my Norfolk.

Dear Sir or Madam

In the particular version of the story I heard—and I wager there must be fifty—the locale was Cairo and the protagonist a young subaltern in the Eleventh Hussars, the crack British regiment dubbed the Cherry Pickers because of the brilliant striping on their dress trousers. Lieutenant Cyprian Coutts-Habirshaw, the officer in question, had been given an evening's leave and, attired in full resplendent uniform, sallied forth into the town in quest of adventure. Spying a *boîte* whose elegant yet discreet façade pleased him, he entered and beheld a bar untenanted save for a strikingly lovely brunette in evening dress, contemplating an empty champagne glass. Coutts-Habirshaw responded as to the call of bugles; he swung onto the adjacent stool, signaled the barman, and demanded to know his choicest vintage.

"Lanson '26, effendi," was the unhesitating answer.

"Splendid," said the young man. "Hurry along a bottle, and fill Mademoiselle's glass. She looks rather parched, if you ask me."

Nobody asked him, least of all the lady, who remained detached and aloof while the wine was broached and the lieutenant essayed a few initial pleasantries. She sipped her drink, allowed her glass to be refilled, and gave not the slightest indication, by word or glance, of his existence. Confronted with so total a rebuff, Coutts-Habirshaw began to experience a sense of panic, but he rattled on gamely, hopeful that his charm and the grape would thaw her *froideur*. Midway through their second bottle the officer's aplomb had faded and he was starting to plead. Unconventional his behavior was, he admitted, but it was born of loneliness; he was a stranger in a distant land, at bottom a decent chap, who longed merely for feminine companionship. Was that a crime? The beauty studied her reflection in the mirror with cool composure, unmoved and quite anesthetic to his presence. Together, yet worlds apart, they finished the champagne, and then Coutts-Habirshaw, on the verge of tears, decided to storm the redoubt. Commanding a third bottle, he waited until the inflexible creature had drained a glassful, and forcibly enclasped her waist. The lady stiffened, patted a stray wisp of hair into place, and, with an almost imperceptible movement of her lips, addressed him in an unmistakable masculine bass. "My name is Derek Inveigleman, of Her Majesty's Secret Service," she murmured. "In two seconds your hand will encounter a shoulder holster. Evince no surprise; we are being watched."

The anecdote hurtled back into my memory a day or two ago as I was reading *Museum Piece*, the autobiography of James Laver, the English novelist, expert on costume, and former curator of the Victoria and Albert Museum. Reminiscing about Gwendoline Otter, a celebrated hostess, who I suspect was Lady Ottoline Morrell, he wrote as follows: "Gwen's luncheon parties were never without interest. I met *chez elle* Alec Waugh and Evelyn, not yet famous, and Ernest Thesiger, whose aristocratic nose, stylized gestures, and superb enunciation had already impressed themselves on my mind when I saw him play the Dauphin in the original production of *St. Joan*. Ernest asked me to lunch and when, at the end of the meal, he suddenly poked a finger inside his collar and brought out the string of pearls which he always wore around his neck, I knew I had been accepted into his circle of friends. He was one of those actors whose stage personality and real personality seem to coincide."

Mr. Thesiger's pearls obviously were no more than an innocent affectation, somewhat akin to the single gold earring flaunted by hairy young men in the Village nowadays to proclaim their defiance of convention. What really riveted my interest in the foregoing, though, was Laver's implication about the intermixture of stage and real personality in theater folk. It happens that I had the opportunity, through a quirk of circumstance, to witness this phenomenon at close range several years ago, and the permutations were so curious that they may be worth a brief recap.

The mechanism that set them in motion was a play I wrote as a vehicle for a comedian named (for present purposes) Smiley Grimes. One of the few remaining clowns of the stature of Willie Howard, Bobby Clark, and Victor Moore, Grimes had had a long and distinguished career in every medium of entertainment—burlesque, vaudeville, musical comedy, pictures, and television. He was a serious and dedicated artist, a perfectionist who worried endlessly about every role he played, and in the dramatic bouillabaisse I had confected he had reason for anxiety, for he was to play six parts: a millionaire philanderer, a Hollywood agent, a Cambodian émigré, a septuagenarian restaurant tycoon, a Los Angeles judge, and a female magazine oligarch.

On our first day of rehearsals, in a tenebrous cavern over Ratner's Restaurant on Second Avenue, he drew me aside to confide that he had devoted extensive study to the psychology and mannerisms of his characters. "The millionaire's a pipe," he said. "Him I know inside out—a cross between Tommy Manville and Otto Kahn. The agent likewise—Swifty Lazar, Myron Selznick; he's no problem. Your restaurant tycoon is a mean old bastard who sees a Red under every bed, and the judge in L.A.—well, you copped him from the Irish Justice bit in burlesque. Now, on the Cambodian

I'm still a little foggy. He's just a Chink laundryman—*nicht?*"

"Oh, sure," I said. "No tickee, no washee—that sort of bilge. There won't be enough Cambodians in the audience to squawk."

"Fine," he said. "Well, that leaves the lady magazine editor, which, to tell you the truth, I'm kind of nervous about her. I'm fifty years in the business and this is the first time I ever played anything in drag. Berle, Hope, Skelton—they've all done it, but not me. We have to get every detail right—the clothes, the hair, the walk. It's a real challenge."

I promised to move heaven and earth to help him meet it, and he went away reassured. A day or two later the costume designer brought in preliminary sketches for the company's wardrobe. Smiley nodded approvingly as he examined his various changes, but when he came to the woman's costume I saw his brow darken.

"Hey, what gives here?" he complained. "This is the editor of a fashion magazine? She looks like a welfare worker—a cashier at Stouffer's!"

The designer's claws flashed. "That happens to be a very smart basic-black faille, Mr. Grimes," he snapped. "Exactly the kind a person in her position would wear. The cut is classic—stark, dramatic, pure. And I chose the accessories with utmost care—the brooch, the shell earrings, that stunning Italian bag—"

"It's a funeral dress, for Chrisake!" Smiley burst forth. "You expect me to get comedy out of *that?* I need some props—a string of beads, a feather boa, or a parasol."

"My dear sir," the other rejoined, his face flaming, "if your conception of the part is Sadie Thompson, I can dress you like Jeanne Eagels. This playwright, whatever his name is, specified a chic, high-style *femme du monde,* and I will not compromise my standards, sacrifice my entire reputation, become a laughingstock in the profession to wring a few cheap boffos from the public. I'd rather go back to Himmelfarb's on Seventh Avenue and design play togs, sell chestnuts on street corners . . ."

or Madam

The altercation reached such a pitch that the producer, snatching a hasty blintz in Ratner's, four floors below, had to be summoned to mediate, but even he was hard put to it to restore harmony. A chance suggestion from our ingénue that culottes were in vogue impressed Smiley, and he began urging hostess pajamas for the character. These the designer icily rejected for office attire with the haughty assertion that the scene would take on the aspect of a knocking shop. Ultimately the two agreed on a gold lamé suit with little fur accents at wrist and collar, to be worn with a matching turban, and all hands resumed work visibly refreshed. The sole victim of the contretemps was the producer, whose blintz had unfortunately ossified in the meantime.

Inside the week Smiley started fretting over the footwear his costume entailed. To cultivate the grace and fluidity of movement a lady oligarch would display, he contended, he needed some high-heeled slippers to practice walking. The playwright being least indispensable to the production, I was automatically assigned to procure them. In a vast shoe salon on Thirty-fourth Street, as garishly lit as a delicatessen, I skulked around inspecting the available merchandise, and, frustrated, waylaid a fox-faced salesman.

"Size eleven?" he repeated in an unnecessarily loud voice. The half dozen women within earshot turned and regarded me transfixed. "Who are they for—your wife?"

"No, no," I said, with a pitiful attempt at nonchalance. "She buys her own. Another man."

He gave me a long, speculative glance. "Oh, Mr. Kay," he called out to the floorwalker. "Would you handle this customer? He wants some outsize opera pumps for another guy."

Bloodied but bowed, I eventually sequestered a pair in an uptown emporium patronized by giantesses, and, after a pratfall or two, Smiley learned to teeter about quite creditably, though balancing a book on his head to improve his carriage overtaxed him.

There was also another flareup between him and the costume

designer when the latter, understandably seeking to exhibit the gold *tailleur* to advantage, proposed that a foundation garment of sorts be worn beneath it. "Mind you, nobody's disparaging your figure, Mr. Grimes," he added hastily. "All we envisioned was something to suppress the hips and give you a svelte, modish line."

"Now look, Fegelspan," said Smiley impatiently. "It ain't the corset I'm fighting—I wore one as a Hussar with Rose Sydell and her Bounteous Belles in 1920, a living statue in the Vanities, I forget the shows. The bind is, I got to make a lightning change from the woman to the judge."

"Then don't take it off. Keep it on under your robes."

Smiley surveyed him aghast. "*What?*" he exclaimed. "You think I could hand down a legal decision in that courtroom knowing I have on a girdle?" He tore off the old tweed cap he wore at rehearsals and flung it on the stage. "That tears it!" he shouted. "One thing I won't stoop to, and that's a mockery of the whole judicial system! Better I should be a roustabout in the circus, sell frankfurters at the Polo Grounds . . ."

The producer, who had stolen down to Ratner's for another blintz, was again yanked back to intercede, but this time he brought the delicacy with him, and through a mouthful ordained that no restraint, physical or otherwise, was to be laid on the star. Since Smiley was already wrenching my lines out of recognition, the edict chilled my heart, but I submitted for the sake of amity.

The next crisis to arise involved the spectacles appropriate to the lady editor's costume—a pair of harlequin glasses richly encrusted with sequins and seashells the designer had chosen at a Madison Avenue optician's. They proved too small for Smiley's face, in addition to containing the wrong lenses, so I accompanied him to the store to insure an adequate fit. Before I could explain their purpose to the prim fusspot who waited on us, Smiley had donned the glasses and was vainly striving to read aloud the extract from Richard Henry Dana's *Two Years Before the Mast* on the test card.

The salesman gaped at him in consternation. "Good God, who ever sold you that frame?" he sputtered. "It's resort wear—the type of thing ladies buy for the Caribbean. You'd be ejected from a restaurant if you wore those here."

"Mind your own beeswax, friend," Smiley retorted. "They suit me fine, except I want them bigger and clearer." He snorted in disgust. "I'm blind as a bat in these lousy cheaters. Can you imagine me fumbling for a lipstick or a comb in my purse when I do a piece of business?"

The entire staff was cataleptic when we took our leave, but Smiley had the glasses he required, and swagger indeed they looked as he browsed through *Variety* in the penumbra of the work light.

No more dilemmas of a transvestite nature occurred until the dress rehearsal in New Haven, where the editor's wig emerged as wholly out of character. The short pageboy bob, while suitable for a breezy sophomore at Bryn Mawr, did nothing to soften Smiley's craggy features. Added to his gold lamé suit with the tufts of fur, it made him resemble one of King John's nobles at Runnymede rather than a pillar of the *haute couture*. The fat hysteric responsible for the error was banished to New York to effect repairs, and Smiley played the scene sporting his old tweed cap. Luckily, that foolish consistency said to be the hobgoblin of little minds failed to bug the little minds who were present.

Anguish predictable attended the tryout of the show in Philadelphia, heightened by the producer's inability to find the type of blintz he subsisted on. Smiley's female characterization, if tentative at first, rapidly gained momentum, and in the final week out of town became captivating—hoydenish, acid-sweet, tyrannical by turns. The New York opening certified his personal triumph—to such a degree, in fact, that even the fashion press hailed his *brio* as the lady oligarch. Sad to say, however, an unforeseen waterspout struck the production amidships; it foundered, the mighty ocean rolled on as it had five thousand years before, and I alone, Ishmael, was left clinging to a spar.

On the anniversary of the debacle a year later, Smiley and I had lunch at his theatrical club. At the conclusion of the meal, when our post-mortems were finished, he shrugged philosophically.

"Well, it wasn't a total loss," he said. "I got something out of it. Here—have a cigar." From his breast pocket he withdrew a gold lamé purse I had cause to remember, and plucked out a panatela. "I never could find the right size case for these till I played that dame."

Mistaken or not, I thought I detected a sudden hush from the box-office men at the adjoining table. "No, thanks," I said hastily. "I—I have to run. My bank closes at three."

"Wait a minute, kid." He stopped me. "You can't go like that. There's a piece of coleslaw stuck to your chin."

"Never mind—I'll remove it in the taxi," I said, and bolted. I was afraid he might offer me a compact.

I Dreamt That I Dwelt in Marble Halls

If anybody in the Paris Branch of Merrill Lynch, Pierce, Fenner & Smith had swiveled his gaze from the stock ticker into the Champs Élysées of an October afternoon last year, he would have witnessed the culmination of a dream. The culminator, just extricating himself from a taxi at the curb, bore no particular resemblance to Apollo, or any such modern avatars of the Sun God as Warren Beatty, other than a radiant visage. His fat little shoulders laid no claim to Herculean strength, and from the gooseberry flush he exhibited as he sprang out of the vehicle, he seemed a likely candidate for a milk farm. Indeed, the proprietor of a Normandy milk farm who happened to be passing, a Monsieur X, paused as if to recommend his establishment, but hastened on with a typical Gallic shrug. To the sharp-eyed reader who will already have guessed my identity, the question arises—what was the special significance of the address I had sought out? Why should the sight of a brokerage office—even a French one—produce a singing in the ears like an exaltation of larks?

The answer, of course, is that behind Merrill Lynch's prosaic exterior stood one of the most ornate, improbable structures in France—the mansion where La Paiva, the celebrated courtesan, had reigned during the Second Empire. Into its completion her Prussian lover, Prince Guido Henckel von Donnersmarck, had poured the inexhaustible wealth stemming from his Silesian mines and industrial holdings. History, though, had taken an ironic revenge; this temple love had built was now consecrated as a refuge from predatory females, a masculine stronghold—the headquarters, in short, of that paragon of all men's clubs, The Travellers. And the ambition I had so long cherished to sojourn under its roof, saturating myself in the atmosphere of *la belle époque*, was at last about to be realized. It had taken rivers of ink to arrange, wheedling in high quarters, endless assurances of my probity and social fitness, but here I was, a temporary member of the most exclusive fellowship— The voice of my taxi driver sharply brought me back to earth.

"M'zoo!" he was saying urgently. " 'Ave you forgot ze grand parcel?" I stared at him uncomprehending. "Zis vast *objet* you carry from ze airport—zurely you recall heem?"

The package he thrust into my arms, four feet square and sheer dead weight, was a crushing reminder of my fatuity and a prime example of feminine guile. A week earlier in London, I had received an anguished phone call from an American crumpet I knew domiciled in Paris. It appeared that thieves had made off with the canvas top and side curtains of an MG she had borrowed. Through a London source she had secured replacements, which she had ordered sent to my hotel, and she was counting on me, her darling boy, to bring them over on my plane. I remonstrated loudly, painted myself as an invalid, a rakehell on the verge of collapse from alcohol and gluttony, but nothing availed. Sobs and vituperation greeted my every excuse, and at length I acquiesced with a groan.

Unwieldy as it was, the package would have been no more than a nuisance except for a newspaper item I read en route to my flight. Owing to the theft of some highly valuable paintings in Britain, the police were closely watching all harbors and airports. By the time I arrived at Heathrow, I was sweating with fear. What guarantee was there, really, that I was transporting side curtains? For all I knew, the sweetmeat who had inveigled me was affiliated with a ring of art thieves, or worse yet, dope peddlers. Slinking across the departure area, I momentarily expected trench-coated figures to materialize and clap the darbies on me. That hurdle surmounted, I then decided Interpol would be lying in wait at the French *douane*. Altogether, the trip was an affliction, and now further humiliation loomed. Instead of the suave, nonchalant image I had of myself registering at the club, I looked like a grubby furniture mover, a minion of United Parcel. It was demeaning; in the Flaubertian phrase of that foremost of all etymologists, Bert Lahr, it was cheapening.

Fortunately, no exalted personages were on hand to observe my arrival; the premises were hushed in majestic gloom, and within minutes I was installed in a period top-floor room, where a period manservant resembling the immortal Passepartout unpacked my traps. The first item on the agenda, obviously, was to familiarize myself with the geography of the club—and awesome it was. The main lounge, gigantic as that of an ocean greyhound, was a symphony of marble, porphyry and gilt inlay. On its enormous mantelpiece a life-size panther crouched, nuzzling a succulent nymph, some of whose dimensions were larger than life. The ceiling mural, its theme Day chasing away Night, showed half a dozen mythological ladies with similar full-blown charms. Ornament galore, reminiscent of the harems of the Ottoman Empire, decorated the other public rooms, such as the bar, the card room and the billiard salon. The prize exhibit, though, was a central staircase two stories high of solid onyx that led up to La Paiva's bedchamber, now the club's dining room. The most striking feature of the former chatelaine's snuggery was her bathroom, also a vision of onyx and marble and containing a tub of solid silver with vermeil chasing.

Spectacular as these treasures were, the effect they produced was that of having gorged oneself on a three-pound box of marzipan. I felt as I had on first seeing the loges of the Paramount Theater in Times Square—peevish, overstuffed, and resentful at the bombardment of schlock masquerading as elegance. The one remedy for my condition was an ice-cold Martini, and I went in quest of it posthaste. By now the bar was crowded with folk of obvious distinction, and from the chitchat I overheard, I judged I was the sole person present below the ambassadorial level. To banish my inferiority, I ordered a second cocktail and a third, and well before I had sampled my fourth, I was treading on air. I gave some shrewd financial advice to the white-haired Belgian banker on my left, discussed the horseflesh in the upcoming Longchamps races with the stable owner on my right, and generally acquitted myself as a worldling and *bon vivant*.

Just as I was at my most winning, the hall porter broke in to summon me to the phone. The caller was Charlotte Russo, the cream puff whose auto accessories I had air-lifted across the channel. Her remorse for the duress I had undergone was so sincere, her apologies so profuse, that the reproaches froze on my lips. It is a characteristic of mine that once somebody evinces penitence, particularly a shapely young colleen, I bend over backward to be magnanimous. An hour later, therefore, the canvaswork safely deposited with Charlotte's concierge, the two of us were tête-à-tête in a Russian restaurant on the Left Bank, consuming quantities of sturgeon, borscht, *piroshki, côtelettes* Pojarski and blinis, and toasting our reunion in repeated draughts of vodka.

"Do tell me more about that fascinating club you're staying at," Charlotte urged. "This La Paiva character of yours—was she a great beauty?"

"Not by my standards," I confessed. "Her mouth was much too sensual, and her body—well, I suppose it might appeal to coarse-grained people who like a voluptuous figure."

I Dwelt in Marble Halls

"Was it as good as mine?" she asked, and twisted around in her chair to enable me to make a comparison, which, of course, was impossible under the circumstances. I mean, to answer her question a person would have needed all kinds of calipers and tape measures and equipment rarely found in your average Russian restaurant.

"Why—er—I imagine La Paiva's legend was a matter of personality rather than looks," I hedged. "Every celebrity of the time used to frequent her salon—Gautier, Alexandre Dumas, the Goncourts, all the leading statesmen. And her exploits were the talk of Paris. She fought a duel in the Bois de Boulogne, for instance, with Cora Pearl, another famous courtesan, in which the two of them were stripped to the waist and employed whips."

"How dreadful," Charlotte breathed, her eyes shining. "Where was she from? What was her early life?"

"Well, it was sort of a rococo version of the Horatio Alger stories," I said. "She was born Thérèse Lachmann in the Moscow ghetto, married a tailor, whom she left for a concert pianist, and through him met and lavished her favors on a number of the French aristocracy. Then she married a Portuguese noble named the Marquis de Paiva. After ruining him with her extravagances, she spent 300,000 francs snaring Guido von Donnersmarck, her German Midas—"

"Wait a minute," Charlotte broke in. "Where'd she get the 300,000 francs? There weren't any finance companies in those days."

"No, but they had women known as 'ogres' who advanced money to various Grand Horizontals like La Paiva, Blanche d'Antigny and Mademoiselle Maximum to buy wardrobes and jewels with which to attract rich protectors. Once the prey was caught, the huntress split fifty-fifty with the ogre. Anyhow, von Donnersmarck was so infatuated that, besides this mansion, he gave his plaything a splendid château at Pontchartrain and married her. His last words on his deathbed were, 'Everything I am, I owe to La Paiva.' "

"Too, too divine," said Charlotte. "Look, angel, I've just had an absolute inspiration. Let's you and I go back to The Travellers and have a brandy so you can show me all the statuary and stuff."

"Sorry, my dear," I said. "Members of the fair sex aren't allowed in the club under any conditions."

"Oh, you're such an old crab," she said resentfully. "Couldn't I have one teeny-weeny peek? After all, it's not as though I were asking to take a bath in her silver tub or something. I just want a look at the onyx staircase and the ceiling."

"Honey, I wish I could do it," I sympathized, "but it's out of the question. I'll tell you what, though. Why don't we go back to your pad for a brandy? You can look at the ceiling there."

Charlotte's face clouded over; it seemed that she had promised her mummy never to entertain a man in her digs without a chaperon. Indeed, I retorted, how far would La Paiva have got if *her* mummy had extracted such a promise? The upshot was that we bickered all the way back to her doorstep, where she denied me even a sisterly good-night kiss. There was, in fact, a vindictive note in her voice when we parted.

"OK, go on back to your old club," she snapped. "But you wait and see, wise guy—you'll be sorry for this, you mark my words."

In the taxi that bore me homeward I chuckled at the absurdity of her threat, but as events proved, I had occasion to remember it soon enough. About four o'clock the following afternoon I was seated in the club's writing room inditing several notes to my laundryman, dentist and dry cleaner—creditors who I judged would be sufficiently impressed by The Travellers' stationery to overlook my trifling bills. Suddenly, a bolt out of the blue, came word that Inspector Dugong of the Sûreté was waiting to speak to me in the visitors' lounge. On the instant I was assailed by the darkest forebodings. So the parcel I had been duped into transporting *was* con-

traband, and now the police—tipped off by Charlotte herself—
were closing in. Fool that I was—why had I forgotten to what
lengths a woman scorned would go to wreak revenge? I saw myself
cowering in the dock, vainly protesting my innocence as three mag-
istrates straight out of Daumier condemned me to servitude on
Devil's Island. A sob welled up in my throat. Well, they might
railroad me, but by Jupiter, I wasn't going to give up like a sheep.
Squaring my fat little shoulders, I strode out to the lounge, where
an elderly bearded gentleman in a claw-hammer coat was seated, a
briefcase on his lap.

"Inspector Dugong," I said before he could open his mouth.
"We've never seen each other, but just let me say one thing. I'm
rotten to the core. I'm ready to lie, and cheat, and bear false witness to get out of this jam. In fact, I'll do anything to save my
neck."

"Spoken like a man," the inspector croaked, and rose to his feet.
"Well, Cuddles, now that my disguise has fooled the staff and
yourself, suppose you show me around this mausoleum."

My jaw sagged as I heard Charlotte's voice issuing through the
official's luxuriant whiskers. "L-listen, are you out of your living
mind?" I demanded. "Take off those clothes—I mean, don't take
'em off—I mean, get out of here! They'll bastinado me if they
catch you inside this club!"

"Well, they won't, because I'm using you as a shield," she said,
coupling her arm with mine. "Come on, where's this onyx staircase
you were fluthering about last night?"

Caught in so painful a dilemma, I had no option but to accede,
and for the next half hour Charlotte propelled me through every
nook and cranny of the building, from the wine cellars to the roof.
Such clubmen as we encountered, particularly in the washrooms,
were visibly startled at the spectacle of a fellow member, pinioned
by a graybeard, conducting a tour, but eccentrics were no novelty at
The Travellers, and we went our way unmolested. Had Charlotte

stopped there, all might have ended tranquilly; success, however, emboldened her and she overreached herself. Removing her beard and wig, she extracted a camera from the briefcase, posed before the sculptured mantelpiece and ordered me to take a snapshot—as proof incontrovertible, she said, that she had actually invaded the club.

"In Heaven's name, Charlotte, don't make me do this," I pleaded, my teeth chattering. "If anybody walks in here—"

Barely had I emitted the words when two dignified oldsters, members of the Chamber of Deputies at the very least, crossed the threshold. Simultaneously, I pressed the camera release and there was a blinding flash. Squealing in terror, the pair flung themselves behind armchairs, obviously believing they were the target of a political assassin. The ensuing hour was a mite confused, inasmuch as I was busy making alibis, the staff was stuffing my possessions helter-skelter into my pockets, and the hall porter was booting me into the Avenue des Champs Élysées. It was a pretty abrupt transition from *la belle époque* into the Space Age, but ish kabibble. I can always brag to the boys at the livery stable about the time I slept with La Paiva.

In Spite of All Temptations/To Belong to Other Nations

There were some good art exhibitions [at the Edinburgh Festival] . . . and a large showing of Corot, a painter's painter and en masse rather drained of light (or perhaps too many gray-haired ladies in tweeds between you and them).

In the lift in my hotel a complete stranger from Texas said, "Taken in the crows?" She meant Corot and accented the last syllable to the loss of the first vowel. We got it straight in time for me to say as she disappeared on to her floor, "Here today and gone to Corot," which may not have improved international relations but was irresistible.—Manchester Guardian Weekly

Calmness above all, I tell myself—I must under no circumstances succumb to childish fury. Yet why not? The whole thing is so absolutely galling, so *diminishing*, that I can hardly bring myself to record it, and, of course, never would if Ayscough, my solicitor, hadn't insisted. The old fossil obviously is too potters to understand the simplest facts; not once, despite my detailed explanation, did he grasp what a shattering experience I'd been through or intimate whether we could recover damages for the mental and physical anguish I sustained. Well, inveighing against the legal mind is a footling enough pursuit, I suppose. I may as well narrate the events to delineate, if nothing else, the lengths to which women will resort to wreak their vindictiveness.

I daresay several of my older colleagues on the *Scrutator* bristled when Titheradge, the features chief, assigned me to cover the big Post-Impressionist show in Paris, but they knew in their hearts I was the only possible choice. True, I was the youngest on the staff, newly down from Oxford, and a novice by Fleet Street standards; still, wherever you went—Annabel's, the Caprice, the Mirabelle— people kept calling my art reviews the most authoritative in England, reported our circulation soaring to the skies, lionized me all over the place. As Mummy said, "Stop being an ostrich, dear boy— you've taken London by storm. Everyone lives for your Friday column. They're using words like Ruskin and Berenson." To be sure, the Mater *would* exaggerate, owning 80 per cent of the paper's shares, but nonetheless it indicated which way the wind was blowing.

At any rate, there I was at the Jeu de Paume in Paris, undergoing, between ourselves, a frightful attack of *déjà vu.* There wasn't a single surprise—just the same shopworn canvases I'd known from nursery days, and, indeed, I had the very sensation of ennui that old *Chatterbox* annuals used to give me in youth. If only one Seurat overlooked by connoisseurs, one unfamiliar Signac, had been included to pique the jaded appetite, I thought, and decided, *ruat caelum,* that I really must rap the committee's knuckles in my review. Well, just as I was quitting the gallery, a grubby little *nouveau riche* in an absurd bonnet, with those terribly yearning eyes American culture-seekers have, blundered into me. She gushed apologies in that nasal accent that defies imitation, then proceeded to take advantage of the situation. "Isn't it divine?" she caroled. "I'm all agog about the Van Goghs!"

It took a superhuman effort to restrain my mirth. The poor soul had rhymed the painter's name with her emotional state, too benighted to know that it was pronounced "Kok," with soft "k"s, or, alternatively, "Go." A delicious tidbit to regale the chums with at Annabel's *boîte*, and the impulse to cap it was uncontrollable. I lifted a quizzical eyebrow. "Money makes the mare go," I said, "but Monet makes the van Go." The quip indubitably torpedoed British-American amity, but I would have thought less of myself had I not put her in her place. "Good afternoon, luv."

Perhaps it was an access of euphoria at scoring off the Philistines so neatly, but I felt I deserved a treat, and, yielding to my shameful secret passion for sweets, I hared off to my very favorite *confiserie* in the Rue de Rivoli. *Gourmandise*, I fear, rather got the better of me. After two huge *gâteaux* frosted over with hazelnuts and whipped cream, I sank into such blissful satiety as might a lizard basking on an ivied wall in Provence. Suddenly a voice unmistakable twanged through my marrow, and I beheld the transatlantic succubus who'd captured me at the exhibition. "Do forgive me for disturbing you," she said breathlessly. "I really owe you an apology for mispronouncing Mr. Van Gogh's name. You see, this is my first trip to Europe, and we Americans don't savvy the foreign lingo, but I'm very glad to be corrected, because that's how one learns, isn't it?"

Well, had I sent the creature packing it would have taught her a salutary lesson and averted ultimate grief. Instead, all the tiresome noblesse oblige instilled in one by generations of breeding and education bubbled to the surface. As patiently as possible, I replied that she wasn't responsible for being American any more than my family could help tracing its lineage back to William the Conqueror.

She seemed truly grateful for the explication. "How marvelous to encounter somebody with genuine Old World courtesy," she said, plumping herself down. "I knew you were a thoroughbred the moment I saw you. Your hands are so sensitive and artistic. Are you a sculptor?"

Her naïveté was enchanting—pure Fenimore Cooper. "In a sense," I said. "My medium is words rather than clay. I'm an art critic not altogether unknown in this hemisphere."

"Just imagine," she said, overcome. "Won't the folks back home be green with envy when I tell them! It's a pity my Alonzo never lived to meet celebrities like you. He was so busy running our six-hundred-thousand-acre ranch in the Panhandle and amassing his millions that neither of us had much time for culture."

Great sentimental booby that I am, something in her manner—the appeal of a lonely human being for sympathy?—touched a chord, and I reexamined the woman. My first impression had been wrong; albeit tacky, her suit was tailored of quite respectable material and the furs were unquestionably sable. Her visage, furthermore, while no longer young, still bore evidences of beauty, and even distinction.

Any lingering suspicion that she was a nobody vanished with the entry of the chasseur to announce that Mrs. Huffaker's Rolls was waiting. As she gathered up her bag and gloves, she paused awkwardly. "I hope you won't think me forward," she said. "If you're not otherwise engaged this evening, could you—would you—escort me to the opera? It's a dream I've cherished all my life, but the thought of being alone in that box . . ." She fought to master the catch in her throat. "Please say you will. It'd mean so much."

Why, oh why, do we let ourselves be victimized by the weak? I suppose it was compassion, the knowledge of the luster my presence would shed on her future reminiscences, that swayed me, and I chose to be magnanimous.

In fact, the episode was far less poisonous than I had anticipated. To be sure, my companion made several delicious *gaffes*, such as shaking hands during the interval with the Aveyron-Plutarchs, scions of a very old family who never shake hands when presented, but she insisted on giving me supper afterward at Maxim's, and the *direction*, overjoyed as always to see me, exhumed a quite potable

Krug. Under its influence I promised Moline—named, she told me, after some celebrated American plow, as is apparently their custom on the prairie—to accompany her on a shopping tour next day. The rigors of squiring her through a score of *maisons de couture*, jewelers', and millinery shops were, needless to say, unimaginable, and the constant appeals to my judgment depleting. As it turned out, however, my gesture bore unexpected fruit. I was about to emplane at Orly for London when she pressed on me a truly sumptuous gift—a return-flight ticket, first class, to Texas.

"No, no—not a word," she said, silencing my protestations. "I owe you a debt I can never repay. After all, you rescued me from myself, so to speak. I'd have remained such an ignoramus, a hopeless barbarian, if you hadn't taken me under your wing at the gallery as you did. Come and visit real soon. I guarantee you an experience you'll never forget."

And, indeed, the prophecy was being fulfilled, I reflected sardonically a month later as her chauffeur sped me from the Houston airport to Mrs. Huffaker's residence in the suburbs. What architectural banality, what excrescences of concrete and stucco had bloomed from those arid plains outside the car window! The acute desolation that had attended my brief stopover in New York welled up anew. Everything I'd encountered thus far seemed designed to outrage the senses—the clothes our *soi-disant* cousins wore, their language, their food, their pastimes. Worse than the ostentation, the crudities of taste and behavior, though, was the pervasive noise. The smallest activity, it appeared, demanded a rich musical obbligato. Banks and supermarkets, bookstores and hotel lobbies throbbed with light opera and similar glucose; gone was the tobacco juice spurted at the visitor's feet in Mrs. Trollope's day, and in its place cacophony. No wonder America's contribution to literature and the arts was negligible—it was impossible to concentrate. As for the vaunted standard of living there, that, too, was an illusion. Breakfast kippers were totally unheard of, ordinary toffees of the sort found in any English confectioner's unobtainable, and the mere mention of gooseberry flan evoked stupefaction.

My forebodings lessened somewhat as we swung past a set of ornate gates, wound through masses of shrubbery, and came to a stop before a vast Renaissance-style palazzo. Moline, a breath of French chic in lounging pajamas I had selected for her at Dior's, gave me an effusive welcome. She apologized for the light repast we were to have; her entire staff was absent that day for some complex reason—perhaps one of their native corn dances.

"You won't mind an informal lunch, just the two of us?" she queried. "I didn't ask anyone, knowing you'd be exhausted from the trip, the excitement of New York—"

"On the contrary, I'm delighted," I assured her. "And I can't wait to have you show me over the house. It—ah—looks fascinating."

Her eyes sparkled. "I've waited for this moment too," she said, with an emphasis that rather puzzled me. "You'll see it all, never fear. One thing in particular, that'll make a lasting impression, I hope."

My fleeting glimpse of American décor en route must, I suppose, have partly inured me to what followed, else I believe I never could have withstood it. The atrocities the Huffakers had surrounded themselves with beggared description—the bogus Italian painting, the Mid-Victorian statuary, the objects of virtu rifled from a hundred auction rooms. Mixed into the mishmash were oddments of Spanish, French, Early American, and modern furniture, not to mention Moorish tabourets inlaid with mother-of-pearl, armchairs of steerhorn, and hassocks fashioned from camel saddles. Such a kitchen midden would doubtless have posed a dilemma for the average visitor, but in matters of aesthetic opinion I always make it a principle to speak forth. I told Moline as succinctly as I was able that her home was a chamber of horrors. To my surprise, she agreed.

"I know," she said humbly. "I'd feel the same if I were in your shoes. I mean, you've been conditioned by centuries of European civilization, haven't you?"

"To say nothing of birth and superior schooling," I added. "Yes, dear lady, in that respect I'm afraid we rather have the 'jump' on you, as you say in your argot."

"Oh, that reminds me!" she said, taking my arm. "The object I said I was sure you'd remember? Come this way—it's out in the garden."

I followed her along a rocky path bordered by greenery to a secluded patio dotted with outdoor furniture. In the center stood a rustic well curb of quite unremarkable design, arched over by a roof of moss-covered shingles. To my alien eye it possessed only the most transient charm, but, explained Moline, this was a memento of the Huffakers' early struggles, the original well that had watered their ranch house in the Panhandle.

"Alonzo used to stand here by the hour gazing into it," she told me reminiscently. "It's so wonderfully cool and mysterious down there. Look inside—go ahead."

Rather to indulge her whim than from any real curiosity, I complied and bent over the edge. In the next moment the most appalling catastrophe in my memory overtook me. I felt a sudden vigorous thrust from behind and toppled headlong into the dark, flailing wildly for a purchase as I dropped. Somehow, inexplicably, I managed to clutch the chain the bucket was suspended from and partially braked my fall, though the screech of the mechanism and that lurch into oblivion will haunt me forever. A second afterward I plummeted into freezing water up to my hips. The shock acted at least to dispel my vertigo. Gripping the chain for dear life, I regained my balance and peered upward. Framed against the sky, Moline Huffaker, that unutterable serpent, was leaning comfortably on her elbows, regarding me with a glee I can only describe as diabolical.

"Tallyho, old bean!" she called out. "How's everything Gauguin? It's a right smart climb out of there, luv, but don't be a Sisley—you can make it. Well, toodle-oo for now; I'm off to the Caribbean. Any time you're Pascin by, do drop in, won't you? Pip-pip."

Well, I believe that covers the salient points I outlined to Ayscough in his chambers at Lincoln's Inn. As for the pain and suffering I endured in my imbroglio and the compensation I am entitled to therefor, those will be assessed in full measure by Her Majesty's courts. For the present I have but one thing to add—a word of warning to Britons everywhere. Beware a country that can produce harpies like Mrs. Moline Huffaker, a country without a scintilla of taste, clamorous with cheap music, and loyal to one tradition only —vengeance, derived from its aboriginal Red Indians. Shun it, I implore you. Those people are *fiends*.

Turn the Knob, Doc, You're Obsolete

"Make a fist, like a brave little man," said Dr. Prognose's nurse, brushing a stray tendril of hair under her cap and selecting a disposable needle. I was undergoing the routine preliminary tedium of an annual checkup, alleviated in part by the fact that Miss Bustanoby's sumptuous figure threatened to escape momentarily from a uniform that must have shrunk in the washing. "Here, let me massage your palm," she offered helpfully. "Now we're in business."

We were, though not of my choosing, and after the quick lethal stab, I watched her manipulate the pipette.

"Enough there for the Gram stain and the slides?" I queried. "Remember, you've got to estimate the hemogoblins—that is, if you still use the Spencer Brightline counting chamber."

"Goodness, that's a surprise." Her lovely eyebrows widened. "I didn't realize you were a physician."

"Well, not really," I said modestly. "I took the pre-med course at Brown for a few months back in the twenties before I switched to hotel administration. And right after Pearl Harbor I trained six weeks as a medical assistant, but the government wrote me a special letter asking me to stay out of that branch. I guess they wanted me for some secret mission."

"I guess," she concurred. "All right, you can go in—the doctor's ready for you."

Prognose, as always, was the soul of brisk efficiency. He auscultated my chest, savaged my nose and ears, struck my ankles with a tuning fork, and clucked at the sight of my midriff. (His own, for that matter, was no chocolate ice-cream soda.) When it came to the electrocardiogram Miss Bustanoby was to supervise, which required me to be topless. I feared lest she might follow suit, but Prognose sensed my anxiety and conducted it himself.

"Fit as a fiddle," he pronounced moments later in his consulting room. "You're in magnificent shape." As was everybody around the office, I thought wistfully. "Yes, absolutely textbook. Now, any problems? Anything at all troubling you?"

"Look, Morris," I said. "You don't have to feed me that soothing sirup—I'm not a baby. I've a pretty extensive knowledge of medicine, and I know when my system's out of whack. So let's discuss this as colleagues rather than doctor and patient—agreed?"

"Right," he said, eying me pensively. "Only try not to use too many technical terms, will you? They confuse me."

"I'll make it as simple as I can," I promised. "OK, digestion first. I take it you've watched enough television to comprehend how stress and turmoil produce acidosis?"

"Well, I've seen the juice trickle down those conduits . . ."

I smiled tolerantly. "That's oversimplification, Morris. You see, the thorax, or chest cavity, up here contains kind of a latticework, a whole lot of rods, or ropes in the case of some individuals, crisscrossing every which way, like the cash tubes you find in old-fashioned department stores. Should one of these pencil rods snap or the ropes fray out, it causes a booming in the head, and the resultant fluid drips into a flask—the stomach—where it bubbles . . . What are you bending down for?"

You're Obsolete

"I'm just tying my shoelace," he said, his face scarlet with exertion. He straightened up. "Go ahead—I visualize it. How does one offset this distress that I gather you suffer from?"

"By coating the stomach wall with any good white emulsion," I explained. "It has to be done orally, of course, since that area doesn't permit easy access. I use some foamy tablets whose name escapes me at the moment. This strip of denture material illustrates how they act."

"Then, what's bothering you?"

"You don't think I'm liable to develop an ulster?"

"Not unless there's tweed in the pills," he reassured me. "No, you're quite safe. And by the by, you show an amazing knowledge of the body structure. Very impressive in a layman." I shrugged and said it was available to any student of Gray's *Anatomy* or, for that matter, anyone with a TV set. "They didn't have either in the diploma mill I went to," he confessed. "I learned the little I know from the *Orange Book of Fairy Tales*. But getting back to you— what else seems out of kilter?"

"Well, I feel awful listless every afternoon—washed out," I said. "I eat a perfectly normal lunch—lentil soup, *rinderbrust*, red cabbage, potato pancakes, *rote gritze*, and two bottles of lager—but I can barely hoist myself to my feet afterward."

"Nothing there that should slow you down particularly." The man's face betrayed manifest bafflement. "Perhaps in the light of your wider experience, though, you have a theory."

"I do indeed," I said. "In my opinion, it's an open-and-shut case of rust-poor blood. I don't know how closely you follow the literature, Morris, but for some time doctors have suspected that persons with rust-poor blood, or no blood at all, are prone to be torpid. I wager if I went out to your lab and stared at my slides with Miss Bustanoby, we'd find no rust in the microscopic field."

"Stay where you are," he said coldly. "Have you tried any medication to counteract this—er—zombie syndrome?"

I admitted having taken one or two specifics, advertised on the air, generating such excessive vigor that I had sprung into my tuxedo, executed a furious tango around the living room with my wife and demolished several lamps. Prognose, however, was inclined to pooh-pooh my qualms. He felt there was enough latent rust in *rinderbrust* to fully supply me with the mineral ingredient I lacked, and that the condition would subside in time.

"Other than these minor—er—derangements," he pursued, "I assume you feel tolerably well. Your weight's constant, your tissue tone—"

"Hold on," I interrupted. "I haven't mentioned the blocked nasal passages, the devastating headaches and the insomnia. All of those are danger signals, bear in mind, and thanks to television, I've learned to recognize and cope with them."

"Yes, we medical men know they could be indicative of brain fever or something too ghastly to designate," he said. "To separate them for a moment—when did you become aware of this sensation of blockage in your bugle?"

"Shortly after duplicating a test I witnessed in a commercial," I said, endeavoring to focus events in proper scientific fashion. "It showed part of a patient—he was split in half, like a bloater—breathing into a football bladder. The message was clear to even the most benighted: none of the beneficial air in the bladder was feeding back into his sinuses. Of course, this party had a very low forehead."

"Unlike yours, whose frontal development reminds one of Professor Moriarty's," he complimented. "So, having ascertained the same condition in yourself, how did you remedy it?"

"With these vapor capsules they advertised, which discharge purified steam into the bronchial tubes. It's the headaches, though, that I'm worried about. I don't have any, but from a diagram I saw recently in a shampoo commercial, it looks as if they're caused by hair follicles growing too close to the brain."

"Well, your concern *is* somewhat justified," he acknowledged. "It's like English ivy clinging to a brick wall, and the effects can be equally disastrous. At the first sign of pressure in your temples I'd consult a good mason. . . . Excuse me." He arose and, opening the door, called into the anteroom. "I shan't need you, Miss Bustanoby. Run along to lunch."

"All by her lonesome, Doctor?" I protested. "Listen, I'll be glad —I mean, I know a little place on East Fifty-fourth Street—"

"She can find it, thanks"—he stopped me, and added, I thought disparagingly, "she's got a perfectly adequate map." He drummed his fingers on the desk top. "You spoke of insomnia, as I recall. Does it recur at regular intervals?"

I nodded. "From eight in the evening till eleven-thirty," I said. "I used to settle down after supper with a book—the works of Elbert Hubbard, Ridpath's *History of the World,* or whatever—and sleep right through to bedtime."

"Whereas now you're glued to the tube, studying your materia medica," he deduced. "You keep threshing around, twisting and turning, building up a chain of frustrations, and as a consequence don't get the rest so vital to the human organism. I'm surprised that with your keen analytical powers, the explanation shouldn't have occurred to you."

Despite myself, I had to marvel at the man's acuity. "Gee whillikers, Morris, you're right—but what's the answer? There must be something I could do."

"I don't believe in easy solutions," Prognose said austerely. "In any case, I'd hesitate to propose one until I knew all the factors involved. You sure you've told me everything that's worrying you?"

"Well, to be candid, there is a problem of a sort, psychological in nature, I should elucidate," I said. "It involves a certain dichotomy, and to help you extrapolate its essence and form a viable rationale, I think I ought to sketch in the background first."

"And I think you ought to have one more test before you leave here," he advised. "You may have a trace of susskind poisoning. Carry on, but watch your syllables."

"The thing is," I began, "as a writer, I've always been obliged to smoke a pipe—you know, for those rugged photographs that publishers require on book jackets. Well, I recently switched to cigars, and soon after, I noticed that every time I lit up, a white bird of prey, or rather a girl dressed as a bird, appeared and batted her eyelashes at me. . . . You're taking notes on all this, I presume?"

"I'd prefer not to," he said. "If the building burned down and some fireman happened to spot them, it might prove embarrassing to you. Er—how would you describe this intruder's attitude toward you?"

"Gee, Doc, at the risk of sounding boastful, I believe the poor thing's in love with me," I said sheepishly. "Mind you, I never encourage her—in fact, I look away as though she weren't there."

"Has your wife ever seen her?"

"Luckily, no," I replied. "But I live in continual fear she might, and knowing how jealous she is, I've had to resort to smoking in the shower."

"A most ingenious subterfuge," he approved. "Obviously the feathered stranger wouldn't dare follow you in there."

"Who knows what a bird is capable of?" I exclaimed distractedly. "I'm not an ornithologist and neither are you. In whatever case, my wife objects to cigar fumes in the bath, she's constantly upbraiding me, and it's reached such a point domestic-wise—"

Prognose held up his hand. "That's quite sufficient," he signified. "I get the over-all picture, and it demands assistance beyond what I can furnish. I'm referring you to three different specialists on this slip of paper, which you can read on the sidewalk. And now, if you'll pardon me, I'm late for an appointment."

I did as he directed and saw the names of a Mexican divorce lawyer, a shrinker counseling those beset by nonexistent birds, and a man with a pickup truck who hauled away TV sets. I also saw a certain so-called healer erupt from the side door of his office and bolt off in the direction of a bar on East Fifty-fourth Street. I hate to run down a member of my profession, but I'll bet you there's something between him and Miss Bustanoby.

Three Loves Had I,
in Assorted Flavors

There it lay in a dusty recess of our Pennsylvania attic, atop a pile of other discarded records—Cole Porter's "Experiment," played by Ray Noble and his orchestra—and there I crouched that winter's day, heart-stricken, simianlike, to avoid concussing myself against the rafters. To think that a quarter of a century had elapsed since I used to play it over and over, marveling at the smooth precision of the brass, the buoyant lines in the refrain so characteristic of Porter: "The apple on the top of the tree/ Is never too high to achieve./ So take an example from Eve./Experiment!" Heavy with nostalgia, I bore it downstairs, and when our laundryman peered through the window ten minutes later, he saw his customer, eyeballs capsized, gliding about with a broom in his arms, an unreasonable facsimile of Fred Astaire. Why I was thus engaged, or what associations the song held for me, I could never explain to such a hayseed, but I can do so here. "Experiment" was the outstanding tune in *Nymph Errant*, an English musical I labored to convert into a Hollywood film back in the thirties, and now that TV's jackals roam where once I fought and bled, the sorry tale may finally be told.

The architect of my misfortunes was, in actuality, a very decent bird—a producer named Sonny LoPresto, who himself was a successful songwriter and Broadway celebrity. From the outset his attitude was refreshingly candid and succinct; he made no effort to minimize the problems ahead. "Kid, I'll be honest with you," he said through his knees. (The armchairs in his office were so deep that we could hardly discern each other's face.) "This property was wished on me by Wingfoot Shaughnessy, the head of the studio. He saw it in London, with Gertie Lawrence in the lead, and he flipped—bought it on the spot. Now, it's a great Cole Porter score, a crackerjack, but the book— Well, it's going to need lots of elbow grease to get a picture out of it. Which is why I'm teaming you with Cy Horniman on the screenplay."

"Cy Horniman?" I repeated incredulously. "But his specialty is hoods. He wrote all that underworld stuff for Cagney over at Warner's."

"Damn right he did," said LoPresto, beaming. "He's got a terrific plot sense—he'll give you enough situations to make a hundred musicals. So what if the guy only thinks in terms of blood and guts? Use him—milk his brain!"

It baffled me that, of the twelve hundred and fifty members of the Screen Writers' Guild, LoPresto couldn't have picked a pen with a daintier nib to complement mine. However, professional ethics enjoined silence, and I acquiesced—not without foreboding.

Horniman was hours late for our initial conference the next morning, and when he did totter in, unshaven and half asleep, he looked pretty shopworn. His face, which bore remnants of the starry-eyed beauty typified by Nell Brinkley's Adonises in the Hearst press, was puffy with dissipation, and a resentful scowl, as of one persecuted beyond endurance, corroded his forehead. As he fell back on the davenport in my office, racked by yawns, I noticed he was wearing a suede tie spattered with food stains. It was an unimportant detail, but I had a premonition our union was going to be shortlived.

"Christ, what a hangover," he murmured, combing his hair with his fingers. "We must have killed two quarts of tequila last night in Olvera Street, this Mexican cooz and I. My head is so hot you could fry an egg on it." He paused—I suspected, waiting for me to produce a skillet—but I registered polite concern and said nothing. "Well, anyhow," he resumed, "I wish I'd met Conchita ten years ago. I wouldn't be paying alimony to those two vampire bats I married. They stripped me of everything but what I've got on."

I could understand why they had left him his tie; nevertheless, I pretended commiseration, and delicately inched around to our project. Horniman confessed he had not yet read the basic material, but he said he would digest it that evening.

Two days passed by without any word, during which I built up a substantial head of steam. On the third he phoned to propose that we work at his home to escape the distractions of the studio. His lair, when I ultimately found it, thirteen miles below the Signal Hill oil fields, turned out to be a bungalow in a heavily wooded canyon—a refuge, he explained, from leeches like process servers and federal tax agents.

"Hell, it's too late in the day to talk script," he said, and cracked his knuckles. "I had Conchita prepare us lunch before she left for the cannery, so we'll just have a little snort and relax. Do you drink Moscow mules?"

I never had; nor, judging from the effects, will I ever be induced to again. After a purely nominal intake I experienced a feeling of exaltation, in the course of which I gobbled quantities of cold frijoles washed down with muscatel. There ensued a sudden thunderclap, as though I had been hit with a broadaxe, and then I was face down on the patio listening to my collaborator, garbed in a sarape and sombrero, pick out "Las Cuatro Milpas" on a guitar. The subject of *Nymph Errant* did not arise, needless to say, and our two subsequent meetings at the studio were similarly fruitless. Horniman was in a strange comatose state on both occasions; his conversation rambled, and I detected a sickly-sweet odor, unfamiliar to me at that time, emanating from his cigarettes.

A day or two afterward LoPresto summoned me to his office. "Don't bother to tell me how the yarn is going," he said. "I'll tell you. Your partner's on Cloud Nine and I've decided to replace him. From now on, you work with Byron Burrows, the author of *Dead on Arrival.*"

"Sonny, this is a *musical*," I protested. "What kind of casting is that? Burrows is Horniman all over again—another gangland expert!"

"Yep, and a first-rate story mind," he said. "He's just the man to supply the skeleton for your brittle, sparkling japes. So get over there pronto and huddle with him—he's in that adobe villa across from Wardrobe."

Whereas most scenarists were housed in buildings like the Irving J. Thalberg Memorial, at Metro—whose façade doubled as an apartment dwelling or a high-grade mortuary on occasion—Burrows was permitted his own bower, and it was a lulu. To paraphrase Dashiell Hammett's dictum "The cheaper the crook the gaudier the patter," it was a case of the cheaper the scribe the gaudier the pad. The décor was a mixture of schools—the pecky-cypress walls adorned with pewter, fusing La Cienega Boulevard with Louisburg Square; an English kneehole desk; *toile-de-Jouy* curtains; and even a ceramic fox of the sort found in Madison Avenue antique shops. Burrows, a pallid, bespectacled chap, arose to greet me from a swollen red-leather lounge chair. In a community where facial tics were a commonplace, his were exceptional; they literally pursued each other across his features like snipe. The source of his turbulence soon became apparent—he was the most fearful hypochondriac I had ever met. We had barely started to discuss an approach to *Nymph Errant* when Burrows chanced to emit a slight cough. Instantly he was on his feet, groping toward a shelf crammed with medical books. He thumbed through one of them, hurriedly consulted an illustration, and collapsed into his chair.

"Finished," he croaked. "I've had it—I'm done for. Oh, my God."

I took the volume—Koch's standard work on tuberculosis—and looked at the plate, a detail drawing of lymph nodes in technicolor warranted to freeze the marrow. In my naïveté I sought to persuade the man that his alarm was unfounded, but he was impervious to reason. Throughout our association he was forever swallowing lozenges, spraying his throat, scanning his fingers for nonexistent pustules, and palpating his abdomen, and much of the time he was so busy taking his temperature that he was speechless. Like all imaginary invalids, he felt he had evolved a regimen that catered to his special needs. At 11 A.M. our secretary brought him a tall glass of buttermilk and half a glass of bourbon. At four the dosage was reversed—a large bourbon followed by a small buttermilk. During our fortnight together there was no visible change in his condition, but we managed to eviscerate *Nymph Errant* and construct a species of framework. Though we had minor disagreements—like his insistence that Dion O'Banion and Bugs Moran would quicken the action—our relationship was amicable. One Monday, though, the secretary greeted me with chilling news. Burrows had suffered an attack of the rams over the Sabbath and had been removed to a rest home in Tucson to dehydrate.

"Buck up, my boy," Sonny LoPresto counseled as I sat in his quarters, profoundly discouraged. He quoted numberless ordeals out of his Broadway past that had ended in triumph. "I know how rough it's been, but we're out of the woods at last. I've been combing the agents' lists and I've got you the perfect teammate—Lothar Perfidiasch, the noted Hungarian playwright."

"And plagiarist," I supplemented. "He's been sued for every play and movie he ever wrote—or, rather, didn't."

"Granted, but a great constructionist," he emphasized. "After all, there's only six basic plots in the world, and it's up to you, with your shrewd nose for the unusual, to winnow out his ideas and select the least obvious. He's waiting for you in the commissary."

As indeed he was, over a third *Schlagobers*, his crafty eyes atwinkle above the white carnation he always sported; he was well aware of the disarming influence of flowers. The usual anecdotes about Ferenc Molnár and Budapest tricksters consumed our first afternoon. Subsequently Perfidiasch started bunting plots at me one after another, all too familiar to steal—*Fifty Million Frenchmen, Lady, Be Good, Roberta, A Connecticut Yankee,* along with everything Maugham and Sherwood and Coward had written. In the end I consented to one I couldn't identify—a farce of Georges Feydeau's, I discovered years later—and we fell to work.

Some seven weeks thence, just as we were nearing the final sequence of the screenplay, LoPresto called us in. He was pink with embarrassment. "Men, it kills me to break the news to you, but there's been a terrible mistake," he said. "Wingfoot Shaughnessy is convinced that the *Nymph Errant* he saw in London was about some dames who open a charm school for sourdoughs in the Klondike. Maybe it was, or maybe he ate too many liqueur candies that night. Anyway, he's the boss, and when I told him our version he blew his stack and canceled the picture. Turn in your kimonos."

I was eastward bound aboard the Chief the following noon, and it was many months before I heard the coda to our *Phantasiestück*. On the day I left, a young novelist, freshly arrived from New York to adapt his book, checked into the studio and was assigned my office. In rummaging through the desk, he came upon our script and, eager to absorb the technique of screenwriting, lay down on the davenport to peruse it. Uninured to the damp chill of southern California, he switched on the petcock of the gas radiator, nobody having warned him that it must be lit manually. He was slowly drifting toward the Final Fadeout when, by the happiest of coincidences, salvation appeared in the form of my collaborator. Perfidi-asch, in search of his cigar case, threw open the door and beheld the recumbent azure-faced stranger. His behavior, if indefensible by medical standards, at least saved the young man's bacon. He pummeled and shook him violently back to consciousness, and, before the other could rally his thoughts, began excoriating him. "What are you doing, you idiot?" he shouted. "Are you crazy? They find you here, a stiff with these dialogue pages on your chest, and the next thing you know, my friend is dragged off the train at Needles on a murder rap! . . . *Say*—could this be an idea for a picture? Excuse me, I must call up Sol Wurtzel at Fox right away. . . ."

Call Me Monty, and Grovel Freely

Baron Teviot of Burghclere, 33, who until his father's death Sunday was Charles John Kerr, plans to go back to work as a trainee supermarket checker. "We are the same people whether I have a title or not," he told reporters. "And the rent still has to be paid. I shall go on working for a living." . . . He wants customers to go on calling him Charlie.
— New York Post

All right, so Marcy and I were cornball, a couple of Americans on our first trip to England and doing the whole tourist bit. Windsor Castle, the Tower, Portobello Road, Hampton Court—you name it, we saw it. I said to Marcy when we got to London, "Look, angel," I said, "if there's one thing that bugs me it's somebody who's afraid to be mistaken for a square. I'm an ordinary person— maybe a little luckier than most. Just because I happen to be a big wheel back home, a junior assistant associate of a top news magazine, with my name on the masthead, I'm not going to throw my weight around. Our bureau chief here could show me a lot of inside stuff, but we'd never get the feel of the country—you follow? We're foreigners—let's behave like it." Which we did, and you never saw such red-carpet treatment. The British excel in Old

World courtesy. You can't walk down a street without some bobby, twirling his nightstick, pointing out a quaint pub or a monument from the Wars of the Roses. The very stones under your feet seem to be saturated with tradition.

And the shopping! I don't know if anyone has commented on this before, but London is a man's town—I mean, it caters to the masculine sex. You wouldn't believe the wealth of hats and sweaters and shirts on view along Piccadilly and Bond Street; the two of us used to come back to the hotel every night dead tired, loaded with bundles. Marcy got some nice things, too—a cute leather address book to fit in her purse and a box of those chocolate-covered mints women love. I hadn't planned on buying any clothes except a tweed jacket or so and a few pairs of slacks, until Tom Greshler at the bureau talked me into having some suits made in Savile Row. Well, sir, it was one hell of an experience. His tailor's was like a cathedral, all walnut-paneled and Dickensian sporting prints, and three different cutters to measure the coat, weskit, and trousers. I got into a real bind with the man in charge of the coat, though. He kept nagging me to let them pad the shoulders and nip in the waist, and I finally had to straighten him out.

"Listen, what do you think I am—a gigolo?" I asked him. I wasn't aggressive—just firm. "Next thing I know, you'll have me wearing a monocle. I can't afford to look like a freak at the office, Algy—we're a conservative outfit. Either copy this Brooks model of mine or knock it off."

That did the trick, and from then on they were as sweet as pie. They yessed me to death, arranged to mail over my duds without fittings and all that jazz, and never even asked for identification for my Express checks. Tom thought it'd be a good idea work-wise for me to see the inside of an English club while I was there, so he and I went around to the Cheesemongers, which extends guest privileges to our staff. One tradition of this male stronghold still observed from yesteryear, I learned, is a washroom where the brushes and combs are chained to the wall to prevent their being stolen. As luncheon fare, we partook of a cut off the joint, two vegs., and a pint of bitter, and after I lay down in the reading room for a spell I felt OK again. While drenched in the atmosphere, I dashed off a couple of notes to our researchers in New York, with gags like "Well, slaves, here I am in jolly old Lunnon," etc. Their eyes must have popped when they saw the club stationery.

The minute I got back to the hotel that afternoon Marcy was bursting with some kind of news. In that typical feminine way, it was upside down and backward, but I finally pieced it together. An hour before, in the tearoom at Harrods, she'd run into Ailsa and Jock Beasley, who belong to our country club in Smoke Hills.

"You remember Montague Pauncefoot, don't you?" Marcy reminded me. "The English checker at the Val-U-Mart—the thin blond boy?"

"Sort of a washed-out character, with a smirk?"

"Yes, but very nice," she said. "Well, he's suddenly become a nobleman—Lord Grubstone. The papers were full of it—how he was keeping the job in spite of his title and preferred to remain just plain Monty and heaven knows what. I guess it was so much talk, though, because hardly a week later, Ailsa heard, he and his wife returned to England."

"It figures," I said. "After all, a peer like that has responsibilities toward his tenants—the gamekeepers and farmers who till his estates. . . . You know, now I think of it, there *was* something rather distinguished about him. His carriage, or maybe the bone structure in his face."

"That wasn't the impression you gave. You said he was an obnoxious little pimple."

"Will you kindly stop putting words in my mouth, for Chrisake?" I said. "Sure, he had a somewhat unusual accent, but they can't help that—it's part of their lineage. No, we were on damned good terms, Monty and I, and I often meant to ask him out to the house."

"Well, you missed the boat."

"Not at all," I said. "Why couldn't we look him up here? He's a democratic guy—he'd get a bang out of a couple of his old customers dropping by."

"Don't be absurd," she said. "I grant you he was always very generous with cartons, and helpful when I couldn't find the horse-radish or whatever, but he'd never remember us, honest and truly. Now let's forget it—I have to change if we're to make the night tour of Soho."

Well, I saw there was no sense arguing, and clammed up. The next morning, though, I called Tom's secretary at the bureau and asked for a quick rundown on a certain titled family, the location of their ancestral seat, and the sightseeing in the vicinity. By the end of the day I had the info I needed and everything in readiness. Marcy was pretty suspicious when I started bleating about this ruined abbey in Oxfordshire we mustn't miss; the old female intuition told her something was cooking, but I snowed her with a lot of doubletalk about Chaucer and Piers Plowman the secretary had pulled out, and she gave in. So right after breakfast we caught a train to a place with a name that broke us up—Leighton Buzzard —and taxied out to the ruins. It was nothing you'd look at twice, of course—half a dozen beat-up arches covered with ivy—and I didn't blame Marcy for crabbing at the trouble we'd gone to. I waited until we got back into the cab to spring it.

"Who owns most of the ground hereabouts?" I queried the driver. "Is it part of an estate or something?"

"Yes, Lord Grubstone's, sir. The Hall is up there, just beyond that copse."

"You're kidding!" I said. "Of all the fantastic—Marcy, did you hear that? Monty, the Val-U-Mart fellow—five minutes away! It's a perfect opportunity to buzz over and say hello—we'd be dopes not to!"

She knew it was a put-up job, but she couldn't squawk with the driver listening, and before she had a chance to we were on our way. The house, instead of the huge, frowning affair with turrets I expected, was on the dinky side, a grayish stone box the size of a branch library, squatting on a half acre of gravel. The butler who answered the door—and he took his time about it—looked like a road-company Robert Morley at the Paper Mill Playhouse. He gave us a frosty once-over, and when I said our name didn't matter, we wanted to surprise His Lordship, he motioned us into a side chamber. It seemed to be only a storeroom, judging from the case of stuffed birds and a set of *Punch* dating back to 1841, but all of a sudden a red-nosed old gaffer, in a stock, shot up from an armchair he was asleep in. The way he reacted, you'd have thought we came off a flying saucer.

"I say, what are you—Australians?" he exclaimed.

I told him, and that really alarmed him.

"Actually? I've never seen any before. Er—excuse me."

He scurried out, and as Marcy began needling me to leave, Monty appeared. For a split second I had trouble recognizing him. He wasn't wearing the white duster and the pencil behind his ear any longer, naturally; he had on like a Little Lord Fauntleroy costume—a velvet suit with a ruffled shirt foaming out of the collar—and he wore his hair in a tomboy bang. But also his whole manner was different—a mixture of peevish and hoity-toity, totally unlike the old days.

"Yes?" he snapped out. "You wished to see me?"

Figuring we might have interrupted him in a game of chess or something, I took the bull by the horns—recalled ourselves to him and congratulated him on his new status.

To my amazement he gave us a complete deadpan. "I'm afraid you're quite mistaken," he drawled, looking down his nose. "I *have* been in the States briefly, but never under the circumstances you describe. If I may say so, the American visitor to our shores sometimes tends to become a bit—ah—*dérangé.*"

I started to get hot under the collar. "Are you suggesting we're unbalanced?" I said. "Why, Marcy and I have seen you at the check-out counter for the past—"

"Sweetheart, let's go," she interrupted. "Lord Grubstone's right —we've made a stupid error, apparently."

His face grew a little more human. "Frightfully sorry to cause you this misapprehension," he said. "You *are* guests in this country, I suppose. . . . Look here—we were just sitting down to lunch with some people. Perhaps you'd care to join us?"

Well, Marcy wouldn't hear of it, but I was so mystified and at the same time riled by his reception that I insisted. Also, for one molding opinion on the foreign-news desk, it was a splendid chance to observe British aristocracy at close range. There were eight or nine persons, mainly oldsters, chattering away in the dining room, and hardly anyone looked up when our host introduced us as newcomers from overseas. I was wedged in next to a horsy old party with porcelain choppers who was lambasting Harold Wilson. Pretty soon he turned and, out of the blue, asked how long I'd been in the Coldstream Guards. I said I never was.

"But you must have done, damn it," he said. "You're wearing their regimental tie."

I explained I had bought it at Turncoat's, in Jermyn Street, the day before.

"Then take it back at once, man," he said, his wattles quivering like a turkey's. "You ought to be ashamed, parading around under false colors. No wonder the country's going to the demnition bowwows."

I was about to pin his ears back when a gargoyle in a beaded hat opposite quickly chimed in. The mischief had started in America, where nothing was sacred, she claimed. "And what do you expect, with that intolerable central heating of theirs? It dries up the mucous membrane, addles one's speech—"

"To say nothing of the swindling," another old buzzard croaked. "The worst bobbery I've met with this side of Shanghai. You put a sixpence in a stamp machine and the wretched thing invariably holds back a penny. The Mafia's share, of course."

That broke the ice, and they all began sounding off. A chap's shoes were likely to be stolen from outside his hotel room, and decent food was unobtainable; you couldn't buy a pilchard anywhere for love or money. I was so burned up by then, what with Grubstone's pretense of not being Monty and his sitting there, the muzzler, relishing us squirm, that I wanted to grab Marcy and blow the joint. Still, I felt I had to unmask the faker, make him admit we knew him when. And just like that, the inspiration came to me—*voom*.

I raised my voice a trifle—enough to carry to the head of the table. "Speaking of stamps, My Lord," I said blandly, "my wife over there and I have a beef that involves you. Why didn't you folks at the Val-U-Mart ever give out any green or blue ones, like the Acme or the Grand Union?" The entire place got deathly still —not a sound. "I'll tell you why," I said, gathering momentum. "Because you were a cheap, fly-by-night outfit, a bunch of chiselers. You handled the crummiest brand names, the most inferior meats, and baked goods you could insulate a roof with, and, brother, what a markup—ten and fifteen cents on each item! . . . No, Marcy, I won't shut up—he knows the score! He knows how they cheated us on the empty bottles we brought back, those flimsy bags that burst halfway to the car. They taught him how to gouge the public, never you fear!"

Well, it was almost scary, the effect of my taunt. I had in mind to jolt the truth out of him, bring him down off his high horse, but I didn't dream the form it would take. His expression slowly changed like Jack Palance's in *Jekyll and Hyde*; one moment he was the smooth, disdainful dandy born to the purple, the next he was out of his chair, a raging fiend. He was practically incoherent. "That's a typical customer for you!" he shouted. "Yes, I know your kind, all right—clogging the express lane with twelve loaves of white bread, mixing up the dog food, mauling the bananas! You're the type that buys a pint of coleslaw after sampling the whole delicatessen case, that cadges free suet from the butcher to save on birdseed, that leaves his shopping cart in a snowdrift at the end of the parking area! Oh, I've seen you altering the prices on the canned salmon, filching beet greens to put in your soup!" He hammered on the tabletop with his clenched fists. "I hate every mother's son of you —do you hear? I rue the day I ever set foot in New Jersey!"

Whether it was the man's humiliation at being exposed in his own home or the strain of his outburst, that settled Lord Grubstone's hash; he was still sitting there, with egg on his face and the company frozen like the waxworks at Madame Tussaud's, as the two of us made our exit. Marcy didn't have much to say until the train had left Leighton Buzzard, and then she opened up. It was pretty personal stuff, but, to tell the truth, I wasn't listening. I was too busy formulating in my mind's eye the story I was going to cable back on swinging London and the decay of the British Establishment.

I Hate Spanish Moss

Whisper-soft and panther-sleek, its sextuple cylinders obedient to the smallest whim of my powerful credit card, the rented 1951 convertible crept into the orchard where the houseboat *Sleepyhead* lay moored in Florida's Lemon River and, shearing a banana palm off at the base as neatly as a toothpick, shuddered to a stop. The dozen passengers assembled for our voyage through Lake Okeechobee's fabled waterways, ranging in age from 70 to 103, abruptly broke off their denunciation of the Red termites gnawing at the Taft-Hartley Act and gaped as I fought to extricate myself from behind the wheel.

"The seat belt, dear, the seat belt," my spouse murmured with the benevolent smile that provokes universal wife-beating. "Why don't you loosen it before you wrench off the floorboards?"

Sooner than sully my lips with a riposte that would have shriveled the creature, had I been able to think of it, I withdrew a penknife, sawed through the nylon straps and descended to appraise the craft that was to house us through the ensuing long weekend. Seventy feet by fourteen, she was a triumph of naval architecture, an authentic cheesebox-on-a-raft in the tradition of the early ironclads. Her gunwales, gently awash in the brown current, afforded easy access for any venturesome 'gator or water moccasin, and the lofty superstructure, cunningly designed to entangle overhanging vegetation, gave every expectation of capsizing at the merest zephyr. To add a further ominous note, an anguished, protracted wheeze like Cheyne-Stokes breathing issued from the outboard motor, currently being flailed into submission by a derelict with a stillson wrench. I directed my wife to carry our luggage aboard, and strolling over, inquired of a wizened bystander on the order of Popeye, whose cap sported an official emblem, what was amiss. He jetted a stream of tobacco juice past my feet.

"Ah hain't the skipper," he said. "He's up in the galley, a-stowin' the lard fer to fry the vittles." I asked if he was one of the tour. "Naw, Ah'm just Jake Vulture, an aged recluse that comes down heah fer chuckles," he said. "Hit's better'n a TV show. You-all fully covered?"

"Er—what do you mean?" I asked apprehensively.

"Nawthin'," he said, moving off rather quickly. "Never said a word. And Ah hain't seen a single body, nary a bone."

In the unavoidable ritual of dry grins and wet handclasps that acquainted us with our fellow passengers, my premonitions, far from being stilled, waxed and bloomed. The patriarchs of the group, two gaffers resident in Saint Augustine, hailed originally from Vermont; Mr. Higbie had been assistant usurer of a finance company, Mr. Sopwith a salesman for rat cheese, and their wives, unbeknownst to themselves, models for Grant Wood's "American Gothic." Messrs. Crump and Futtrell, fresh out of Moline, exuded equal parts of bonhomie and bourbon; the former was a roofing contractor, and his friend a wholesale feed merchant. The sinuses of Mr. and Mrs. Pforzheimer, Far Hills, N.J., were so painfully clogged with refinement as to render their speech inaudible. Of the remaining quartet, Mr. Dutcher was a onetime C.P.A. from Oswego, Mr. Krebs the owner of a Turkish bath in Fall River, and Dr. Alewife a retired osteopath, whose wife was plainly feeding him arsenic in small doses.

The nautical ballet attending the *Sleepyhead*'s departure might have been lifted in its entirety from some Hasty Pudding show whose actors were befuddled with muscatel. When Captain Zack, a marine version of Mr. Coffee-Nerves, and Freckles, his youthful mate, finally unsnarled the lines and we slipped downstream, I already heard the scratch of underwriters' pens and the Lutine bell tolling at Lloyd's. As for the passengers, they behaved with utter childishness. Mulishly ignoring my insistence that the scenery was a sham, a photomural supplied by a display firm in Fort Myers, they hung on the rails extolling the wealth of Spanish moss wreathing the mangroves, the profusion of orchids, herons and ibis. The imposture became apparent soon enough. Suddenly the foliage vanished and we blundered into an endless, dismal network of canals bordering a potash plant. Luckily, just as some of the company were coughing their last from sulphur fumes, the cook's tocsin sounded, heralding lunch, and every man jack of us, even those incapacitated by scurvy, scrambled to safety in the mess hall.

"Remember the menu at our hotel in Bali back in 1949?" my wife asked under her breath, surreptitiously wiping a fork on her underskirt.

"Let me think," I said. "Canned pea soup with frankfurters from Holland, pigs' knuckles and sauerkraut, and preserved pineapple, wasn't it?"

"Yes, and lashings of zwieback," she added. "Well, hold your hat—here come some more of those tropical viands."

Her woman's instinct was unerring. The table groaned under platters of smoking hot wieners flanked by creamed spinach, giant cartwheels of unripe tomato, and biscuits that discharged a miasma of flour as one wrenched them apart. Packed shoulder to shoulder in the moist heat, their eyeballs rolling wildly, our companions ate like famished lumberjacks. Their dialogue, while more aseptic than that in a logging camp, was far less sparkling. Everyone there, it appeared, had a particularly favorite TV commercial. One by one, in neuralgic detail, they discoursed on the myriad detergents and deodorants inhibiting personal and public stench—the compounds that shrink the nasal passages, whiten the baby's laundry, prevent the drip of hydrochloric acid into the stomach and vanquish the smells repugnant to associates. Wearied at length by the hosannas for Ajax's White Knight and Tums, I decided to evoke intellectual discussion. Had anyone present detected a kinship between Robinson Jeffers' *Big Sur* and the early cantos of Ezra Pound? Mr. Krebs emitted a shrill "Whoo whoo!" and Crump and Futtrell exchanged owlish winks signifying I was a closet transvestite. I arose with icy dignity to get a breath of air, but since we were all packed in like sardines, had to subside in hot-faced humiliation till the meal ended.

A succession of absorbing sights and sounds awaited us throughout the afternoon. Dredges innumerable lined the waterway, sculpturing mud into ever-changing patterns on the banks; buzzards flapped overhead, closely scrutinizing our party, and whenever the eye tired of the panorama, it could always rest on a gaunt Brahma grazing in the palmetto scrub. At dusk we warped into Wilhelmina, a decayed hamlet obviously subsidized by Carson McCullers to furnish her with literary material. Eight of its stores were untenanted, the ninth occupied by a waxworks portraying a group of pellagra victims frozen around a pinball machine.

Sleep that night was fitful; there was a scant three-inch clearance in the upper bunk between pillow and ceiling, across which someone had looped a strand of BX that abraded my nose if I threshed about unduly. My wife's situation was relatively idyllic, her only concern the whereabouts of half a dozen spiders she had surprised in the sheets at bedtime.

The next day's progress was marked by a sudden contretemps. Soon after ascending a series of locks into Lake Okeechobee, each more fascinating than the last, our engine expired. Captain Zack, whose mechanical skill barely sufficed to open a jar of olives, thereupon burst into tears and hid in his cabin. With admirable presence, though, one of the womenfolk plunged a broom straw into the gas tank and discovered it was empty. In a trice, panic, which can be fatal at sea, was averted; Freckles was dispatched in the dinghy to the nearest garage, and by midafternoon the *Sleepyhead* was wallowing forward amid an aroma of hot wieners that tickled the salivary glands. Still to come, however, was a feature eulogized in the prospectus—a thrilling ride in an airboat. In due course the propeller-driven scow materialized, churning up a wake of dead catfish that Freckles quickly scooped up to augment our larder. I let myself be persuaded aboard, and hand in hand with Mrs. Alewife, hurtled off into the reeds. The wind whistling through her porcelain dentures provided a most romantic obbligato, and I might well have stolen a kiss had not a blade of saw grass dislodged my glasses. By the time we returned shipside, the opportunity had passed—perhaps just as well, for the carnal side of my nature, once aroused, knows no restraint.

The small talk during dinner that evening, due to our enforced intimacy, disclosed some unsuspected idiosyncrasies in our number. Mrs. Sopwith and Mr. Dutcher, whom I would have guessed off-hand to be partial to radishes, disliked radishes because they repeated. Mr. Futtrell asserted that Harvard beets, unless taken in moderation, induce heartburn. Mr. Krebs nursed a prejudice against eating baked potatoes in restaurants, a maternal uncle of his having strangled on a piece of tinfoil at a Boston chophouse. I was about to describe my wife's aversion to baked dog and fire-water, the result of her childhood among the Ogalala Sioux, when an unmistakable kick under the table sealed my lips. It occurred to me afterward that I might have been wrong; could Mrs. Alewife, under a pretense of administering arsenic to her husband, have possibly sent me an amorous signal? But it was too late to turn back the clock. On such gossamer threads does one's destiny impend.

Our anchorage for the night lay some fifteen miles distant at

Glen Gravel, a settlement built around a stone quarry and a sugar mill operating around the clock on some mysterious exchange basis. They were linked by a bridge under which we moored, and all night long the trucks rumbling between sifted a fine rain of grit mixed with unrefined sugar into the *Sleepyhead*'s hatches. Everyone was a trifle edgy, therefore, when one of the trucks drew alongside the next morning and a phony wrangler out of a TV western boisterously herded us inside. The vehicle, it developed, was a so-called swamp buggy, a furniture van with low-pressure tires adapted for picnicking in marshlands.

"I loathe marshlands," my wife snapped as we jolted along over an interminable highway. "I loathe picnics, too, for that matter. This is typical summer-camp sadism. You wait—before the day is over, they'll chop down some kind of bush and make us eat it."

Stunted as is her intelligence, the woman has a prophetic gift. No sooner had we reached our goal, a federal game reserve, than our guide felled a cabbage palm, extracted the pith and boiled it up with bacon and onions to the consistency of warm linoleum paste. Armed with platefuls of the goodge and charred hamburgers, we all stood about gazing apathetically at the hundreds of gnarled roots protruding from the savanna. These cypress knees, it was explained, are much prized for their artistic beauty; given three coats of orange shellac, they make lovely tie racks and bases for lamps, or alternatively, can be placed on a coffee table as conversation pieces.

"Those things wouldn't start a conversation between anybody but urologists," I observed to the guide. "Most of them look like bladders and kidneys. I wouldn't give 'em houseroom."

"Nobody asked you for houseroom," he retorted with asperity. "All we want out of you, brother, is a big, fat silence. Now, friends, lemme show you how us swamp denizens whittle a turkey call, and then I'll play some country hoedowns on my li'l ole gee-tah."

A malarial fog was shrouding the marshes and all of us were sneezing our heads off when once more we trooped aboard ship.

Spanish Moss

Except for a Phi Beta Kappa key Mr. Pforzheimer alleged to have lost on the outing, there had been no misadventures. The moment he was out of earshot, though, Mr. Higbie expressed doubt that Pforzheimer had ever owned such a thing; he was merely giving himself airs. Krebs, on the other hand, claimed to have seen the missing object but said it was a Playboy key. Quite a few present felt that since there was a diversity of opinion, a public debate should be held in the mess hall that evening on the topic "resolved, that Pforzheimer is an old fibber." I was urged to captain the affirmative team but declined, inasmuch as it was late and I still had a sizable area of my nose to scrape on the BX before we docked.

While the return journey would have been less of an anticlimax if someone had bothered to add a few new dredges, Captain Zack's cornucopia still managed to yield up a last-minute surprise or two. Our farewell lunch of hot wieners and catfish was enhanced by a regional delicacy, hush puppies encrusted in sturdy little jackets of lard. One of them rolled off the table during the meal and struck Mr. Sopwith in the foot, nearly fracturing his instep. Fortunately the pain abated and the former cheese merchant was left with an interesting anecdote he could spin to his cronies in Saint Augustine. About an hour later, as the vessel was re-entering the Lemon River, Mrs. Sopwith accidentally locked herself in the *cabinet d'aisance*, or head. Unavailing were her piteous appeals for rescue, useless the blows she showered on the door; the latch was jammed, and it seemed likely that the poor lady might be permanently entombed. At last a desperate solution was evolved. Two groups were organized, the first to batter down the door and the other, in a concerted action, to hurl itself against the cabin wall opposite. The scheme succeeded beyond expectation. With an apocalyptic crash, six people fell inward on Mrs. Sopwith in a melee like the Marx Brothers' stateroom in *A Night at the Opera*.

Others have achieved riches, renown, the love of fair woman; mine, contrariwise, has been a lifetime crammed with beauty. I have seen Angkor Wat at dawn, the Valley of the Kings at sunset and the Taj Mahal by moonlight—yet all paled beside that potash plant on the Lemon River as the houseboat crawled home to its landing. So overcome was I at our deliverance that I almost, but not quite, forgot to pinch Mrs. Alewife goodbye. Then, hurdling the gangplank with a song on my lips, I knelt down on my non-cypress knees, kissed the greensward, and gave it all back to the Indians—Okeechobee, the *Sleepyhead* and its walking dead, the whole shooting match. Henceforward I intend to weekend on terra firma, and north of the Mason-Dixon line.

Come, Costly Fido,
For I Am Sick With Love

Some five years ago *The New York Times* published an article on the drama that ensues in auction rooms, larded with an anecdote whose significance, I confess, I was too obtuse to grasp at the time. Mr. Louis J. Marion, of the Parke-Bernet Galleries, was recalling an auction thirty-five years earlier "when bidding for copper pots and pans electrified an audience." William Randolph Hearst and Francis P. Garvin, it appeared, were vying through representatives for kitchenware valued at two hundred dollars. "The bidding climbed relentlessly and shockingly, he said, to $3,500, because the respective agents had been ordered to buy 'at any price.' At that point, Hiram H. Parke, the auctioneer, stopped the sale and retired to his office with the agents in tow. After reprimanding them for their foolish stubbornness, he decided that the lot should revert to the estate so that neither could have it."

This frosty rejection of the clients' money, and the wigging administered by the auctioneer, seemed to me capricious, if not downright inexplicable, but three years later I ran up against another example of scorn for mere lucre—an advertisement for Merrill Lynch, Pierce, Fenner & Smith, the brokers. Headed "The Check We Didn't Take," it read thus: "He wasn't used to dealing with brokers—that was obvious—but there he was, sitting in a Merrill Lynch office talking with one of our Account Executives. All he wanted was to buy $7,000 worth of a certain stock, and he laid a check for that amount on the desk. Simple request. Easy sale. But the Account Executive asked him a few questions first about himself, his financial circumstances, his reasons for buying that particular stock. It didn't take long to find out that the man really knew little or nothing about stocks, bonds, or investing. And that's when the Merrill Lynch Account Executive politely refused to accept the check."

Here was a switch indeed—a customer of unimpeachable solvency being kissed off because he had failed to prove his competence as a shareholder. True, the suppliant wasn't castigated for his presumption, like the bidders at Parke-Bernet, but you didn't have to be an entomologist or an otologist to know that he slunk out with a flea in his ear. The whole relationship between buyer and seller, I began to surmise, was undergoing an upheaval—a suspicion confirmed not long ago by an advertisement in the pet section of the *Times*. Its tone was succinct and uncompromising: "Super Special for Dog Purchaser with the perfect background of love and knowledge of dogs who passes our approval. We have on display the son of———, 8 months old, 2½ pounds. Price $1,500. (Money alone will not qualify the purchaser.)"

Whereas the two previous items had only occasioned perplexity, I felt a surge of resentment at this newest bit of *chutzpah*. The dealer wasn't advertising a pet; he was hurling a defi at animal lovers in general, taunting them to shape up to his standards and clearly implying they hadn't a Chinaman's chance. The longer I thought about it, the more it struck me as a personal challenge. Frankly, I couldn't think of anything I needed less than a poodle weighing two and a half pounds, but that was irrelevant. What *was* imperative was to demonstrate that no power on earth could prevent me from owning the creature, and I resolved to prove it, come hell or high water, if it took my last penny.

Mr. Lupus, the official to whose desk I was directed in the loan department of my bank, had twin gimlets in lieu of eyes, and they bored into me as I wrote out my application. Thinking to ingratiate myself while he was scrutinizing it, I essayed a guess about his antecedents.

"Very unusual name that—Lupus," I said. "It means 'wolf,' doesn't it?"

His nod was superfluous, for as he moistened his lips to speak I caught a glint of yellow fangs. "What's the purpose of this loan?" he asked. "Home improvement? New automobile?"

"Why—er—not exactly," I said. "I'm figuring on buying a dog. That is, I'm not buying him, but I don't want anyone to think, or not think, that I can't *not* buy the dog, or conversely buy him, if I want to, or don't want to, as the case may be."

Mr. Lupus extended his hand and shook mine warmly. "Sir," he said, "I'd like you to know how unusual it is meeting a man who can express himself in a forthright, unequivocal fashion. You sit here day after day listening to people bumbling on until you're well-nigh frantic, wondering what in tarnation they're driving at—and then in comes a chap like yourself, who in a few crisp words clarifies his needs so even a child can understand."

"Thank you," I said. "I think you're pretty special, too, Mr. Lupus. Now, where do I go to pick up the bread?"

"To the moon," he snapped. "Do you suppose that's how a bank stays in business, loaning money to moochers to not buy dogs? Get out of here before we hit you with a vagrancy rap."

To encounter a setback at the very outset was a bit daunting, but I wasn't going to let it throw me. When the time came to pony up the fifteen hundred dollars for the animal, I told myself, I'd manage somehow—hadn't the advertisement specifically stated that the money was secondary? Still, it was essential to create an impression of affluence; from the moment I walked into his premises, the shopkeeper must recognize me as a man of substance, one capable of indulging any passing whim. I accordingly repaired to a theatrical costumer in the Times Square district and bade him supply me with a cutaway coat and pencil-striped pants, an ascot tie, a silk hat, and a pair of red socks. Garbed in the classic raiment of Jiggs, the lovable Croesus of "Bringing Up Father," and with a cigar stub clenched between my teeth, I was satisfied I projected an image that would impress even the most highfalutin tradesman. The vehicle I engaged for the trip to the dog boutique, a cream-colored Rolls phaeton, was not ideal for the purpose; there was about it a hint of *nouveau riche,* accented by the chauffeur's gold livery, that could be construed as vulgar opulence. However, since we were not going to drive into the store itself, I finally decided it was inconsequential. Le Chien Chic was a small, elegant establishment in the East Sixties whose doorman viewed our equipage with icy indifference as we drew up at the curb. The sight of my red socks did ruffle his composure a whit, for few of the clientele, I judged, ever called in their stocking feet, but he made no effort to bar my progress. The interior of the shop was a carpeted salon tastefully decorated in Louis XV style, altogether devoid of the wire cages, leashes, and canine playthings usual in such places. A young lady in a surgical smock, seated at a desk near the entrance, languidly surveyed me up and down and inquired what I wanted.

"The fifteen-hundred-dollar pooch you people advertised," I began, handing her my card. "Who do I see—"

"Please," she said, with a pained grimace. "We never use terms like that here. All our animals are individuals, each with his own clearly defined qualities and characteristics, and to permit any of them to be so labeled would be a cheap and gratuitous insult."

"My dear young woman, I don't propose to argue semantics with you," I said impatiently. "I'll have you know I left a very important board meeting to come here, involving the consolidation of several TV networks, an airline, and numerous chain stores. Furthermore, should you need added proof of my fiscal stability, I have in my breast pocket here a list of the securities in my portfolio, totaling upward of twenty-seven million dollars."

"I doubt if that makes a particle of difference," she said haughtily. "You'll still have to take your place with the other applicants back there." Only then did I notice the ribbon of folk queued up at the rear, who, judging from their patrician scowls, were not the sort accustomed to be kept waiting. "Just get in line, Mr. Gotrox, and your credentials will be processed in due course."

Lacking any alternative, I complied, and discreetly took stock of my fellow candidates. They were clearly upper-drawer—a dowager with a swelling port like a ship's figurehead, a horsy young matron in a shift lettered "Ethel Walker School, Simsbury, Conn.," an effete fashion plate with lace cascading down his bosom, and a scarlet-faced old plutocrat, redolent of brandy and fine cigars, restlessly swishing a hunting crop. Forbidding though he seemed, I thought he might enlighten me about the likelihood of qualifying for the poodle. He was far from optimistic.

"Better not raise any false hopes," he warned. "This is the third time I've tried to buy a dog from these chaps, and I haven't a clue yet whether I'll make the grade. They're sticklers—absolute perfectionists—and, take it from me, you can't bulldoze them."

"We'll see about that," I said grimly. "I'm a pretty influential cuss in my neck of the woods, Mister. The name Irving Gotrox opens a lot of doors east of the Mississippi."

He smiled pityingly. "Look, friend, get this through your skull," he said. "You could paper these walls with greenbacks for all they care—money only antagonizes them. Why, I've brought in diamonds of the finest water, twice the size of the Koh-i-noor; airplane views of my estates in Tuxedo Park, Upperville, Puerto Vallarta, and Kenya; notarized transparencies of my yacht proving it to be

91

fifteen feet longer than J. P. Morgan's *Corsair*—and they still won't consider me. I haven't given up hope, though," he went on, lowering his voice to a whisper. "I'm trying a whole new approach today."

"What's that?"

"Self-development," he said. "I've been taking a course in the great philosophers at the New School for Social Research. It's given me a breadth of vision I never had before."

"Do you think it'll raise your status with these people as a dog owner?" I asked, endeavoring to contain my skepticism.

"Search me," he said helplessly, "but I've got to do *something*. I can't go on this way, a scarlet-faced old plutocrat, redolent of brandy and fine cigars."

The line of aspirants had meanwhile dwindled, and those who had preceded us were emerging chopfallen, failure writ large on their countenances. I bade the old party take heart when it came his turn, but the verdict was all too evident as he reappeared, his shoulders bowed in defeat.

"It's no use—they won't have me," he said brokenly. "And I can't say I blame them. What does a two-and-a-half-pound puppy know or care about Spinoza, Locke, and Schopenhauer? He wants to be cuddled, caressed, fussed over—not smothered in pelf. Ah, well, no sense blubbering; go ahead in, sir, and the best of luck to you. You deserve it—you've a heart as big as all outdoors."

The two individuals confronting me in the cubicle I entered were not the type to bolster one's self-confidence. The unwavering, flinty eyes under their razor-cut manes had an intensity, a pitiless zeal that reminded me of Savonarola. To attempt to overwhelm fanatics such as these with cash, instinct told me, would be folly; I must match wits with them. I held up my hand before either could speak.

"Let's set the record straight at once, fellows," I began. "More than likely, from these clothes I'm wearing you've already categorized me as an uncouth parvenu of illimitable wealth. Well, nothing could be further from the truth—I'm as poor as a church mouse."

"What's that you say?" one of the partners inquired, frowning. "You mean you don't even have the requisite fee to purchase our animal?"

"Not a farthing," I said firmly. "But if it's character, and wisdom, and—yes—nobility you ask of his purchaser, then yours truly has them aplenty. I'm a wonderful human being, gentlemen—the sort you don't often meet nowadays. All kinds of creatures, great and small, take an instant shine to me—it's a blend of sweet and sour in my makeup they can't quite put their finger on. Withal, I'm as smart as paint, as neat as a pin, and as sharp as a tack, though I can be as dull as a hoe if occasion demands."

"Hmm, this is refreshing," the other partner commented. "He seems to possess a grace, a benevolence all the previous applicants have lacked."

"A saintly quality, almost," his colleague agreed. "I get the feeling of terrific magnanimity. Am I mistaken?"

"On the contrary," I replied. "It's my outstanding trait, and I can promise you it'll be expended without stint on that beast of yours if he becomes mine. Yes, sir, little Toto—little Froufrou—what the devil *is* his name?" It was Toodles, they signified. "Right," I said. "Well, from here in, he's never going to want for a thing, believe me. He'll sleep on snowiest damask, he'll dine off caviar on silver plates, he'll be petted and cosseted within an inch of his life. OK, friends, what's your decision?"

The pair regarded me thoughtfully for a moment, then put their heads together in a whispered colloquy. When they revolved back toward me, it was pikestaff-plain I had won the day.

"Maybe we're just two sentimental fools, Mr. Gotrox," said the first. "Still and all, your features radiate such benign good will, such tranquillity of spirit that we can't bear to gainsay you. Take him, and as for the money—well, forget it. Nobody could begrudge so small a price for meeting a man of your stature."

"Most trenchantly put," I acknowledged. "However, and much as I hate to look a gift horse in the mouth, I've got news for you—I can't use the animal. I already have two dogs, and they're driving me up the wall. The last thing I want is another varmint yapping at my heels and unraveling the carpets. So let's leave it there, boys, and watch it—the next time you have a litter, I'll thank you to keep a civil tongue in your advertising. Good day."

And watch it they did, for nary another pygmy poodle have I seen offered since, with or without owner's pedigree. It just goes to show how inessential—in fact, what a positive handicap—money's become these days. That is, to everyone but Mr. Lupus at the bank, may a pox fly away with him.

Be a Cat's-Paw!
Lose Big Money!

Anybody can be a wiseacre after the fact, so let's get one thing straight at the outset. In chronicling the complications that arose from a note I found this spring in a bottle on Martha's Vineyard, I am not whining for sympathy or seeking to condone my behavior. If a totally unselfish gesture to a stranger—a benefaction, really—is wrong, then I was culpable and richly deserving of what I got. Impulsive, overly sentimental I may have been, but never throughout the ensuing imbroglio, I contend, was I prompted by base or ignoble motives. On the contrary, I like to think that, though an innocent dupe, I acquitted myself at all times with a dignity, a gentility, few other dupes in my position would have displayed. That is what I like to think.

The circumstances under which I discovered the note couldn't have been less dramatic. I was strolling along South Beach on the Vineyard one morning midway between Gay Head and Zack's Cliffs, and there, squarely in my path, lay a flask of the sort that usually contains stuffed olives. On the scrap of paper inside, in a clearly juvenile hand, was the following: "My name is Donald Cropsey. I am twelve years old. I live at 1322 Catalpa Way, Reliance, Ohio. I have been visiting on Nantucket for a week. I threw this bottle off the ferryboat between Nantucket and Woods Hole, Mass., on Saturday. Please write me a note telling me when and where you found it."

Now, twelve-year-old boys, and especially those who litter the shoreline with glass, invariably raise my hackles, but somehow this message disarmed me. Its style was direct and unaffected, there was nothing cringing or subservient about it, and it exuded a manly independence characteristic of the wide-awake youngsters that Horatio Alger and Oliver Optic used to portray. I therefore pocketed the note—figuratively, that is, since I wore only bathing trunks—and later in the day complied with Donald's request. After recounting how it had reached me, I felicitated him on his vigorous, clean-cut rhetoric and his astuteness in modeling himself on such masters of English prose as Hazlitt and Defoe. Lest his ego become inflated, however, I hastened to point out that his handwriting was sorely deficient. "You will forgive me if I speak quite bluntly, my boy," I wrote, "but this progressive-school script of yours demeans you. I cannot stress too strongly the importance of good calligraphy in molding your future. A firm business hand with well-shaped capitals is a prerequisite in every field, be it the counting house, a mercantile establishment, or a profession like law or medicine. I suggest, accordingly, that you proceed with all dispatch to perfect yourself in the exercise known as Hammond arm movement, keeping the wrist flexible at all times and practicing the letter 'l' lying on its side."

As I weighed the foregoing prior to sealing the letter, it struck me that a few words of counsel to the lad on his reading would not be amiss. I recommended, hence, that he familiarize himself with all the works of Henty, with the stories of Harry Castlemon (*Frank Before Vicksburg, Frank on a Gunboat*, etc.), with Ralph Henry Barbour's *Around the End*, and with anything by Altsheler he could find. He might also browse through the files of Hearst's *American Weekly* with profit, I added, quoting examples of the curious lore to be found there—the S.S. *Vaterland* posed vertically against the Singer Building to contrast their size, the eye of the common housefly magnified a hundredfold, the milk baths and other beauty secrets of Lina Cavalieri and Gaby Deslys, the advice on physical fitness from Jess Willard, and the disclosures about high society's Four Hundred by Count Boni de Castellane. In closing, I extended warm wishes and urged him to put his best foot forward, his shoulder to the wheel, and his nose to the grindstone—a pose guaranteed to excite the compassion of influential folk who might help him in his career.

I had quite forgotten the episode when, a month later in New York, I received a letter from a Mrs. Rhonda Cropsey. Writing on the stationery of a midtown hotel, she identified herself as Donald's mother and thanked me effusively for my epistle. She had taken the liberty of opening it, inasmuch as her son was in El Moribundo, California, visiting his father, from whom she was estranged. So brilliant, so truly inspired was my letter that before forwarding it she had made a copy, which she reread daily until every syllable was engraved on her heart.

"What a wonderful person you must be," she went on. "A kind of saint, I imagine. Who else would trouble to reply to a child they didn't know, or bother to outline a program of studies to enlarge the little fellow's horizon? Never in all my twenty-eight years—yes, I am that young, even if I sound like an old fuddy-duddy—have I felt such gratitude to an individual. I really would do anything to reward them. . . . But here I am wasting your valuable time with my silly-billy compliments; I guess I just can't help 'fessing up to hero worship if I feel same. Anyway, the reason for my contacting you at present is that I am in your bailiwick a day or two shopping for some feminine 'frillies' and wonder could we meet for five minutes to discuss little Don's next educational step. Won't you ring me very soon, pretty please?"

Well, that put me on the spot for fair. Here was a doting mama, undoubtedly a frump from backwoods Ohio, thirsting to talk me deaf, dumb, and blind about her precious darling, and yet to ignore her appeal would be tantamount to a slap in the face. I stewed over the problem for a good ten minutes and finally had an inspiration. I'd humor the woman and phone, but avoid any confrontation, wheedle or coax me though she might.

"Hello? . . . Yes, this is Rhonda Cropsey." The voice wasn't at all what I'd expected. It was low-pitched and cool, and there was a delicious tremor in it that made one's spine tingle. "O-oh, can it really be *you?*"

"Who else?" I stammered. "I mean—hello. Yes, it's me. Look—er—I've just had a cancellation. I'm terribly busy as a rule, but I could be at some central point like the Plaza bar in half an hour, if that's not inconvenient for you."

Not in the least, she quickly assured me—that would be ideal. I then gave her painstaking, explicit instructions as to which bar I meant, in case she blundered into the Palm Court or the Edwardian Room. Actually, my fears were groundless; far from a flibbertigibbet, Mrs. Cropsey proved to be not only alert but a demure and strikingly attractive young matron. If her figure was a shade too sensual for true beauty, it was compensated for by features that some Pre-Raphaelite painter—Burne-Jones or Dante Gabriel Rossetti—might have limned. Under a wealth of corn-colored hair worn in a snood, a pair of blue eyes looked out at the world with such trustful innocence that it wrung your heart. Her lack of sophistication became further evident when I asked what beverage she fancied.

"I-I've never tasted anything stronger than fruit juice," she confessed shamefacedly. "That cocktail you're having—a sidecar—what is it?"

I explained it was a mild digestive, compounded of the merest trace of brandy and a drop of Cointreau, and, reassured, she ordered one also. In a few moments our initial constraint had vanished and we were chatting away like old friends. It seemed hardly possible, I remarked, that one so girlish could have a twelve-year-old son, and she was equally incredulous at my laughing admission that I was past thirty. From the wisdom, the magnanimity implicit in my letter to Donald, she was prepared for a man twice, if not thrice, my years.

"Gracious, what a difference between you and that husband of mine!" she murmured, a shadow of pain contorting her lovely forehead. "Do you know that that swine used to beat me black and blue?"

Since I had never laid eyes on the swine in question, I felt ill-equipped to pass judgment, so, limiting my reaction to a pitying headshake, I ordered another round of drinks and deftly steered the conversation to her son. Precisely what advice did she seek from me about his schooling? A guilty blush suffused Mrs. Cropsey's cheek, and she hung her head penitently. Concerned as she was for the boy's welfare, she admitted to an ulterior motive in approaching me. She had tentatively selected a number of frocks, suits, and coats at a Fifth Avenue store and wanted me, her sole friend in New York and a man of faultless discrimination and taste, to choose the most becoming from among them. She realized it was a dreadful imposition, she was already indebted to me beyond measure, but this one final boon would forever enshrine me in her affections, elevate me to Olympus. . . . In vain I protested my inadequacy to judge feminine fashions; the more vehement I grew, the more insistent she became, and at last, succumbing to a mixture of cajolery and sidecars, I broke down and assented.

In actual fact, the decisions Mrs. Cropsey exacted of me turned out to be trifling enough. I ran my eye expertly over the garments she was considering, compared various details of design and workmanship, and unerringly chose the best. The salesladies were frankly awed at my acumen, doubtless supposing that I was some biggie from the garment center. So harmonious was the atmosphere and so obliging the staff that my companion bought a few other articles—an expensive negligee, a couple of imported handbags, six pairs of shoes, and some diamond clips suitable for sportswear. At her request, and for a bumper fee, all the purchases were dispatched by messenger to her hotel, and a floorwalker, rubbing his hands and bowing obsequiously, escorted us to the credit office, where she was to make payment. Suddenly, as she was rummaging in her bag, she emitted a startled exclamation. "My traveler's checks!" she gasped. "They're gone—they've been stolen! No—no —wait! I remember now—I left them behind at the hotel."

Drumming his fingers on the desk top, Seamus Mandamus, my lawyer, regarded me fixedly for several seconds over his glasses. "I see," he said with infinite sympathy. "So you helped her out, I take it. You wrote a check for the amount and then returned to her hotel so she could reimburse you."

I stared at him nonplussed. "How did you know?"

"Oh, just instinct." His smile radiated sheer benevolence. "Now, let me guess. When you got there, Mrs. Cropsey remembered something else. She *hadn't* left her checks in the hotel safe, as she thought at first, but in her room. So you accompanied her upstairs —right?"

"It wasn't a room—it was a suite," I corrected. "She had a living room with a pantry, a bedroom—"

"Yes, yes, I know what a suite is," he said impatiently. "Anyhow, there was a fifth of Scotch and some ice in the pantry, so she invited you to fix a drink while she went into the bedroom to fetch the checks."

"This is uncanny!" I exclaimed. "I swear, you sound as though you'd been there the whole time."

"If I had, Buster, you wouldn't be sitting here now with an ashen face," he rejoined. "One minor point, though. How did you reconcile the bottle of hooch with the lady's earlier statement that she never drank anything stronger than fruit juice?"

"Why—uh—it didn't occur to me," I said. "I may have been a little fuzzy from the sidecars."

"And the strain of shopping and all." He nodded beningnly. "But I imagine the fuzziness evaporated pronto when Mrs. Cropsey reappeared, eh? Weren't you startled that she had slipped into something more comfortable—something clinging and filmy?"

"Great, Scott, man, you must be clairvoyant!" I marveled. "Matter of fact, I *was* bowled over. But then, on top of everything, before I could catch my breath, those two hooligans with the camera burst in. There was this blinding flash—"

"You needn't go on," he interrupted. "It's cut and dried, a standard procedure. Did the fair one break into hysterical sobs after they left and lock herself in the bedroom?"

"You took the words out of my mouth," I said. "I hammered on the door for over half an hour, but not a tumble did I get. That was the last of Rhonda Cropsey."

"Not quite," replied Mandamus gently. "In case you still don't know the score, it becomes my painful duty to enlighten you. You are currently a co-respondent in the divorce action of Cropsey *v.* Cropsey, and a large, angry department store whose check you stopped is suing you for eleven hundred and eighty-five dollars in merchandise. I wonder whether you've learned anything from this experience."

I certainly had, though I wouldn't admit it to *that* shyster. The next time I see a bottle on a beach—or anywhere else—I intend to compress my lips in a thin line and kick it out of my path. And that goes for all twelve-year-old brats on the Nantucket boat and their blasted mothers.

She Walks in Beauty—Single File, Eyes Front, and No Hanky-Panky

It was nigh on dusk that autumnal London afternoon when I came abreast of Whelp & Cunliffe's in Conduit Street and, as was increasingly my habit, paused to examine their famous waterproof shoe. Whelp & Cunliffe, if anybody needs to be reminded, are one of Britain's outstanding stocklists of rainwear, specializing in Inverness capes, riding aprons (as approved by the late Earl of Lonsdale), Newmarket boots, and custom leggings. For the past four years their window had featured a man's Scotch-grain brogue sitting in a shallow pan of water to demonstrate its moisture-repellent qualities. As usual, not even a bead of humidity shone inside the shoe, for all the colonies of algae on the water's surface and the penicillin mold encrusting the pan. A triumph of the bootmaker's art, indisputably, and I was wondering just how they achieved it— whether, in fact, they hadn't chiseled and rung in a few virginal shoes—when someone clapped me familiarly on the back. Revolving, I beheld a young squirt in a Carnaby Street version of a military greatcoat, his tempestuous inky curls surmounted by a Dutch bargee's cap. He had the sly, hateful face of those imps in Beardsley's illustrations for *Under the Hill,* and I knew with absolute certainty that I had never seen him before in my life.

"*Comment ça va,* baby?" he crowed. "Remember me—Pierre Flatulin, public relations, All-Gaul Airlines? We met in Julie Newmar's lobby eight years ago. No, I'm a liar—it was nine years. *Qu'est-ce que tu fais ici?*"

The appropriate answer—that I was minding my own business—froze on my chops, and, mumbling some evasion about salmon fishing north of the Tweed, I made off toward Regent Street. To my dismay, he ignored the snub, linked his arm in mine, and skipped along with me, resisting my most pointed efforts to dislodge him. He adored walking in London—the atmosphere was so *vif,* the girls such goddesses—and he'd be delighted to offer any advice as to shopping or directions. Did I need a gift for friends overseas, like perfumes or scarves? He had a connection in the duty-free area at Heathrow, a porter with access to damaged cartons, who for a slight *pourboire* . . . Or perhaps, he suggested with a critical glance, I might like to have my hair styled in a more becoming fashion; a mere call from him would set Vidal Sassoon athirst to transform me. Clearly, the only way to rid oneself of an incubus was to feign an emergency, and with a plea that I was overdue at my urologist's, I fled into a cab.

Undaunted, he thrust a large engraved card through the window. "Tomorrow night at the Commonwealth Institute!" he bawled in at me. "A marvelous party—don't miss it! My airline's annual reception for the Miss Globe contestants—sixty-six beautiful girls from all over the world! Where are you staying, so I can remind you?"

I threw him the name of a Turkish bath in Jermyn Street, and we veered away. That anything short of a cataclysm would impel me to attend an out-and-out leg show was, of course, unimaginable, but, incredibly enough, events on the evening in question conspired to. Minutes before I was to join a Welsh couple taking me to an eisteddfod in a Nonconformist chapel in Dorking, I received word that a gas main beneath the church had exploded and reduced the place to matchwood. Crestfallen and yet in a measure relieved, I repaired to a highly touted Indian restaurant and to an equally noxious film about Swedish inverts, and at eight o'clock found myself rigid with despair in the Tottenham Court Road. The thought of immuring myself in a hotel room with the biography of Prince Metternich I had bought in a cultural upsurge was so odious that I whimpered in self-pity. At that instant, clenching my fists in my pockets, I encountered the invitation Flatulin had forced on me. Sixty-six lovelies from as many lands—it was a deliverance, a miracle! My cheeks flamed in anticipation as I raced toward the Commonwealth Institute in Kensington.

The raffish turmoil of an Atlantic City beauty pageant that I had envisioned soon turned out to be a chimera. Several thousand spectators of both sexes, the majority in full evening kit and painfully decorous, were massed in the well of the Institute—a structure resembling a surgical amphitheater—sipping champagne and rubbering down at an illuminated dais. At periodic intervals the threescore and six claimants to the beauty crown, each wearing a chaste ball gown and a fixed paralytic grin, undulated out of the darkness, performed a curtsy, and daintily withdrew. The whole spectacle was so singularly bloodless, so devoid of ribaldry, that I was about to fling out, cursing Pierre Flatulin for a blackguard, when a voice on the PA system bade us join the contestants for a buffet supper and dancing. Instinct whispered that if I were to procure food and wine for one or two of the hopefuls my gallantry might be rewarded, and so it proved. A quarter of an hour later I was ensconced in an alcove with three—Miss Iceland, Miss Colombia, and Miss Greece—all of whom simpered gratitude for my attentions. Our preliminary exchanges were marked by an air of constraint; eventually, though, Miss Colombia finished gnawing on a chicken wing, wiped her fingers on her locks, and asked what line of business I was in. I replied that I was a member of an anti-caffeine society sworn to assassinate El Exigente. There was an abrupt swish of taffeta as she disappeared into the throng, and her colleagues resumed simpering gratitude for my attentions.

I removed a shred of carrot from my tie and cleared my throat. "You know," I said, addressing Miss Iceland, "I recently read an article about smoked fish or something that would have fascinated you—I mean, as an Icelander. I forget what it said or just where it appeared, but I remember how groovy it seemed at the time. Did you happen to read it?"

She shook her head, but my query reminded her that she had promised to phone her mother in Reykjavik, and, with a demure smile, she lumbered off. To be candid, I was not at all sorry, as the last of the trio was easily the comeliest. A bewitching creature, whose trim black bob awoke memories of the immortal Louise Brooks, Miss Greece was dressed as befitted her origin in a simple white wool chlamys secured at the shoulder with a gold lover's knot, and such was the purity, the calm wisdom of her demeanor that she might have stepped straight off a Grecian vase. My exultation, however, was short-lived, for I quickly discovered that we shared no common language. I tried her in French and a few halting fragments of Italian and German, but she stared at me without a glimmer of comprehension. Suddenly I had a magical, heaven-sent inspiration—the three years of classical Greek through which I had been keelhauled in high school. All I could remember was a single orotund line from the *Iliad*, but anything was better than this damnable lockjaw. I arose and drew a deep breath. *"Ton d'apamé bomonós,"* I intoned sonorously. *"Prosephē nephelēgeratá Zeus."* I paused, and translated helpfully, "That means 'Thus spake the wine-dark, cloud-gathering Zeus.'"

"Zeus?" she repeated, blinking.

"Yis—yis!" I confirmed, slipping into pidgin in my desperation to make her understand. "Him wine-dark, you savvy? Him plenty noisy fella with the thunderheads—ho, ho!"

Her look of perplexity slowly changed to one of alarm, and she made a furtive movement toward her handbag. In a last frantic effort to detain her, I recalled another possibility—the two semesters I had spent retracing Xenophon's *Anabasis.* I grabbed her arm. " 'The following day, we advanced twelve parasangs,' " I bleated. " 'The Thessalonians were drawn up in a phalanx, with the archers in front . . . the archers in front . . .' "

I was still fluthering away about the archers and Miss Greece was undoubtedly halfway back to Igoumenitsa when a fist smote me between the shoulder blades. Pierre Flatulin, in a luminescent green dinner jacket that extruded a cloud of eyelet lace from his shirtfront, stood grinning at me, flanked by two blond amazons. "Perfidious one, where have you been hiding?" he berated me in French. "I searched for you everywhere! *Voici*—our playmates for the evening, Miss Finland and Miss Yugoslavia!" The pressure of their handshakes was almost crippling. "All right, now," Flatulin commanded, fizzing like a Catherine wheel. "I'm taking you to a really swinging place—*je m'en fiche de cette ambiance.* Come along, everyone—*allons-y!*"

Imbecile though I was, I had sense enough at that juncture to realize that a pit yawned at my feet and that it was time to encase them in bedroom slippers. Before I could formulate the thought, however, the die was cast. The four of us were roaring through Belgravia in a motor so streamlined that we lay tilted like astronauts, our chauffeur, Flatulin, plainly navigating by the stars. Between Hyde Park Corner and Charing Cross he narrowly missed three traffic stanchions and the statue of Eros, and at last, seizing any pretext to slow him down, I observed that his Jaguar was overpowered.

"What Jaguar?" he said irritably. "This is a Jensen—can't you see?" All I could see was a jetliner knifing across the London sky, and I wished I were aboard it. "I also keep a Lamborghini, a Facel Vega, and a Maserati," he added, "and I'll tell you why. I have a silly aristocratic streak in me—I refuse to drive the same car two nights in a row. . . . Aha, here we are, *mes enfants*. Prepare yourselves for the most exclusive *boîte* in Europe."

The Splendid Silver Spoon—so named, Flatulin explained to us, because its patrician clientele had been born with silver spoons in their heads—was a Stygian-dark burrow in which half a hundred lunatics crepitated to the deafening noise of a West Indian steel band. As we wove past the bar, the group of Maltese procurers, layabouts, and spivs ranged before it appraised our partners' anatomies in the most explicit terms. One of them, in fact, leered so unashamedly into Miss Finland's bodice that I was tempted to box his ears, but the fellow turned away with a mumbled "*Scusi, Signore.*" The choice of refreshment, once we were seated, offered no problem; Beluga caviar and Dom Pérignon, it appeared, were the only things left in the kitchen at that hour. With a lordly wave, Flatulin ordered quantities of both and then bore Miss Finland off to the floor, whereupon I applied myself to weaving a spell around her friend. The language barrier reared anew; I managed to ascertain that she hailed from Belgrade, but since all I could recollect of it was that I had contracted fleas there, our conversation dwindled. In an effort to revive it, I seized upon the gold band gracing her finger. "*Coniugale?*" I queried, simulating horrid jealousy. "Marriage bells? You 'ave 'oosband—Liebchen?"

She nodded enthusiastically and fumbled out of her reticule a snapshot of a Cro-Magnon party astride a tractor—the father, she coyly signified, of her three children. Unable to reconcile motherhood with her aspirations to the throne of beauty, I lapsed into a moody silence. Seconds later Miss Finland rejoined us in high dudgeon. Flatulin, she reported, her magnificent bosom heaving, had precipitately abandoned her on the dance floor and pelted into the street. If this was a sample of our vaunted southern chivalry, she was content to remain in Helsinki forever, she declared, and, gathering up her fecund companion, she stormed out. As I was vainly trying to decipher what had happened, the maître d'hôtel approached with the request that I proceed to the manager's office at once.

In a malodorous cubicle at the rear, a Cypriote with a face crisscrossed by razor scars, who could only have sprung from the imagination of Mr. Graham Greene, lounged behind a desk. "This is Inspector Sculpin, of Scotland Yard," he said, indicating a craggy figure in a mackintosh. "'E wants to ask you a few questions."

"Purely routine—nothing to worry about," said the Inspector suavely. "Are we reliably informed that you arrived here tonight in a 1968 Jensen drophead coupé operated by a French gentleman? . . . Quite. Did he give the impression the car was his?"

"W-why, yes," I faltered. "He also said he kept a Lamborghini and a slew of other cars."

"He has—briefly," Sculpin corroborated. "All of them stolen, of course, as were his three passports. Did you happen to notice what he was wearing?"

I described his finery as best I could.

"Ah, yes," the Inspector said. "That checks with the description of the articles removed last night from Mr. Fish's premises in Savile Row. Well, sir, I needn't detain you any longer. Should you encounter the bleeder again, you might ring me up at the Yard. We'd rather like to return him to Wormwood Scrubs."

An hour later, recumbent on my bed at Fledgling's Hotel, I finished totting up the charges at the Splendid Silver Spoon and exhaled gratefully. Ninety-seven pounds sixpence—a picayune price indeed for having come through such an evening unscathed. I was snug in my haven, beholden to nobody. No Rubensian pink-and-white females whining to be caressed, no lingerie or hose flung about, no lipstick on the counterpane—everything was neat as a pin. It was phenomenal what disorder, what complications I had been spared. I picked up the phone, called room service for a double order of hot cocoa, and, with a sob, opened the biography of Prince Metternich.

Five Little Biceps
and How They Flew

CARAMANICO, *Italy (Reuters)—Some people are literally allergic to work, according to a report submitted to an Italian medical conference here. The report said that muscular activity could release an excessive amount of histamine, a powerful chemical stimulant in the body tissues, to cause rashes and allergies.*—The Times

HOUSTON, *Tex. (AP)—An Illinois psychiatrist says this country is being swept by an epidemic of work addiction. Dr. Nelson J. Bradley said work addiction has all the characteristics of alcohol or narcotics addiction. . . . The work addict has a driven craving for work, develops an increasing tolerance for it and suffers withdrawal symptoms without it, Bradley said. He said one sure sign of the work addict is habitually working overtime. He said another likely one is the man who says he has not taken a vacation in 17 years.*—New York Post

It was the kind of Pennsylvania Dutch barn immortalized by Andrew Wyeth and Charles Sheeler, a soaring nave of fieldstone to which various wooden transepts—a wagon shed, a granary, a fore-

chute, and a silo—had been added across the past century and a half, and every time I drove up our lane the sight of it dominating the ridge and the adjacent fields gave me a renewed sense of stability and peace. While wholly ornamental nowadays—a receptacle for firewood, discarded bookcases, and rusting pickaxes—it symbolized continuity, and the hex signs on the façade were a placatory gesture to destiny that was highly comforting. During the last couple of winters, however, time and the weather had made visible inroads. The paint had flaked off most of the siding, patches of stucco were missing from the gables, and overnight the picturesque had suddenly grown shabby. When a gossipy neighbor stopped me in the post office to observe with acid sweetness, "I hate to see the old landmarks disappear," I knew the community was buzzing. The barn had to be painted—sixty-five mortal gallons, I remembered from the past—and it was fruitless to sulk. I went in search of a contractor.

Mr. Trautwein, universally recommended as a wizard in his profession, lived thirty miles distant in a trim Mennonite hamlet in the back country. The houses flanking his glistened with fresh paint; their shutters glowed like cut velvet, their porches sparkled. Trautwein's residence, in distinction, was the most neglected dwelling I had seen outside the Gorbals in Glasgow. No trace of pigment showed on the weathered clapboards, the gutters sagged dispiritedly from the roof, and the yard was littered with turpentine cans, splintered glass, drop cloths, and similar detritus. Dismayed by these portents, I was about to clear off, but, recollecting the axiom that cobblers' children traditionally go unshod, I decided to persevere. Trautwein, a needle-nosed citizen with a Chester Conklin mustache, was immersed in a TV western he reckoned would occupy him for the remainder of the week, but he finally consented to drive over in a day or two and give me an estimate. With the instinctive timing of countryfolk, he materialized one evening just as my wife was extracting a soufflé from the oven, and the atmosphere when I bolted off to inspect the barn with him became abruptly charged. Trautwein's face lengthened at the magnitude of the task confronting him.

"Too far gone," he said gloomily. "Them boards'll suck up paint like a sponge. If I was in your shoes, I'd pull the durn thing down and use the wood for kindling."

I rejoined somewhat loftily that I had not been appointed chief minister of this domain to preside at the dissolution of my barn. The reference was clearly lost on him.

"Okeydoke," he said indifferently. "It's your money, not mine. You want a spray job or do we brush her on?"

"Hand work," I said, my voice resonant with admonitions gleaned from the *Consumers' Guide*. "The old-fashioned, painstaking way. Coat every nook, every knot with the best stuff obtainable, and damn the expense. This building was here when the red man roamed those woods, brother, and, by Godfreys," I vowed emotionally, "it'll be here when he returns!"

Assuring me that the mandate was graven on his heart, Trautwein took off, and a month passed without any word from him. I phoned his home half a dozen times, on each occasion falling into long, frustrating causeries with what were either children or chimpanzees; possibly both were being reared together as an experiment. Ultimately I cornered the man, only to be bombarded with excuses. The weather was too humid to paint and the insects too numerous, there was a nationwide shortage of ladders, and arthritis was epidemic among his help.

One August morning, long after my hopes had faded, a panel truck bearing no identification, like those used to merchandise hot furs, drew up at the corral and discharged two persons in white boiler suits and matching berets. My first supposition, that they were Andrew Wyeth and Charles Sheeler, yielded when they disclosed themselves as emissaries of Trautwein—Russell Mullch and Howard Compost by name. As they started off-loading their gear, I was immediately struck by the difference between them. Compost's vigor was well-nigh manic; he whisked up five hogsheads of paint at once, threw scaffolding about like jackstraws, and flung a block and tackle with such force that it defoliated half the nasturtiums in our dory. Mulch, contrariwise, seemed to be tottering on the brink of invalidism, a pallid lymphatic shade whose every step threatened to be his last. Watching him struggle to open a can of putty, beads of perspiration the size of Catawba grapes dewing his forehead, I was appalled. To anyone with a professional eye like mine—and, as a onetime premedical student, I knew my way around pathology—the man was suffering from iron-poor blood. He was a gone goose.

At the moment, however, I had other matters engaging my attention—notably, dipping sprays of Queen Anne's lace in whitewash to make floral arrangements for our hall—so I exacted a pledge from the duo to preserve the fine old Pennsylvania Dutch flavor of the barn and withdrew. An hour or two later, it proving unfeasible to watch them through field glasses from our bedroom, I sauntered out to investigate. Compost, in a display of almost inhuman energy, had singlehandedly primed two-thirds of the exterior, nailed fast all the battens, replaced the corrugated iron on the silo, given the hardware an undercoat of red oxide, and now straddled the roof in suicidal fashion, batting away pigeons as he daubed the crevices in the forepeak. His partner, Mulch, was nowhere in evidence, and, horrid as the surmise was, I wondered whether he had crept off into the fields to die. My fears were shortly assuaged; he was stretched out in our hammock under the maples, sneezing convulsively and disfigured by angry red blotches.

"Touch of ragweed, eh?" I said, expertly sizing up the dilated pupils and the flaccid wrists. "Still, it could be the shellac fumes— I recall some mention of that by my preceptor in pharmacology class. Well, stiff upper lip—we'll soon set you right."

I compounded a weak solution of bicarbonate, sirup of figs, and

Dijon mustard—which I would have preferred to administer intravenously, but pulse and respiration (my own, that is) dictated otherwise—and he managed to ingest it. Distressing to report, his symptoms persisted; and I was thoroughly nonplussed by the time Trautwein appeared at dusk to check on his workmen. He betrayed marked evasiveness at my queries about Mulch, but eventually unbosomed himself. The man was totally allergic to work; if he so much as picked up a brush, in fact, wave after wave of histamine surged through his system, utterly devitalizing him.

"It happens on every job," he confessed. "Sometimes he can't even get out of the truck, poor bastard. It's the exact opposite with Howard, though." He pointed up at the ridgepole, where Compost was balanced like Bird Millman, frenziedly smearing away at his perch in the half darkness. "Now, him, he's liable to go on all night. I wouldn't dare stop him, else he'd come down with withdrawal pangs. You got to know how to handle these fellows."

"Well, I'll tell you one way," I suggested. "Why don't you put on *two* work addicts? They'd finish the chore in half the time."

"You mean, leave Russell go?" he asked incredulously.

"Er—only temporarily, until the job is finished," I said. "Fair is fair, but to pay someone for lounging in a hammock—"

Trautwein's lips tightened. "I ought to report you to the authorities," he said, outraged. "Aren't you ashamed, preventing a man from working just because his tissues are sensitive? He's got dependents, little kiddies that you're taking the bread out of their mouths. I never heard anything so heartless."

I was tempted to point out that if the kiddies, like his own, were hanging on the phone giving out misinformation, they were too busy to eat, but I forbore. At length, we hit on a *modus vivendi*; Compost would be asked to paint with two brushes to compensate for his colleague, the other's wages to be reduced by half. It was an equitable solution, and one, I felt, that would enable us to dwell together in harmony.

and How They Flew

An hour before daylight next morning the dogs set up a hideous brouhaha. Compost had driven in, trained a searchlight on the barn, and, to the accompaniment of the "Washington Post March," was scraping the accumulated rust from the spouting. Mulch, on the other hand, failed to surface until eleven. After a few nerveless brushstrokes, he fell head foremost into the hollyhocks and had to be transferred to the screened porch, on which I could supervise his temperature more closely and supply him with barley water and magazines. As a small token of appreciation for Compost's zeal, my wife made up a picnic basket containing a block of foie gras, a Cornish hen, and an excellent Mâcon, but the gesture was futile; he insisted on working through lunch. His partner, though, got down the collation, and, indeed, revived sufficiently to sip a *vieux marc* and smoke a cigar. Improvising a sphygmomanometer from a bicycle pump and the gauge off an old hotwater heater—we medical people are trained to use the materials at hand—I took his blood pressure and found it encouraging. We were not out of the woods yet, but, provided Mulch had plenty of rest and never lifted a finger again, there was every indication he would pull through.

The picture up at the barn, however, was less reassuring. By nightfall Compost's exertions, far from slackening, had redoubled; temporarily forswearing his brush, he had hauled aloft half an acre of slate and was patching the roof. At ten-thirty, as my wife and I sat before Pandora's box, grinding our teeth at Susskind's euphuisms, it suddenly dawned on me that the chap had labored seventeen hours without surcease. My conscience rebelled and I jumped to my feet.

"Who the deuce are we—Simon Legree?" I exclaimed. "Folks'll drive by and see him up there, with the bats squeaking around— I'm stopping him this minute!"

"Are you out of your senses?" she asked, paling. "The fellow's hooked—you break it off and he'll go right into shock! And the next thing you know, you'll have a million-dollar lawsuit on your hands."

Though the woman's conception of immunology was primitive, there was no denying she had a certain legal instinct. In whatever case, the issue was resolved for us the very next day. Neither Compost nor Mulch showed up, and the place was as deserted as the Hadramaut. I let twenty-four hours elapse and began phoning Trautwein again, with the usual baffling results. Eons later he called back. Mulch had suffered a relapse while wielding a toothpick and was in traction.

"But where's Howard Compost? He's the one that matters," I expostulated.

"Oh, that two-timer," he said wrathfully. "I fired him. He was moonlighting between you and a job in Perkasie. But don't worry—your barn'll get done in a jiffy. I'm bringing over three crackerjacks bright and early tomorrow."

He was as good as his word. Hardly had I finished spraying the antrums for rose fever, oat fly, and horse dander—my own membranes are pretty delicate, but I don't beat my breast about it— when Trautwein roared up in his shooting brake and threw down the tailgate. Out sprang a trio of needle-nosed youngsters easily identifiable as his—the eldest of them seven. Whooping and brandishing their brushes, they swarmed over the building like the followers of the Mahdi at Khartoum, but they delivered the goods, all right. There are those in the neighborhood, I hear, who claim the thing looks like a finger painting. Well, I should worry, I should fret, I should marry a suffragette. It sheds water, which is a hell of a lot more than you can say for most of your quaint old Pennsylvania Dutch barns.

To Err Is Human,
to Forgive, Supine

Whenever I see hordes of women clawing their way into a mid-season clearance sale, the veins pulsating in their necks and their eyes protuberant with greed, I always wonder why so few novelists, apart from Zola in his scarifying *Au Paradis des Dames*, have chosen the department store as a theme. Is it because the purgatorial atmosphere in these places is better suited to the imagination of a Hieronymus Bosch, capable of portraying the cannibalistic fury of the customers, the crucifying boredom and malignancy of the staff? Anyone who has ever worked in a department store, surely, must have quailed under the hauteur of petty satraps like buyers and section managers; their medieval harassment of inferiors, the constant espionage, and the penalties exacted for any infraction of the rules, reflected in the lickspittle servility of underlings, are enough to sicken a goat. I speak from intimate knowledge —at a formative period of my life and for nearly six months, I was a teen-age vassal, the lowliest, in a department store. Only one endowed with a Sicilian capacity for vengeance, as I was, could have emerged from the experience unscathed. I did so by clinging to the same resolve that sustained Edmond Dantès—some day, I swore, I would repay. Forty years elapsed before I squared accounts a month ago, and let's eschew all pious cant to the effect that it turned to ashes in my mouth. Not on your tintype—it was nectar.

Back in 1899 a couple of Transylvanians named Schwimpf and Grosbart, from Bistrica, the native heath of Count Dracula, founded an emporium in Providence on a shoestring (which they proposed to use as a tourniquet) and a proverb revised to read, "You can *too* get blood out of a stone." At the end of two decades, when I entered its employ, the Beehive was a grim, five-story bastion occupying a full block on the city's principal thoroughfare. Trade there on a weekend was so tumultuous that the store had to send out a press gang to shanghai part-time help, and inevitably the crimps reached my high school. I happened to be at a loose end, the lady for whom I had beaten carpets at fifteen cents an hour having made improper advances, and when I was offered a whole dollar for a Saturday job at the Beehive I jumped at it.

Initially a stockroom boy in the men's footwear section, I submitted to the usual pranks visited on a novice. The shoe salesmen, then as now a dismal lot of human beings, were wasp-waisted sharpies akin to Percy and Ferdie, the Hallroom Boys in the comic strip of that era. It convulsed them to send me on errands like fetching a pail of steam and a left-handed monkey wrench, and their guffaws at my naïveté reduced me to jelly. To my overwhelming relief, I was reprieved after a fortnight and dispatched to the rug department, where I imagined that my proficiency with carpets might give me a certain cachet. Even an elephant, however —one of those trained to work teak logs in the forests of northern Siam—would have recoiled from the task assigned me. I and my coworker, a derelict with a wet brain recruited from a waterfront flophouse, were required to tote giant rolls of Axminster and Brussels to an entrepôt two blocks distant and haul them back again. What commercial purpose this served—whether it aged or mellowed the rugs in some mysterious way—we were never told. Nor was our portion eased by the floorwalker, a bull of a man like the tyrant Gessler, who continually denounced us as loafers and lashed us on with imprecations. After several weekends, fatigue and dust took their toll, and I fainted dead away one morning in algebra class. The teacher, apprehensive lest his own brand of sadism had laid me low, investigated. A note went forth to the personnel manager of the Beehive, and the next Saturday I was transferred to the men's-clothing division to fold boxes.

Irksome as my earlier posts had been, they at least provided the companionship of fellow mortals; now I was as remote as a prisoner in the dungeons of the Cheka. From seven-thirty until six I toiled in a windowless basement lit by a naked electric bulb, kneading the boxes into shape and passing them upward to the parcel desk through a trapdoor. Since the half hour allotted for lunch made it impractical to leave the premises, I usually gulped a homemade sandwich and read one of the Haldeman-Julius five-cent blue books, preferably the diatribes of Brann the Iconoclast or Colonel Robert Ingersoll. To add to my tribulations, the departmental head, a sallow fiend imbued with more spit-and-polish than a British sergeant-major, demanded the strictest esprit de corps of his subordinates. I was obliged to wear a blue serge suit with knickerbockers at all times, presumably because Messrs. Schwimpf and Grosbart might pop in on a tour of inspection. Both the suit and my long black stockings, the latter rendered greenish by repeated washing, tended to polarize the lint that sifted down from above, so that I appeared to have rolled in swansdown, but once the boss caught me in shirtsleeves I numbly obeyed regulations. To anyone seeing me in my lazaret—a virtual impossibility, what with the 40-watt bulb—it may have seemed that I bore my lot with stoicism. Inwardly I seethed with fury, clenching my teeth as I worked and composing bitter tirades, patterned after Brann and Ingersoll, against retail merchandising. One day, in an apocalyptic revelation, it dawned on me that I had been exploited: a dollar for ten hours' work was less than I had earned as a free lance. That night I tore my pay envelope to shreds, chalked a gargoyle likeness of the section manager on the trapdoor, and walked out of the Beehive— as I thought—forever.

The heaven-sent opportunity to revenge myself came this past June, when, attending a class reunion and quahaug roast in the area, I was invited to participate in a morning TV show sponsored by the Beehive. The program, I was overjoyed to learn, emanated from the store itself, and, *mirabile dictu,* no less a personage than the founder's grandson, the present head of the company, was to interview me. A bulbous, self-satisfied princeling in a Pierre Cardin suit, Schwimpf was all greasy affability as he presented me to the audience. What nostalgia this return to my early haunts must evoke, he speculated, crinkling up his eyes and twirling his side-burns. Quite, I admitted—the more so since I had worked at the Beehive in youth. His nostrils dilated pridefully at the scent of an unsolicited testimonial. No doubt the experience had ripened me, afforded many psychological insights one was privileged to glean in a great department store. Would I care to recount my memories of that period? I dimpled suitably and began.

To give the viewers a frame of reference, as it were, I sketched in several vignettes out of the past—Dickens' boyhood in the blacking factory, the maltreatment of adolescent females at Bryant & May's matchworks, and the inhumanities prevalent in the naval hulks at Portsmouth. Nevertheless, I continued, let nobody take refuge in sanctimony and pretend that such oppression was confined to Victorian England. I myself had undergone as much in this very building, I announced, and went on to particularize. I had to talk swiftly, for a glance at Schwimpf, whose face had gone the sickly color of pork fat, told me that the moment he rallied his faculties, I was off the air. I therefore gave only highlights, restricting myself to details that I felt would rivet the listeners. I did emphasize one point, though—viz., that nothing seemed to have changed at the Beehive across the years. The same pallid employees were visible in the same abject state of peonage, cringing under the whiplash of overseers. Unfortunately, before I could urge the wretched creatures to seize the premises and set up a commune, Schwimpf got to the engineer. My exit might have been more effective had I not tripped over a cable, but at any rate the cameras had stopped grinding by then.

Altogether, I felt so rejuvenated by my little talk, so filled with a religious sense of purification, that a week later in New York, a show-business colleague of mine, one Arthur Balthasar, commented on how radiant I looked. On learning the cause, he agreed that sweeter than honey is the catharsis that springs from belated vengeance, and proceeded to narrate a similar instance out of his own past. Soon after the First World War he and his brother Irving, both of them fledgling playwrights, shared a decrepit studio near Washington Square in the Village, where they eked out a submarginal existence writing verses for greeting cards. Their pad was little more than a hovel; arctic blasts whistled through the skylight, the floors sagged dangerously, and gobbets of plaster scaled from the walls at their merest breath. Amid the desolation the Balthasars huddled over a jackstove, their noses waxen with cold as they strove to compose joyous rhymes for Thanksgiving and the Yuletide. The greeting-card tycoon on whom their livelihood depended was an individual named Federbush, a callous brute who battened off poets like themselves and drove merciless bargains for their product. The maximum payment for any verse he accepted was one dollar, but he was hypercritical; more often than not, when the brothers brought him a holiday paean, he rejected it as substandard. "It ain't *merry*," he would grumble, drawing on his perfecto. "Go back to your hutch and sparkle it up. Put in some chuckles, some jollity."

Sick at heart, the Balthasars would return to the jackstove and labor to inject gaiety into their verses, but Federbush inevitably responded with the same hateful comment. One winter's day the pair seemed to have reached the absolute limit of their endurance. Famished and on the edge of collapse, they bore their week's output to Federbush, whose brows contracted as he read it. "This stuff's no good," he pronounced. "How many times do I have to tell you—it ain't merry! But here's what I'll do," he proposed, as they snuffled weakly. "Out of the kindness of my heart, I'll pay you a quarter apiece for these. Take it or leave it."

Starvation being the sole alternative, they took it and went their way, bitterly vowing to even the score with him some day. Ten years passed, and Irving Balthasar, now transformed into a lyric writer, managed to achieve the dream of his profession—a musical comedy smash on Broadway. Wealth and the adulation of fair women poured in on him, ostensibly encapsulating his early wounds, and on a balmy autumn evening, as patrons thronged into the theater containing his hit, he stood in the lobby puffing a Havana and benignly surveying the crush. Suddenly a hand gripped his shoulder and he wheeled about to find Federbush, accompanied by a woman, beaming at him. "Irving, my boy!" the arrival exclaimed, oozing bonhomie. "Remember me? You should—I gave you your start. . . . Well, you're on top of the world, hey?"

Balthasar stared at him hypnotized.

"Oho!" Federbush observed cynically. "Maybe you're so bigtime you forgot the old days."

"I never forget anything," the other said slowly.

"Good," said Federbush. "Then how about a couple of passes to your show for the missus and me?"

"Hold my cigar," Balthasar directed, handing it to him. He turned as if toward the box office, and then, flexing his muscles, bent down and picked up a great china jardinière filled with sand and cigarette ends. "*It ain't merry!*" he shouted, and brought it down full force on Federbush's sconce.

Oh, well, *autre temps, autre moeurs,* as the saying goes. Personally, I deplore such violence, and if, as Arthur Balthasar added, the victim recovered without a scratch, the gesture was futile anyhow. Nowadays, and thanks to the wizardry of electronics, we've a much neater tool for settling ancient feuds. If you don't believe me, just ask a party named Schwimpf who's foaming at the mouth of the Beehive in Providence, R.I. Or was, the last I saw of him, I sincerely hope.

Naked in Piccadilly, W.1

"What a perfect union!" said everyone who knew Urban Sprawl, the architect, and the bride he took late in life. "Godfreys, what a devoted couple! It's a marriage made in heaven." Yes, they really warmed the cockles of one's heart, that pair, and when their idyll blew up within a year all the wiseacres, including yours truly, were confounded. I daresay I still would be if Lydia Sprawl, long after the event and lubricated by half a dozen Margaritas, hadn't seen fit to unburden herself to me. It was money that caused them to split up, she confided mournfully; not money in the usual crass sense but a battered amulet her husband had kept in his pocket for years—a Greek coin he called his lucky drachma.

Sprawl's fetishism, apparently, was quite innocent—no more bizarre than anything in Frazer's *Golden Bough*. All through his apprenticeship as draftsman and junior architect, his first important competition, and his emergence at the pinnacle of his craft, the talisman had never once left his person; yet, paradoxically, he was ashamed to flaunt it. Did Lydia mildly suggest converting it into a watch charm for safety, he was aghast. That would practically *insure* theft, said he, and stubbornly continued to mingle it with the keys and silver in his trousers. Calamity foreordained overtook the Sprawls early one morning as they lay abed in their Manhattan flat,

124

sleeping off a toot. Roused by the whine of the buzzer, Lydia padded to the door and found a mealy-mouthed schnorrer in a nun's habit seeking alms for some nonexistent leprosarium. She scooped up a handful of change from her vanity, pressed it on the woman, and tumbled back into dreamland. An hour later she was awakened by a fearful screech. The room was topsy-turvy, and Urban, his face the hue of plaster of Paris, was clawing the walls. "My coin—my little coin!" he was sobbing. "I can't find my lucky drachma!"

Whether it was her hangover or acute revulsion at his puerility, Lydia made a fatal misstep—she blurted out the truth. Forty-eight hours later, she was en route to the Virgin Islands with a spectacular mouse under her left eye.

While a recent experience of mine was not strictly analogous to Sprawl's, there were, I think, similarities worth recording. Three months ago in London I chanced by a small art gallery wedged in among the antiquarian bookshops, hatters' establishments, and jewelry boutiques clustering around Old Bond Street. Displayed in the window was a canvas of an uncorseted beauty failing to evolve a bikini out of a wisp of chiffon that billowed naughtily in the wind. It was an arresting picture—not so much the subject—a standard pinup in every college dormitory—but the technique, which, I found on close examination (I had to put on reading glasses to corroborate it), resembled embroidery. Ever since 1916, when I won a chromo of "September Morn" at a wheel of fortune in Crescent Park, Rhode Island, primitive and folk art have been a sort of hobby with me, and I naturally entered the gallery to investigate. At least twenty other pictures on the same order, all executed with obvious relish for anatomical detail, riveted my eye.

"Could these possibly be needlework, Miss?" I asked the attendant, a miniskirted wraith absorbed in the *Duino Elegies*.

She nodded. "Made from movie stills," she amplified. "That's

Diana Dors over there, Brigitte Bardot behind you, and Raquel
Welch on this wall. Here's a folder about the artist who did them,
if you're interested."

I was, and, reading it, became even more so. Ted Willcox, I
learned, was a former Royal Air Force gunner who, on recuperating
from his war service, had taken up needlework. "At first laboriously
copying regimental badges," the text explained. "Then graduating
to reproducing Anne Hathaway's cottage. In 1944 came the break-
through, his first pinup, 'Marlene Dietrich' (copied from a photograph). From that date, he has more or less specialized in embroi-
dering rather nubile ladies, the later ones against beautifully patterned abstract backgrounds. Executed in embroidery silk, quite
often on linen tea towels, and they can take anything up to three
months to complete." Adjoining this was a tribute from an admirer
named Peter Blake, who had discovered Willcox's handiwork as
follows: "Just over a year ago, I was having a room decorated by
Mr. Vincent Smith, who, one morning, brought in an embroidery
of Lee Harvey Oswald being shot by Jack Ruby, which he thought
would interest my wife." The folder concluded with a typical British understatement: "The embroideries of Ted Willcox are almost
certainly unique."

Now, it so happened I was headed for Asprey's at that moment,
hunting for an anniversary present, and an inspiration hit me. Why
not buy my wife one of these skillfully ornamented tea towels—a
souvenir that was a cinch to evoke feminine admiration and, at the
same time, attract male connoisseurs? Surely, I reasoned, an authentic primitive would have twice the impact, on the mem, of a
silly old brooch or a bottle of scent. I accordingly selected an embroidery of a full-blown Scandinavian package with goo-goo eyes,
on the lines of Anita Ekberg, crouched in a seductive pose on a
bearskin. She was a trifle steatopygous compared to the starvelings
in *Vogue*, for example, but, after all, that was the artist's vision, and

who was to dictate how he should wield his needle? I mean, it wasn't just an arid photograph—it was a creative *statement*.

Well, everything was tickety-boo until I arrived at Kennedy Airport. The customs inspector who checked my declaration frowned when he reached the item "1 Linen Tea Towel—£30 ($84)." I seemed to have fairly sybaritic taste in towels, he commented (he was a college man, one gathered). Where had I purchased the item?

"Why, it's not a towel, fundamentally—uh—that is, essentially," I said, flustered. "It's more of a painting—a tapestry, like."

"Oh, a work of art, eh?" he said, pricking up his ears. "Well, if it's less than a hundred years old, Charlie, it's taxable. Let's have a look."

Had the man merely gawked at the embroidery, or even cackled obscenely, as did everyone within eyeshot, that would have been humiliation enough; it was the pitying stare he gave me, and the curt pronouncement "Duty-free," that was so wounding. I nevertheless comforted myself with the knowledge that the ultimate recipient, a woman whose taste I knew to be impeccable, was incapable of philistinism, and I was proved right. Her curiosity whetted by hints about an unorthodox anniversary gift, my wife was on tenterhooks when she withdrew it from the box. She studied it for a full minute.

"What is it?" she asked finally.

"What do you mean, '*What is it*'?" I shouted. "It's a folk painting—any fool can see that! An Englishman—and a very gifted chap, what's more—embroidered it on a tea towel."

"So he did," she said, examining the reverse. "Genuine Irish linen—they last a lifetime. Well, this certainly is a lovely wedding remembrance, dear," she acknowledged, and began folding it. "I'll just lay it away with the doilies, and the next time we have tea—"

I stopped her. "Hold on, ducks. Nobody hides an Henri Rousseau or a Grandma Moses in the closet. I bought that to hang in the living room."

"Yes, it *would* harmonize with our Pennsylvania Dutch things," she agreed. "A pity we don't have space—it's so bucolic, a Holstein leering out of a fur rug. O.K., I'll tell you what. Since we haven't a barbershop or a rathskeller on the premises, let's put it in the guest bathroom."

Well, the tapestry hung there over the next couple of months, and it became quite a conversation piece. Whenever people burst into a sudden guffaw at our parties, it was unnecessary to ask why, and the second time a girlie calendar arrived from a weekend guest as a token of appreciation, a rare domestic upheaval shook the household. Personally, these bourgeois gibes moved me not at all. I was concerned for a quite different reason—I was afraid that steam escaping from the shower might cause the design to deteriorate, so one day while my wife was off shopping I surreptitiously coated it with clear shellac. It was this gesture on her behalf, arising from sheer altruism, that sparked a disaster akin to the Sprawls'. Several mornings later, in scouring the medicine cabinet for a Band-Aid, I discovered the picture was gone. I ran panic-stricken to the kitchen.

"The needlework—the Ted Willcox!" I cried out. "It's missing! It's been stolen!"

"No, no, it's all right"—my wife placated me. "Mrs. Reifsnyder, the cleaning woman, found a peculiar glaze all over it, like bacon fat. We sent it to the laundry with the other towels. . . . Honey, what's wrong? Mrs. Reifsnyder, the brandy—quick!"

By the time the two finished burning feathers under my nose to revive me, the impulse to blacken the culprit's eye had subsided, and, in any case, I had to get to the Paragon Wet Wash in Doylestown to pick up the trail. It was a cold one. The most vigorous scrubbing had made no dent in the shellac, reported the manageress, and hence the towel had been dispatched to the firm's dry cleaner in Philadelphia. I needn't have any qualms, though, she added swiftly—Mr. Turtletaub did beautiful work; the article would come back like new. Gripping the counter to retain self-control, I bade the woman take the mush out of her mouth and phone Turtletaub to expect me at his plant inside the hour. Up hill and down dale, snaking and twisting through uncharted reaches of the City of Brotherly Love, I roared at a pace that would have unnerved Graham Hill. My goal, the Nonpareil Cleaners & Dyers, lay hidden up an alley off Locust Street as sinister as any in Limehouse. That I ran the risk of having my weasand slit by some devotee of the poppy was a foregone conclusion, but nothing could deter me now. An obese character in his undershirt, gnawing on a cigar, peered up from his ledger and identified himself as Turtletaub.

"The special order from Doylestown?" he said. "Yep, they phoned me." He reached into a bin and brought forth a small Plio-film envelope. "Listen," he queried, "where'd you buy this here novelty—at some schlock store on the Atlantic City boardwalk? Dint they tell you it would shrink?"

Bereft of speech, my knees trembling, I goggled incredulously at our Willcox original—no longer a lush, exuberant ode to femininity, a paean to Venus Callipyge, but a measly little face-cloth out of a five-and-ten-cent store. Gone those opulent curves that had quickened the artist's needle, gone the languorous marbled limbs for which I as a collector had endured such mockery.

After an eternity I recovered my voice. "You vandal," I said hoarsely. "You—you Visigoth. Do you think for one moment you can destroy a masterpiece and get away with it? Well, disabuse yourself, my friend—you'll pay for this, and dearly. I'm calling my attorney, Otis Vivendi of Schwartz, Quartz & Replevin in Doylestown, this very afternoon, and I'm going to sue you in the highest courts of the land. I'll bankrupt you, Turtletaub. I'll hound you to the ends of the earth. You'll rue this day!"

The fellow's face turned ashen. "Sugarman!" he screamed

through the racks behind him. "Come up from the basement—I need you. Bring the pipe wrench!"

Well, I calmed him down after a bit, and when he finally comprehended what he'd done nobody could have been more abject. Offered to pay for my gas, mothproof my sweater, and so forth, but of course I wouldn't hear of it. *"Finita la commedia,"* I said, and drove numbly homeward, reflecting how dear my worship of Beauty had cost me, wondering if it had taught me anything. Indubitably it had—every woman, regardless of sex, would rather have a brooch than a Brueghel. And I'd learned one other thing also. The next time I go shopping for naïve art, I'll make bloody well sure it's Sanforized.

Moonstruck at Sunset

I believe it was Hippolyte Taine, the historian—or possibly Monroe Taine, the tailor, a philosophical chap who used to press my pants forty years ago in the Village—who once observed that immortality is a chancy matter, subject to the caprice of the unborn. Not every notable wins his niche in the hall of fame on precisely the terms he would have chosen, and for every marbled dignitary in the Borghese Gardens or the Bois de Boulogne there is another who survives only as the trademark of a cigar, an italicized entry on a menu. Could Dickens have visualized himself as the patron saint of a taproom on West Tenth Street, or Van Gogh as the tutelary god of an Eighth Avenue cleaning establishment? Neither Dame Nellie Melba nor Lily Langtry, certainly, would have been content to face posterity as they have, one as a dessert and the other as a foundation garment. Perhaps the most eccentric parlay of this kind I know of, though, was unwittingly generated in the brain of a British novelist named Robert Hichens. When he spun his famous tale of Domini Enfilden's desert love and entitled it *The Garden of Allah*, he never could have foreseen the landmark by that name —or, worse yet, a punning version of it—that would rise one day in Hollywood to perpetuate the glory of a Russian actress.

The actress, of course, was Alla Nazimova, and in naming a cluster of hotel bungalows on Sunset Boulevard the Garden of Allah the builder paid impressive tribute to her talent. (Since the builder happened to be Nazimova herself, there was never any question of her sincerity. With the passage of time, unfortunately, Nazimova's reputation waned and the Islamic cognomen prevailed.) As Hollywood architecture went, the place was fairly restrained—a sprinkle of tile-roofed, Neo-Spanish villas centered about a free-form pool—and its clientele equally so. Most of the hotel's guests were migratory actors, playwrights, and similar gypsies with tenuous links to the picture business, and if they reveled, they did so discreetly and in whispers. This was a source of perplexity to the press, notably a Manhattan columnist I once encountered on the grounds. It was his conviction that debauchery was mother's milk to screen folk, and he had selected the Garden of Allah as a vantage point to study it. Unable to find any orgies, he became morose, drank an immoderate amount of whiskey one night, and dove headlong into the pool in his dinner clothes. After his return to the East, he wrote a description of a couple of saturnalias he had attended in the Garden which would have shocked Petronius out of his toga.

The time was 1931, and my wife and I were recent arrivals in Hollywood, unfamiliar with its mores and domiciled in a sleazy bungalow court near the studio where I was undergoing my novitiate as a screenwriter. Our flat was less a home than a bivouac. The walls were plasterboard, the pastel-tinted furniture the flimsy type found in nurseries, the rugs and draperies tawdry, and the kitchenware minimal. As for the conversation of our fellow residents that filtered through the walls, that also promoted no feeling of stability. They seemed to be constantly staving off bill collectors and betting on horses that never finished, exchanging symptoms of incurable diseases and rehearsing roles inevitably excised from films in the cutting room. But the rent was nominal and our discomfort somewhat allayed by the usual will-o'-the-wisp delusion that we were saving money hand over fist.

at Sunset

One evening I came home to find my wife dissolved in tears. After crystallizing her over a Bunsen burner, I managed to elicit the reason. A matron in Beverly Hills whom she knew had visited the premises that afternoon and pronounced them sordid. Ostracism, swift and pitiless, loomed in Filmdom unless we moved at once, her friend declared; the only possible locale that might restore the face we had lost was the Garden of Allah. I spurned the idea with such vehemence that the neighbors beat on the walls to quiet me, but their protests went for naught. In rhetoric that must have reminded them of Edmund Burke denouncing Warren Hastings, I poured vials of wrath on suburban snobbery; I blasted the colony's *nouveaux riches* until the welkin rang. When its strains died away, I realized the futility of argument and meekly started packing.

Since all the villas at the Garden were chockablock at the moment, we were lodged for an interval in a two-story annex overlooking the pool. The prospect from our windows was a soothing one—barbered lawns and shrubbery, emerald water rippling in the balmy California sunshine, and over all a genteel hush that bespoke affluence and contempt for vulgar display. Guests were rarely visible on the walks; occasionally a seamed old plutocrat in canary-yellow slacks doddered forth to exercise a Pekingese, or a European movie director in overtight satin shorts, mistakenly believing himself on the Riviera, would dog-paddle cumbrously about the pool, but otherwise the drowsy, peaceful scene was seldom marred. The first intimation of anything unusual came the second night after our arrival. Fire broke out in an apartment house nearby whose name immortalized still another celebrity—the Voltaire Arms—and some two dozen occupants of the Garden converged excitedly on the grass to watch. Among them were several screen personalities of both sexes whom we had no trouble identifying, as well as a number of prominent playwrights, executives, and agents. They were all officially married, but not to their present roommates.

While startling, there was nothing indecorous about the assemblage; its members looked like sleepy children as they stood knuckling their eyes and gaping at the fire engines. One wondered if their faces would reflect the same dewy innocence in the divorce court.

Once ensconced in a villa of our own, it soon became evident that our neighbors, if more solvent than those in the bungalow court, were as peculiar. The man next door, for example, was a wizened homunculus who had edited one of the New York tabloids during the Peaches Browning era. Behind the smoked glasses that hid his saffron-colored face his eyes were on continual alert for some unseen enemy. I thought that perhaps he feared reprisals from gangland chiefs he had exposed, for he never ventured out except in a polo coat with upturned collar, and then only a few steps from his burrow. The explanation given my wife by our maid was more mundane: he was beset by process servers trying to collect the alimony he owed five women. His misogyny one day bore fruit. He wrote a book chronicling his vicissitudes, a best seller that became a hit play and eventually a musical smash—but his wives triumphed. They garnisheed his royalties, and he ended his days a bankrupt on a New Jersey goat farm.

In the cottage adjoining his was another enigma, a celebrated character actor whose behavior also occasioned intense speculation. A suave, courtly leading man popular on Broadway and in films, he was married to a society beauty no less distinguished than himself. Always arm in arm and solicitous of each other, they seemed a devoted couple, except that she often appeared in public with a black eye. He and I developed a nodding acquaintance, and one afternoon, quite without prompting, he confided to me that his wife had fallen the night before and struck her eye on a birdbath. A few days later she exhibited another shiner, contracted, he told me, in the same manner. The third time it happened I was tactless enough to ask if there was a birdbath in their villa, as I had seen none on the grounds. Our friendship curdled abruptly, which may have been providential. There were probably more black eyes where his wife's had come from.

Gradually, as time wore on, other transients whose actions defied analysis passed through the Garden—a gray-haired poetess who strummed a lyre outside her door for inspiration while composing her verses, a nautical couple who hung out a mess flag whenever they dined, and an Englishman who owned what appeared to be a haunted Rolls-Royce. The car, a vintage model, persisted in rolling out of the garage with nobody at the wheel—a habit he vainly sought to curb by keeping chocks under it and tying the gearshift with clothesline. It was obviously no easy task to minister to the whims of such diverse folk, and how Virgil, the hotel's one-man staff, accomplished it I could never understand. A stoop-shouldered, overworked wraith with an air of patient resignation like that of Zasu Pitts, he doubled as clerk, bellhop, and Florence Nightingale, forever in transit to Schwab's drugstore to fetch midnight sandwiches for the tenants, searching out bootleggers to allay their thirst, and nursing them through their subsequent hangovers. Whatever the commodity or service one demanded, whether it was caviar, a seamstress, bookends, or a massage, Virgil was the genie who supplied it, and after repeated demonstrations of his resourcefulness we began to regard him as superhuman. I found out otherwise when, yielding to his incessant entreaties, I bought two tickets to a spectacle called *The Love Life of Dorian Gray*, an amateur production then current at a neighborhood theater. The play was a fearful hash of epigrams torn out of context from the novel and refurbished with homemade apothegms such as "Love is like a lobster trap; those who are in wish to be out, and those who are out wish to be in." It was acted with unbearable elegance by a cast of heavily peroxided young men and one ill-favored girl, who clearly had backed the venture. Such was the lethargy it induced that by the final curtain all five of us in the audience—two drunken sailors, a nine-year-old boy, and ourselves—were petrified in our seats, unable to move. In the light of what ensued, though, I have to admit that the evening was not entirely wasted. The leading man, ranging the rest of the company before the footlights, requested our attention. "Ladies and gentlemen," he said earnestly, "exactly fifty-three years, six weeks, and four days ago, a traveler arrived at customs in New York who, when asked what he had to declare, responded, 'I have nothing to declare except my genius.' May I therefore ask you, my friends, to bow your heads along with ours in one minute of homage to a great playwright and a gallant gentleman—Oscar Wilde."

Though my horoscope failed to reveal that we were destined to revisit the Garden of Allah often in the following decade, one episode in that first tenancy remains forever etched on my memory. The film script I was crocheting at Paramount was a vehicle for a quartet of buffoons whose private lives were as bourgeois as their behavior on the screen was unbridled. Their actual identity is unimportant, but for those who insist on solving puzzles the ringleader of the group affected a sizable painted mustache and a cigar, and his three henchmen impersonated, respectively, a mute harpist afflicted with satyriasis, a larcenous Italian, and a jaunty young coxcomb who carried the love interest. Having supped repeatedly at the homes of all four, my spouse felt obliged to reply in kind, and, in an ill-considered burst of generosity, invited them and their wives to dinner at the Garden. "We'll have drinks and canapés in our place beforehand," she informed me, "and then take them over to the dining room." Overriding my protest that it was a catacomb, she said, "Yes, yes, I know how depressing it is, but Virgil's promised to put in two more forty-watt bulbs, and, anyway, they'll have such a skinful by then that they won't know what they're eating."

"OK, but that's only half the problem," I said. "How about the dog?" We had a fairly unruly pet at the time, a standard schnauzer who ate everything he could get his paws on. "He's never seen people like these—I better keep him locked up in the bedroom so he doesn't bite one of them. After all, they're my livelihood."

Deriding me as a Cassandra and a calamity howler, she went ahead with her preparations, ordering flowers and liquor as lavishly as if for a wedding and mailing elaborate reminder notes to the members of the troupe. On the appointed evening they appeared with their wives, the latter exhibiting noticeably sullen faces. I was not aware then of something I learned much later—that these kinswomen were at daggers drawn and never saw each other socially. While the men stood around glumly draining their cocktails, the ladies began exchanging barbs so venomous that I was afraid homicide might follow.

"I *love* your hat, darling," one complimented another who was wearing a cloche composed entirely of feathers. "You know something? It makes you look exactly like a little brown hen."

"You don't say," her sister-in-law replied sweetly. "Well, it's a long time since anyone called *you* a chicken."

As the tension mounted and the atmosphere became charged, I grew panic-stricken, and I may have mixed stronger drinks for the company than was prudent. At any rate, I, for one, was sufficiently expansive by the time we were midway through dinner to nourish the illusion that the party was a roaring success. In my relief at having averted mayhem, it mattered not that the food was inedible, the service appalling; I skipped about in the murk lightheartedly refilling everyone's wineglass, joshing the men and charming the ladies—I was, in a word, the perfect host. Indeed, my gaiety was so infectious that the assemblage sat there openmouthed, whether in wonder or overcome by yawns it was too dark to determine. Finally, however, my cornucopia of badinage and jollification was emptied, and the guests trooped back to our villa to retrieve their wraps. I strode ahead of them, giving my version of Richard Tauber interpreting the "Song of the Volga Boatmen" and, as I threw open the door, was confronted by a startling tableau: Cradled in the mink coat that belonged to Mustachio's wife lay our schnauzer, with an object I dimly recognized as her cloche bonnet between his forefeet. He had just stripped the very last feather from its surface and was smirking at us with the pride of an artisan whose work is well done.

Gone is the Garden today, and on its site there stands a curious structure that is either a bank housing an art gallery or an art gallery housing a bank—in Hollywood one never knows. Nowhere inside, though, will the cinema buff find a plaque or any clue to commemorate the shrine a Russian tragedienne erected to herself, and yet none is really necessary. Whenever I traverse Sunset Boulevard nowadays (which, praise God, is hardly ever), I always stop and bow my head in one minute of homage to a great actress and a gallant real-estatenik—Alla Nazimova.

Calling All Moths:
Candle Dead Ahead

Anyone working in close proximity to women, I had always supposed, must be very well aware that his existence, like that of a steel puddler daily exposed to the blast furnace, is fraught with peril. Even a veteran—a floorwalker long accustomed to their vagaries, say—knows that the frenzy of a white sale can so unhinge him that he may round on the customers and chew them out unmercifully. Contrariwise, if one's contact with the sex is professional, such as a physician's or a chiropractor's, he runs a worse risk; he may, in a twinkling, become hopelessly enamored of his patient and, throwing caution to the winds, commit the most unimaginable follies. It is all the more remarkable, therefore, that not long ago a couple of ostensibly prudent Britons, who you'd think would be alive to this pitfall, should have fallen into it headlong.

The first victim, as reported in the *Times* over there, was a London optician in Shepherd's Bush, who allegedly seduced the wife of a travel agent while fitting her with contact lenses. "During several visits [to his shop], things happened which were outside the scope of an optician's duties," Lord Stormont, the Crown prosecutor, stated with consummate delicacy when the case eventually found its way into court. A cautionary tale indeed; a hitherto sober and level-headed oculist peers into orb after orb with impunity, along come a pair that bulge in a more than usually seductive fashion, and—*voom*—he's standing in the dock. The same kind of fate befell the second chap, a dentist, whose downfall was also chronicled in the *Times*. Haled before the General Dental Council to answer charges of misconduct, he confessed to an infatuation with a female patient that had caused him to write her and her family eight hundred letters. "Pointing to a suitcase containing the correspondence," the account went, "Mr. Geoffrey Howe [attorney for the Council] said he estimated that the letters contained about one million words—four times as long as *The Seven Pillars of Wisdom*." Why Lawrence's classic, which has little to do with the molars, should be selected as a unit of measure is unclear, but, in any event, the affair shows how much anguish can result from a simple prophylaxis. Could this unfortunate, on first looking into his patient's gums, ever have prophesied the *furor scribendi* about to engulf him? Obviously not. And yet it underscores the need for eternal vigilance in those plying such hazardous occupations.

Curiously enough, the threat isn't confined to men alone; women so employed are equally vulnerable, as was borne out by a recent experience of my own in New York. Sojourning briefly at a Forty-fourth Street hotel, I had started to shave one morning when I discovered that the Durham-Duplex blades supplied with the razor back in 1919 were exhausted. In consequence I was forced toward evening to apply to a barbershop close by that I hadn't patronized before. Only the boss was in evidence, working with visible haste on a customer, and he shook his head when I voiced my request.

"I have to run over to the Garden in a minute," he said. "I got a white bull terrier in the dog show they're judging at six o'clock. But siddown anyway—the other barber'll be right back. Say, Mr. Weiskopf," he broke off distractedly, "do you mind if we leave the other sideburn go till tomorrow? Buddy Boy's cooped up in a little cage—"

"Well-l-l," the customer deliberated, "I look kind of lopsided, but it don't matter, I guess—I'm staying home tonight."

Scarcely had he gone and the barber whipped into his overcoat when a sultry-eyed redhead, in a tunic molding a figure that verged on the opulent, hurried in from the lobby. As she began railing at the service in the coffee shop, the boss cut her short.

"Skip it," he said impatiently. "Listen, Marvene, do this fellow and then close up. And remember to lock the register, for Chrisake."

She murmured some inaudible sarcasm about its contents, and bolted the door behind him and drew the shades. A premonition stole over me that I would have done better to disguise my beard with talcum than entrust it to someone whose dexterity, at least with a razor, was questionable. I decided to investigate her qualifications to the fullest.

"I—er—just wanted a shave," I said, as I hesitantly settled back into the chair.

"That's what we're here for, Mister," she returned, propelling me into the horizontal. "There, now—relax. This your first time with a lady barber? . . . I thought so. Well, don't worry. I know my business."

"Of course you do." Still seeking reassurance, I cleared my throat. "You must have gone to a Berber college," I ventured, and instantly fell into confusion. It was an unpardonable *gaffe*; nobody could have less resembled a smelly Saharan nomad.

Luckily Marvene was too busy fishing a hot towel from the metal ball to take offense. "No, I didn't," she said, draping it over my face. "I learned the trade from my husband—that is, when he wasn't playing the horses, which was seldom. He's probably at the track right now, blowing our rent money on the sixth."

141

"Oh, well," I philosophized through the steam. "It keeps him out in the open air."

"Only in the stretch," she said. "The rest of the time he's in the clubhouse, guzzling beer with some hooker or other." She rubbed the lather vigorously into my chin, selected a razor, and began to strop it. "Man, does he swing! I've seen chasers in my day, but he's Endsville."

So painful was the recollection of his gallantries, apparently, that she fell silent, working for an interval with a deftness and speed beyond my expectations. During the penultimate stage, though, as she was laving me with bay rum, I thought I detected a very subtle pressure, akin to a caress, emanating from her fingertips. I half opened my eyes and beheld hers ten inches distant, rimmed with mascara and shedding a candlepower almost like Joan Crawford's.

"Forgive me," she said in a low, throaty voice quite unlike her own, "but has anyone ever told you what lovely skin you have?"

"I do?" I felt a faraway buzzing in my ears, as though I were sinking into anesthesia. "It—it always seemed kind of leathery. You know, from the wind and the frost in the country."

"That's *crazy*," she said. "Why, it's as smooth as a baby's. Here," she invited, placing my hand against her cheek. "Feel. Yours is even softer than mine."

Limited as my experience with the lovelorn has been, I knew enough in that instant to beware; one false move on my part and this person could turn into a destroying angel, equipped to do fearful damage with her razor. I disengaged myself as gently as I was able to, arose, and reached for my jacket. But Marvene was not to be disposed of so easily.

"What do you use on your face? Mudpacks? Beauty clay?" she pressed me. "How do you keep it that way?"

"I don't know—honest," I said, plucking a bill from my wallet. "Look, I hate to rush off, but I'm going to the theater, and—"

"It's early," she said. "Couldn't we have a drink somewhere and talk about our skins?"

"But your husband . . . Don't you have to go home and cook supper?"

She snorted. "For that muzzler? Time he gets back from the track, he's full of popcorn and hot dogs. I should make soufflés for *him?*"

"Well, I'll stop in some other time to chin—I mean, to shave," I promised idiotically, and wrenched open the door. As I fled into the street, Marvene cast after me a look of such naked yearning that my scalp crawled. A tide of relief surged up within me at my escape—a liberation, I was to learn soon enough, that was merely a prelude to the onslaught to come.

About four days later I was in Brunschweig's, a cutlery store in midtown, returning a birthday gift some well-meaning dunderhead had given me—a rosewood box from which a flamingo on the cover professedly extracted cigarettes when a button was pressed. What did emerge, in fact, was a mishmash of paper and tobacco of no earthly use, and I said so without equivocation. Just as the clerk was rending the package in a fury, Marvene, her eyes alight, appeared at my side.

"Well, stranger, where've you been?" she greeted me. "Why didn't you come back like you said?"

Startled, I pleaded that my beard hadn't warranted it.

"Applesauce," she scoffed. "Why, you need a shave right now. Doesn't he?" she appealed to the clerk.

"He needs a lot more than that," he declared.

"And you need a good biff in the snoot," I was about to retort had Marvene not interposed. She was there to reclaim some scissors left to be sharpened, she explained, and went on to cajole me, despite my misgivings, into having coffee à deux at a drugstore in the vicinity. The half hour we spent together was an affliction.

Throughout, Marvene kept rhapsodizing about my complexion, exclaiming over its peachlike texture, and speculating about what it would look like under a lens. She confessed that ever since seeing me she had been sunk in daydreams; wouldn't I, couldn't I, allow her to shave me once more? It was sickening, and yet her ardor was so guileless that I was loath to censure her. Finally, however, I could bear no more.

"Damn it, woman, pull yourself together!" I burst out. "You're married—you've got responsibilities. You can't go on being infatuated with a person's skin!"

"Why not?" she demanded quickly. "Does it belong to someone else?" At my reluctant nod, her face contorted with jealousy. "Can she shave you like I do? Ha-ha! I bet she uses a Gillette—a Schick—"

Goaded beyond endurance, I sprang up to depart, but in my haste I spilled a quantity of mail from my overcoat pocket. Marvene bent down to retrieve it. Not till afterward did I realize what her gesture was to cost me, for it furnished the clue she sought to my whereabouts. From that moment on I was an easy stalk, defenseless as a gazelle before a swift-springing lioness. There were half a dozen phone messages in the box when I regained my hotel that evening, each more urgent than the last. The next day I learned that a lady had hung about the lobby for an hour awaiting me. It was unnecessary to read the note she had left—I could visualize its contents. Paralyzed by the sensation of a noose closing about me, I refused to accept any calls, had my meals sent in, and crept out only at night. And then, as if my cup wasn't already running over, the letters began. Every post brought some communication from Marvene, whose preoccupation with my skin seemed to intensify by the hour. In dithyrambs worthy of a lovesick schoolgirl, she compared it to damask, to alabaster, to rose petals; drunk on metaphor, she decked me with garlands of poesy that put to shame the effusions of Julia Moore, the Sweet Singer of Michigan.

To find oneself a love object at my age—it was an absurd, a hateful position, and it called for desperate measures. I might, of course, have had her arraigned on charges before the Barbers' Advisory Committee, but that would subject me to personal embarrassment. The only alternative in the circumstances was flight—not back to rural Pennsylvania, where she could easily entrap me, or to any native wilderness, but to another continent. Accordingly I made a plane reservation to Caracas to mislead Marvene in the event my phone was bugged, and secretly booked passage aboard a liner departing for Rotterdam the next morning. Not a soul was in sight when I checked out at dawn; nonetheless I took the precaution of changing cabs en route to the ship, hid below till the whistle sounded, and finally, as we warped into the stream, ascended to the boat deck, where I huddled under the davits, watching the dock recede and luxuriating in my freedom.

Suddenly an elderly fellow passenger nearby, who was observing the departure through field glasses, emitted an exclamation. "Fighting!" he said excitedly. "Look there—on the pier!"

I took the glasses and adjusted them. A turmoil of some sort was indeed in progress, and as it swam into focus I recognized the chief participant—a sumptuously formed lady with hennaed hair, clutching a barber's satchel and struggling in the arms of two longshoremen. Though I could not hear what she was calling to me, I knew every syllable; it was something of a private nature that wild horses can never force me to divulge. This much I will say, however, and without a particle of remorse. The poor thing brought it all on herself. She just happened to be working too close to me.

Shamrocks in My Head

My salesman was one of those hateful little squirts painstakingly trained by men's clothiers to humiliate their customers beyond endurance, and he was excelling himself. Leaning against a pile of seersucker suits the height of a ziggurat, he burnished his fingernails on his lapel and suppressed a smirk as I strove with bleeding fingers to close the nethermost button of the madras jacket. At length, almost blinded by the rivulets of sweat cascading into my eyes, I shucked off the garment.

"This bloody fabric's impossible," I panted. "It gives me a bulge in the middle like a Rocky Ford cantaloupe."

"That's not fabric, bootsie," he corrected. "That's the pork building up on the old breadbasket. You've got what we call an expensive figure."

"I only wanted something to knock around in," I pleaded. "A yachting coat or a beer jacket like they wear at Princeton."

"Look, old-timer," he said. "You can't camouflage that beanie. Why don't you try Lane Bryant over on Fifth Avenue—some place that caters to expectant mothers?"

Denying myself the drubbing he richly deserved, I flung out of the shop into Forty-seventh Street, bound toward Schrafft's for a chocolate sundae to renew my self-esteem. Scarcely twenty yards on, a sign in the window of a real-estate management firm brought me to an abrupt halt. "Be one of the chosen few!" it urged. "Why not rent an Irish castle for a week or two? Bliss-filled days in the Emerald Isle—smiles and chivalry galore! Inquire within." Still smarting from that popinjay of a salesman's impudence, the idea suffused me like a draught of May wine. Why not a week in Erin indeed, living like a lord amid tenants ingrained with Old World courtesy, sharing their poteen and a wheaten loaf worlds away from this snide, cheapjack metropolis? With a footstep as buoyant as if I had drawn a winning number in the Irish Hospital Sweepstakes, I caromed into the brokers' premises.

Ten minutes later, and thanks to a Mr. Gormley, whose pale, oily visage was indistinguishable from that of a smoked whitefish, I was in full possession of the facts. Sassenach Hall, the demesne in the west of Ireland being let, was the ancestral seat of Marcus, Lord Poltrooney, standing in its own park of 700 acres in County Mayo. All fiefs and appurtenances thereto could become mine for less than the price of a flawed sapphire necklace. No daylight views of the castle were available, regrettably, but Mr. Gormley succeeded in unearthing a moonlight shot, complete with scudding clouds, straight out of the ghost stories of Montague Rhodes James. A butler, cook, and housemaid—the latter possessing the general proportions of Maureen O'Hara, it was implied—would minister to my smallest whim, and for diversion other than the housemaid, there were duck shooting, boating, and salmon fishing in the local streams.

"Have you ever killed a salmon?" Mr. Gormley inquired patronizingly.

"Well—er—I'm not sure"—I hesitated. "I think I once ran over one near Tisbury on Martha's Vineyard. At least, there were some scales on my Chevrolet that the garage said—"

"Quite, quite," he said. "Well, I'll take your application, and if your social references meet Lord Poltrooney's standards, the lease can be drawn forthwith. Now, as to the down payment, we require only a token deposit—as much cash, say, as would fit into the bow of an Oldtown canoe."

Needless to say, my qualifications more than ably fulfilled His Lordship's requirements, especially as I had at one time been junior whip of the Classical High School Debating Society, and a fortnight later my railway carriage deposited me in a pelting rain at Meathead, the market town closest to Sassenach Hall. A ferret-faced youth, ears sprouting like burdock leaves from beneath his cap, slung my bags into a pony cart, and we jounced away to the castle, thirteen miles distant. Seeking to beguile the journey, I essayed a comment or two on the harshness of the Irish Corn Laws and Lord Lucan's savagery in distraining his peasantry for rent. The bhoyo maintained a somber silence, only surfacing to ask whether I had ever heard of a folk rock group in the States called The Scabies, who played on conch shells. Puzzled, I asked how they had acquired such an arresting name.

"Whisht, they've a skin disease of some sort, but it's naught to do with leprosy, I'm told. Just a form of mange."

Our trap was half awash and my dentures rattling like castanets when we finally jogged up the avenue to Poltrooney's manor. Any naïve preconceptions I had entertained of an ivied stronghold bristling with drawbridges and frowning battlements dissipated on the spot. Sassenach Hall was a bleak, late-Victorian structure of gray stone five stories high, perched on a cliff overlooking the Atlantic and resembling the nursery castles that tots construct from Holgate toys. An occasional stab of lightning in the lowering sky, underscored by the eerie soughing of the wind, began to stir dormant memories of *Wuthering Heights* and the Transylvanian didoes of Count Dracula. The cavernous-eyed servitor who answered the bell morosely identified himself as Mulcahey, the butler.

"Did you not bring your guns, then?" he asked, peering at the bags in the cart. Whether he meant my Daisy air rifle or dueling pistols, he did not specify, but the issue was academic in any case.

148

"Divil a duck you'll find hereabouts annyway," he said fretfully. "The leeches is devourin' every blessed wan, alanna. Well, come in, for God's sake, man—don't stand there."

The female remainder of the staff was posed in the entrance hall, curtseying away to the new laird, and I duly curtseyed back. The housemaid's vaunted resemblance to Maureen O'Hara proved in a swift appraisal as close as mine to the Apollo Belvedere, reinforcing a suspicion that there was going to be lots of celibacy in my horoscope. As I sat down to afternoon tea, Mulcahey asked if I had any preference in bedrooms.

"I don't want to be any bother," I said meekly. "Which is vacant?" All seventeen were, except for some trifling ectoplasm, he responded. "Well, then, I'll take turns and sleep in a different one every night."

The prospect of shifting my effects daily caused him visible delight, and he hurried upstairs to unpack me. A moment later he was back with word that as a number of my socks were in shreds, he had given them to Rose in the kitchen to plug up the rat holes.

"And them newspapers you stuffed in your boots," he added. "I put in a pair of His Lordship's trees instead. Have a look when you go up."

I did, and judging from the way the shoes were distended, Poltrooney's feet must have been the size of a cassowary's. I also made a rapid inspection of the upper floors, the plumbing and décor of which appeared to have been lifted piecemeal from some New Jersey hotel near Long Branch. Chilled to the marrow and shaken by volcanic sneezes, I fumbled into the dinner jacket Mulcahey had laid out and made for the dining hall. The half acre of mahogany I presided over between flickering candelabra, while imposing, was not conducive to coziness. Throughout the meal a series of inexplicable noises—doors banging, protracted sighs, and distant moaning —gave rise to a sense of disquiet. Did the castle have any history of ghosts or revenants, I asked Mulcahey. He allowed himself a noncommittal shrug. Then what about pixies, the Little People of song and story, I pursued?

"Ach, well, there's no shortage of them fellas, faith," he said. "Last year, when the circus was held at Nosecandy, they pastured twenty white stallions from Austria in a field where there was a fairy ring. The next mornin', bedamned if the craytchurs' tails wasn't braided into patterns like Kilkenny lace, wan different from the other."

I made a mental note to report the phenomenon to *Old Wives' Tales*, the organ of the Society for Psychical Research, and elbowing aside the savory, a wilted sardine couchant on toast, withdrew to the library. Other than eleven sets of Bulwer-Lytton and a tattered copy of the *Almanach de Gotha*, the only work of fiction in evidence was Hall Caine's *The Woman Thou Gavest Me*. Its effect was so narcotic that even had a coven of witches invaded my bedchamber—a contingency I forestalled by jamming a chair under the doorknob—I couldn't have slept more soundly.

Immediately after breakfast I burrowed into the guidebook to learn what sight-seeing the neighborhood afforded. Cairns, dolmens and similar megalithic souvenirs of the Bronze Age abounded, also an islet nine miles offshore where Meyer Lansky, an eleventh-century necromancer, had cast a spell on a herd of swine. Mindful of several attacks of strangulated ennui in the past from too much archaeology, I decided to visit a couple of renowned ancestral estates in the vicinity, Mealymouth and Breakbone Court. Mulcahey, in whose aged Morris I was to set off, vetoed the former, which had been taken over by a Japanese transistor factory, but assured me that Baron Gristede de Bohack always gave callers at Breakbone Court a warm welcome. His words were prophetic. When I floundered through its gates four hours later, drenched to the skin, and started across the terrace, a hail of buckshot greeted me from an upper window. Before I could scramble back into the car, a scarlet-faced individual with a cavalry mustache in a dressing gown—the first time I had ever seen a cavalry mustache in a dressing gown—flew out of the portal and caught my arm.

"Frightfully sorry, old man," he apologized. "I mistook you for a bailiff—you've the same hangdog look." Nettled, I replied that I was Lord Poltrooney's tenant. "Sterling chap," he said. "Cashiered from the Irish Guards for shoplifting, but otherwise sound. However, come along—I've something to show you. Most interesting experiment—revolutionary, in a way."

The dusty late-Georgian sitting room into which he guided me was large, uncarpeted, and devoid of furniture, except for a spavined armchair. Ranged along a plank resting on two barrels was a variety of whiskies, aperitifs, brandies and cordials. The research Baron Gristede was conducting involved blending these with oatmeal, paraffin, wheat germ and lemon extract to secure a nonexplosive mixture. Thus far, two had blown up in his face without, however, causing serious damage, and he felt success was just around the corner. There was, he asserted as he energetically ladled out two cupfuls, a crying need for a beverage of the sort, inasmuch as casualties among drinkers cut by flying glass in Eire were mounting daily. Hesitant as I was to sample the brew, I had no alternative. To my surprise, I found it quite potable, and accepted a second draught. Whether in fact I accepted a third I can only speculate, because the next thing I knew, Mulcahey was lifting me from the sidecar of a motorcycle in which I had inexplicably arrived at the Hall, and our progress upstairs was slowed by his insistence on clinging to the balustrade and singing *The Harp That Once Through Tara's Halls.*

The excursion I had planned for the next morning began with an unforeseen mishap; somewhat unsteady on my pins, I inadvertently put both feet into one leg of my trousers as I was dressing. Luckily I had the presence of mind to fall against a fire screen instead of the andirons behind it, and was soon right as a trivet.

My goal today was the wreck of a galleon, one of the ships of the

Spanish Armada, whose keel and ribs were reputed to be visible at low tide. By gingerly adhering to wisps of sedge and clay outcrop, I ricocheted down the dunes that fringed the beach, and in due course came on half a dozen blackened timbers protruding from the sand. It was a wild and forlorn place, and surely the last in which one would have expected to encounter another human. What was my surprise, therefore, when a bucolic type, in muffler and cap, materialized out of nowhere and greeted me.

"I daresay yiz'll be one of them American scholars or museum curators like Paul Getty?" he hazarded, his fox face alight with interest. I said that I was merely a well-to-do tourist poking about for souvenirs, and had he observed doubloons or anything of that nature in the wreck? "Bedad, an' 'tis the fortunate man you are!" he exclaimed. "I'm just afther pickin' up some quaint owld coins like yer worship describes. I was hopin' to save thim to send my eldest boy through Trinity College, but I could be talked out of it."

One glance at the red string bag containing a handful of shiny gold pieces was sufficient to indicate that this was a historic find, worth twice the forty quid he asked. With the deftness of a bank teller, he flicked through the notes, and as he vanished into the dunes, I sat down to gloat over my acquisition. Suddenly a horrid buzzing in the ears overwhelmed me, the faintness one characteristically experiences on discovering that he has been yentzed. Attached to the underside of the bag was a sticker with the legend "Whitman's Gold Coins—The Confection de Luxe." When my anguish abated enough to permit rational thought, I made a vow. Should I ever again be braced by a Hibernian bunco artist, I would sneeringly demand whether he saw any green in my eye and inflict a stunning blow on his pate with my shillelagh.

From the moment I had first set foot on the Ould Sod I had yearned to pick up a typical sample of the local crafts, the knitwear and hand-woven textiles celebrated the world over. A morning in a hosiery mill, followed by a trip to a carpet factory, left such a residue of lint that I easily qualified to mate with the girl in the White Owl Cigar commercial—an alluring idea in itself. Eventually, though, I stumbled on a thatched cottage hidden away up a glen that was all I envisioned. Miss Kathleen Mavourneen, the bonnie, raven-haired lass presiding over the stock of cable-stitched sweaters, mittens, and tam-o'-shanters, shyly informed me that they were her handiwork, and we began searching for a cardigan to fit me. Oddly enough, they all betrayed the same flaw as the apparel I had rejected in New York; the material tended to bunch up in the midsection, giving a misshapen look to an otherwise soldierly figure. The noise of a huge lorry outside momentarily distracted Miss Mavourneen, and she went off to investigate.

"Sure, an' it's only a lad deliverin' peat for the fires," she said, re-entering. "We countryfolk up here don't ask much—just a crust an' a bit of warmth."

It occurred to me to wonder why turf was transported all the way from Manhattan in a truck marked "Nifty-Knit Wearables— Wasservogel & Spink, Seventh Ave., N.Y.C.," but I decided to ignore it. Instead, I suggested we might find the bit of warmth she spoke of at some local shebeen, and dimpling prettily, she assented. In very short order the two of us were on the jolliest of terms, thanks to a mutual interest in palmistry, and it developed from her hand that a romance was imminent with a ruddy-faced Rhode Islander, a writer with steel-rimmed spectacles. As our friendship ripened, my admiration for Kathleen increased by leaps and bounds; her only drawback, if any, was that her nostrils were too sensual, her figure a shade too voluptuous. I was just about to propose that we hie ourselves to a tumbledown shack in Athlone when a behemoth the size of Brian Boru, a great loogan with ropes around his corduroys, clumped into the snug.

"This is my fiancé, Rory McClobber," the fair one announced. Rory grasped my hand in what seemed to be a wine press and squeezed. As he released the mangled members and I sank to my knees whimpering, Kathleen patted his arm affectionately. "He's a broth of a boy, isn't he, now?" she said. "D'ye know, he once picked up an ox and threw it at a fella that was winkin' at me?"

I spent a good part of the next day indoors at Sassenach, massaging my fingers with horse liniment and composing a letter to the *Irish Times* about peasant brutality. On the night before leaving the castle, I had what was perhaps my closest encounter with an apparition. While making my way along a dark upstairs corridor after dinner, I beheld a spectral figure advancing toward me. Its garb of hacking coat and Tattersall vest was the exact duplicate of mine, the face contorted in a loose-lipped grin that froze my marrow. In the light shed by the taper I held aloft I unfortunately did not recognize the reflection in the cheval glass as my own, and, springing aside, tore away a medieval tapestry equal to any on the Atlantic City boardwalk. An arduous job I had of it, scissoring the thing apart and stuffing it up my bedroom chimney, but once I had cleaned off the soot, I fell into refreshing slumber with the knowledge of work well done.

My bags stood packed and ready under the porte cochere, and the pony cart, filled with rain water in readiness for our trip back to Meathead, was drawn up outside. Within, Mulcahey and I were completing the final ritual demanded of every tenant—checking the inventory. A look of profound mistrust overspread his face as he ran his pencil down the list.

"The gramophone, the oyster forks, the tea kettle—no, they're all here," he admitted, and paused. "But wait a bit. You didn't happen to see a spin-drier we're missin' from the laundry room, did you?"

I had not, but it flashed through my mind that an earlier guest somewhat the worse for wine may have stuck it up his chimney. As I anticipated, parting with retainers who had served me with such fierce, unquestioning loyalty for a full week was sweet sorrow indeed. The curtseys, obeisances, and ten-pound notes fluttering farewell brought a lump to my throat, and at the bottom of the avenue I had my jehu pause for a backward look at Sassenach's hoary walls. Then, silently murmuring the motto on my own family escutcheon, "*Nunquam iterum, Carolus* (Never again, Charlie)," I bade him drive on.

Hark—Whence Came Those Pear-Shaped Drones?

I say, would it be indiscreet of a married man to kiss and tell—to confess that the other day he found himself in the same boat with an appealing Englishwoman who stirred his senses? Oh, I can read your mind; you doubtless visualize a blissful pair out of an early Compton Mackenzie novel, drifting lazily downstream in a punt past the dreaming spires of Cambridge, with Cicely trailing the tip of her parasol in the lilies and I, Leslie Howard reborn in my immaculate flannels, poling our craft along and apostrophizing her with a verse of Robert Herrick's. (While all unbeknownst to us, a fanatical Serb in faraway Sarajevo prepares the coup that will end our golden dream forever.) Well, you're wrong—I was merely using a metaphor in a quite prosaic sense. I just meant that when I read a letter in the London *Times* from Mrs. Janet Barney of Pangbourne, Berkshire, appealing for help, my heart warmed toward her because I'd once been involved in a plight almost identical with hers. Mrs. Barney—whose letter, by the by, confirms her as a lovely person, the sort you actually would apostrophize—was imploring the women's page for advice on how to cope with girls imported from the Continent as mother's helpers. "I'd like to appeal to your more experienced readers," she wrote, "for a set of simple rules for 'au pairs.' I'm not sure where I go wrong. I suspect it is my fault that the girls take more and more liberties. By the time they leave us, they are eating us out of house and home, staying out late, using all the bath water, borrowing the children's socks and disappearing when needed most. I do keep my end of the bargain with continuous English lessons, generous pocket money, trips out, special traditional dishes, and so on, but somehow I end up washing dishes while the au pair plays tennis with my racquet with my friends. Who will advise me before I spoil the next one?"

Though children played no part in my own predicament, the complications that arose from harboring two young foreigners paralleled Mrs. Barney's so strikingly that her words gave me gooseflesh. (Well, metaphorically.) I should explain that about a year ago I began to be concerned about the burden imposed on my wife by life in the country. Instead of playing Chopin on the pianoforte or painting skillful, evocative watercolors as I'd envisioned, she was busying herself with a score of menial tasks, as exhausting as they were unnecessary. She was forever upstairs and down, pushing a carpet sweeper into dark corners, suspending rolls of flypaper from the ceiling, polishing the isinglass in the coal stoves, and hoisting hundredweights of ice, which bade fair to slip out of the tongs and crush her foot into our icebox. In addition to whitewashing the hens—a chore whose value, to say the least, was arguable—she had started to fashion souvenir birchbark canoes as a source of pin money, as if the allowance I made her were not already lavish. It offended me that a woman of refinement and intellect, a bluestocking and a product of the best finishing schools, should expend her energy on such footling pursuits, and I said so in no uncertain terms. To my surprise—for I foresaw strenuous objections—she signified her readiness to abdicate at once if I could furnish another drudge.

"Now, wait a minute," I demurred. "Cleaning women don't grow on trees, you know, and they're not cheap. Some of them get as much as thirty-five cents an hour. . . . What did you say?"

"Nothing," she said. "OK. How about a nice couple?"

"Honey," I protested. "It stands to reason that if one person earns thirty-five an hour, two would be twice as expensive."

"Well, then, we'd better look around for a robot," she snapped, with an abruptness that sounded like the slam of a zinc-lined ice-box. "You don't expect anyone to work for free, do you?"

"Hold on—you may have thrown me into an idea," I said. "Why don't we spring for an *au pair*—a couple of European youngsters who'd appreciate a good home in the country, rambles galore, and the chance to brush up their English on our Linguaphone records?"

The prospect of supervising two immature aliens, to be truthful, dismayed her at first, but she finally capitulated, and I called an agency in New York specializing in placements of the sort. Ten days later I was notified that Denise Savoureux and Cosette Oscillant were arriving by bus at Trenton the following noon, and I drove in to meet them. The moment the girls appeared in the terminal, a sensation overcame me as of one who has just put foot in a quicksand (*qui a posé son pied dans un sable mouvant*). Far from being adolescents, the two were young ladies whose conformation caused a perceptible stir at the gates; in fact, our introductions were well-nigh inaudible, due to wolf whistles in the background. Denise was a lush, green-eyed blonde of the type you see ogling sailors on sentimental French postcards, her companion a sultry brunette with a teasing smile that coiled itself around the male passerby like a boa constrictor. Accompanying me toward the exit in their pitiful miniskirts and blouses, the latter plainly woven of cobwebs, they seemed to undulate rather than walk. A hot blush suffused my face, and I suddenly felt myself transported to Marseilles, a trafficker in the South American export trade. Rather than suntans and a madras shirt, I ought to be wearing a gooseneck sweater, a cap, and a quarter inch of Gaulois depending from my nether lip.

Luckily the illusion that I was Pepe le Moko dissipated on our journey homeward, enabling me to correct a few misapprehensions about the girls. The agency's description of them as former students at the Sorbonne was fanciful; Denise had been a coatroom attendant at the Crazy Horse Saloon, on the Left Bank, and Cosette a manicurist in the barber shop of the Hotel Georges Cinq. In consequence, their English, which I had been led to understand was minimal, was far more fluent than mine, and much racier. It had improved as well under the tutelage of their first employer in America, a sportswriter on Long Island—a goatish character whose hands, they confided, smiling reminiscently, were always straying. And where had they worked thereafter, I inquired. Most recently in Las Vegas, in a Lido-type floor show at Caesar's Palace. Pleasant and cool though the ambiance, their costumes consisting of no more than a handful of feathers, they much preferred a home environment like the one I was taking them to. I dummied up and said farewell to the brioches, croissants, and quiches Lorraine I had promised ourselves. How on earth was I going to install a ramp of the kind these babes were accustomed to in our dining alcove?

My wife's reaction to Denise and Cosette was, at any rate, heartening; if she felt either dizziness or an impulse to faint, she concealed it and behaved with signal worldliness and aplomb. She did, however, insist that they be lodged elsewhere than in the house, since, as she lightly explained, our proximity could easily degenerate into a French farce. She conducted the girls, accordingly, to guest quarters in an outbuilding a few yards distant, and, with the injunction to slip into something less comfortable than their peekaboo blouses, invited them to relax and familiarize themselves with the premises.

"They're awfully disappointed we haven't a pool," my wife disclosed in the kitchen as she set about preparing a traditional dish to make the two feel at home—a trout blue with almonds. "Maybe you should get a quotation on what it'd cost to put one in temporarily. Oh, yes, and while you're about it, find out about the barn—I think it would make an ideal casino. This place must be such a letdown after Vegas."

From the restraint shown toward the *pièce de résistance* and the significant glances her aides exchanged, it was clear Madame's cuisine had not swept them away. They displayed tolerance toward the wine, however, deeming a bottle of Beaune I had cherished for twenty years a decent enough vintage. In the hope they would assist with the dishes, I washed a few to acquaint them with the technique, but they retired yawning to the piazza and partook copiously of our Chartreuse. The television set having broken down some weeks earlier, we amused ourselves watching the fireflies. Cosette asked if there were any velodromes in the area, or a discothèque for young folk.

"There's a roller rink open Thursdays in Frenchtown," my wife imparted. "Boys? Hm-m-m, not too many in this section. We have one who mows the grass, but he's just been here."

"Well, phone him to cut it again," said Denise, green eyes glinting like a leopard's on stalk. "*Mon Dieu*, listen to how quiet it is, Cosette. This place is a sepulcher."

The stillness prevailed only until the arrival next day of the milkman, who, after one glimpse of our charges, sped off to rouse the countryside. Within an hour the driveway was choked with vehicles of every description—pickups, tractors, sports cars, scooters, and buckboards. Carpenters and plumbers we had vainly besought for years to make vital repairs swarmed over the place offering their services and undercutting each other's estimates. A truck appeared with Nards and Beck and Reedsworth Smiles, a trio of electricians eager to rewire the house at cost, and farmers who had spurned our fields for years as eroded and sterile clamored to replant them, pressing free seed on us. Amid the cataclysmic uproar Denise and Cosette held court in the kitchen, dispensing cokes by the dozen to their red-faced, perspiring swains and teaching them to dance the java. So distracting was the resultant pinching and squealing that I could abide it no longer and bore my wife off to a barbecue stand, where we could lunch in peace. The girls had taken French leave in our absence, but a note informed us that they had gone swimming in the Delaware, whose many eddies can be treacherous if there are no hands to pull one out. Apparently there were, for when they reached home at 3 A.M., the playful slaps and oo-la-la's that rang through the valley reassured us that they were still alive, if somewhat shopworn.

What with the black coffee, the Bromo-Seltzers, and the icebags their hangovers required that morning, it was small wonder my wife mistook me for Eric Blore miming a sympathetic manservant in an RKO musical, yet the eternal feminine in her would not be stilled; did I linger an extra moment in the guesthouse, she stalked in with arms akimbo and extricated me gently but firmly by the ear. Her casual suggestion to Cosette and Denise over breakfast that they help with the housework evoked only a sullen silence that persisted until two pustular youths materialized with a power boat on a trailer to escort them to the Jersey shore. In the ensuing three days we saw them hardly at all. They flew in sporadically to use the phone or to bathe—with, I may say, reckless disregard for towels, which cost us a mint to launder—and it was painfully apparent from their chill behavior that our attempt to befriend these petrels from an alien shore had failed. One evening, though, their mood seemed to have undergone a magical change; radiant with suppressed excitement, their eyes sparkled mischievously and giggles convulsed their abundant frames. Investigation revealed that our neighborhood art festival, an annual affair, was featuring a revue, the director of which had invited them to participate. It was a splendid opportunity to involve themselves in the artistic life of the community, and I approved wholeheartedly.

"What sort of specialty will you do?" I asked, glowing with pride that the family was to be represented. "Characteristic folk songs—*chansons* from Brittany and Provence? Or plaintive ballads, like those of Edith Piaf and Aznavour?"

"*Oui, oui—peut-être*," they replied distractedly, and rushed off to rehearsals. Instinct told me that it was unwise to catechize them. They wanted freedom to choose their own creative outlet, to express themselves wholly and untrammeled. I respected that. It showed spunk.

It showed much more than that, as it developed. The spectacle attracted a capacity audience—the largest in years—which included many carpenters, plumbers, electricians, and farmers not normally patrons of the theater. We ourselves sponsored a party of friends prominent in the musical world and interested in the *lieder* the girls might sing. The setting of their act was an old-fashioned minstrel number performed by local teen-agers, who rattled their tambourines with engaging professionalism as the end-men exchanged jokes about chicken stealing and wooden razors. When the mirth subsided, an orchestral flourish and roll on the snare drums brought our protégées weaving sinuously out of the wings. They wore deeply incised evening gowns threatening to burst at each breath, opera-length gloves, and aigrettes improvised from broomstraws in their hair. To the strains of "A Pretty Girl Is Like a Melody" the pair began a slow strip as calorific as Georgia Sothern's, interspersed with grinds and bumps that lashed their admirers to frenzy. Urged on by hysterical chanting, they had peeled down to G-strings and pasties and were preparing to discard those when a flying wedge from the ladies' auxiliary shot over the footlights and swept them offstage.

En route to the Trenton bus terminal early next day, Cosette expressed chagrin that our association had withered on the vine (*devénu jaune sur la vigne*). It always happened when there was a bossy woman around, Denise observed with a typically Gallic shrug; actually, they had longed to prepare me a few regional dishes like *cassoulets* and *ratatouille,* but what would you, the mistress of the house would have scratched out their eyes in jealousy. As I was stowing their luggage on the rack I overheard the driver agree to deposit them at an establishment outside Perth Amboy called the Diamond Bikini. I must stop by there sometime. It's probably the only roadhouse in New Jersey, if not the world, that can boast a couple of authentic, dyed-in-the-wool *au pair* girls.

The Hermit Crab

English Lord of the Manor wishes to sell title, no property involved, benefit of ancient documents proving title, including survey carried out during the reign of Queen Elizabeth I. £2000. X8436 Times.—The New York Times

Among harder goods, the vintage firm of Sotheby's is auctioning vintage clothes this Friday. Lot 35, Lingerie, formerly owned by the Countess of Craven, is a collection of cambric and lace Nightdresses, Chemises, and Drawers, slotted with blue ribbon, variously monogrammed C.S.M. and C.C. surmounted by a coronet.—Ibid

She was one of those shrill suburban gasbags marinated in bourbon, those relentless, obsessive bores who swarm like Mayflies at buffet dinners. I had squinched down yogi-fashion under the piano and was striving to juggle my plate, cutlery, and wineglass and to avoid being trampled when she wedged herself in alongside and commenced an interminable monologue about food which finally centered on her love for sandwiches.

"It's a fixation with me, sandwiches," she babbled. "I could make an entire meal off them—I eat them morning, noon, and night. And my husband—he's even worse. Put the finest gourmet-type meal before him and you know what he'll say?"

" 'Give me a good sandwich,' " I said numbly.

"Correct," she said. "Now, the average person gets up and has orange juice, cereal, a slice of toast, and coffee—right? Not Frank. The first thing he looks for at breakfast is his bacon sandwich. 'Isabelle,' he says—that's our maid—'where's my bacon sandwich?' And Isabelle says, 'Coming right up, Mr. Bostitch.'"

Providentially, a woman's earring from somewhere in the crush overhead rolled into view at the moment, and I scrambled to retrieve it. Its claimant was a youngish pouter pigeon in silver lamé, eyes lustrous with mascara in a face like a West African ghost mask, who identified herself as Lady Angela Burwash. She thanked me so profusely that I remarked that the bauble must be an heirloom.

"How observant of you," she said. "Yes it belonged to Robin's great-aunt—Violet, Countess Utmost, you know." I didn't know, but her own accent, I noted, was homegrown—an American married to a British title, plainly. "And this is my husband, madly making love to that beauty on the couch."

Burwash, a bulky, rather foppishly clad individual in his forties, with hair like the Seven Sutherland Sisters' rippling down the nape of his neck, heaved himself upright and shook hands. His languor and his strangulated delivery were characteristic enough, though he, too, lacked any English inflection in his speech.

"Rum little party, isn't it?" he observed. "Where on earth does Gloria find these waxworks—Madame Tussaud's? That orangutan there by the hearth, for instance. I daresay he's one of your typical Chicago gangsters."

I said that he was a renowned attorney whose reminiscences had become a best seller.

Burwash frowned. "You mean a solicitor, do you?"

"Well, maybe you'd call him a barrister."

"My dear man, there's a world of difference," he said pityingly. "Let me explain the distinction." He did, making it the thousandth time I had been so enlightened, and then proceeded to list other curious Americanisms—"elevator" for "lift," "freight car" for "goods wagon," "kerosene" for "paraffin," etc., etc. The longer he went on the more puzzled I grew, for his accent was so much at variance with his identity that I couldn't reconcile them. My hostess, when I alluded to it later that evening, also confessed perplexity.

"I hardly know them, to be honest," she said, "but I'm told the Burwashes are a very old family, dating back to Charles I or something, and Robin and Angela have spent years in Canada, where her father apparently had these vast landholdings. That's why they sound American, though obviously they're English to the core."

I can date the next time I saw Lord Burwash with accuracy—it was Lincoln's Birthday and I was on the Ninety-sixth Street platform of the IRT when an extraordinary figure strode past. He was dressed like the Great Emancipator, in a tile hat and frock coat, his hands affixed to the lapels, and from the brooding melancholy on his countenance you could tell he was weighing McClellan's conduct of the Army of the Potomac, or an equally momentous problem. Since Lincoln's foremost impersonator, Frank McGlynn, was no more, and it was improbable that Raymond Massey stalked the subways in full makeup, I concluded that this must be some homeward-bound journeyman actor out of a TV holiday special. Standing nearby were a couple of sailors, one of whom eyed the passerby with curiosity but no recognition. He nudged his companion. "Holy smokes," he said. "Get a load of that creep with the muff."

Practically in the next moment the doors of an express shot open and disgorged Burwash, garbed in a canary-colored Guards overcoat and enough whipcord to outfit the entire Whitehall barracks. Before I could share the tidbit I'd just overheard, he went into a *megillah* about his presence in the subway. He never let slip an opportunity to ride our Underground; the argot spoken by the commonalty, their polyglot speech rhythms, helped him to a fuller understanding of the American character, which, on the whole, he felt to be fairly childlike.

To stanch the flow, I asked whether he and his wife had been living abroad since our last encounter.

"No, we rarely use the Hall nowadays," he said. "Can't stomach those trippers strewn over the lawns at two bob a head—National Trust, you know. Besides, it's hard cheese on Angela, having to plan meals, oversee the staff, and the rest of it. So my estate agent copes, and we keep a bolt-hole here, a tiny place where we can pig it and get our own breakfast."

"Oh, I say," I protested. "Surely you don't carry your own laundry down to the Chinaman?"

"Er—not quite, I'm afraid," he said, with a shade of hauteur. "Well, must dash—I've an engagement to have a tooth stopped. Ring us up sometime and we'll give you a cut off the joint and a pint of bitter. There's a pub we rather fancy on Columbus Avenue —a saloon, I believe you call it, though that's actually a car model, isn't it? Toodle-oo."

Somehow an evening with *Pilgrim's Progress* in my chimney corner seemed preferable to one with the peerage in a West Side gin mill, so I didn't pursue the invitation. A matter of four months later I happened to be up on Martha's Vineyard, and dropped into a stationery store in Edgartown, looking for a mechanism of sorts with which to run a staple into my thumb. The shop was full of plutocrats bespeckled with liver spots, demanding the *Wall Street Journal* in loud, authoritative tones, and I didn't peg Burwash at first. All at once, however, his voice cut through the din, vibrant with incredulity. "But the smallest kiosk at home carries the *Times Lit. Sup.* and the *Daily Mail!*" he was sputtering. "Don't you people stock any English newspapers at *all?*"

The clerk, a distracted college girl, replied that they occasionally received the *Observer* and the *New Statesman.*

"Well, shouldn't bruit it around," Burwash snapped. "I never read the Communist press, thank you very much. Good day."

I snatched up a nudist magazine to screen myself, but the sweetmeats emblazoned on the cover arrested his eye, and he pounced on me. After a few heavy jocosities about voyeurism, he disclosed that he and his wife had been given a cottage in either East or West Chop for a fortnight, together with a sailboat equipped for fishing.

"Well, I'm glad you got a smack in the Chops," I said heartily. "You deserve it—I mean, everyone needs a rest from the strenuous social round in New York."

"Precisely my words to Angela this morning," he said, proving us to be kinsprits. "Now, when can we capture you for a real slap-up English meal? How about tomorrow—the next day—the day after that?"

Short of submerging myself in a lobster pot off Cuttyhunk, no feasible refuge from his hospitality occurred to me, and I knuckled under. The lunch, true to his promise, was typical—jellied eels, cold lamb garnished with several limp varieties of okra, a milk pudding, and a savory—and the conversation fitful. It had been raining torrentially since their arrival, and the Burwashes were inclined to be morose about the island's charm.

"I can't imagine what you see in the place," said Lady Angela. "We took a stroll along the shingle just now, and the water just seethed with crayfish waving these dreadful feelers. The postman told Robin a boy in Oak Bluffs was devoured by a shark."

"It was his own fault," I said, springing to the defense of the Vineyard. "I heard the kid was teasing it—throwing pepper in its eyes."

"Still, that couldn't happen at our watering places—at Eastbourne or Torquay," Burwash said loftily. "There's something in the Yankee temperament that finds release in violence, don't you think?"

I thought so, but tact prevented me from defining it. To further

168

illumine the gulf between English life and our own, he outlined the idyllic existence they hoped to resume at Burwash Hall when the Labour Government was ousted—a pastiche of backgammon, charity bazaars, improving the local breed of swine, and encouraging the peasantry to retain old-fashioned courtesies like touching their caps. Lady Angela suggested that on my next trip over I might be persuaded to hunt with the district pack. She was confident a pink coat of my size could be borrowed from one of the grooms.

"Speaking of clothes," her husband put in, "would you know anyone who'd like to pick up a rather valuable collection of undershirts and shorts? My neighbor Balbriggan wore them—chap who fell out of the balcony in the Lords during the Suez crisis. The jumpers are top-quality jersey, embroidered with his crest, of course, and the shorts have the original horn buttons made from their stags. There's also a box of his old garters he very much prized. Be a windfall for historians of our era."

"Gee, I wish I could afford them," I said, "but every cent I've got is tied up in my stables." In a small bandanna kerchief under the roof, I deemed it wiser not to add. "Where could they be inspected, if I hear of a purchaser?"

"They're kept in a numbered Swiss account, owing to the high insurance rates," he said. "If your party's credentials are in order and he can post, say, a few hundred quid as an earnest of good faith, I think Balbriggan's widow might be induced to sell."

I promised to alert only persons of the highest probity, like wealthy archimandrites, and presently withdrew.

Once or twice throughout this past winter the matron at whose flat we met asked if I was in touch with the Burwashes, but my failure to unearth a customer for the underthings had given me such a sense of inadequacy that I quickly changed the subject. Then, out of the blue, I got wind of the pair the other day in an altogether unlikely locale—a barbershop in the Grand Central area. I had engrossed myself in a magazine to avoid listening to two fellow patrons—lawyers, from the context, or, more properly, solicitors—discussing some tedious litigation. Suddenly a reference to Burwash pinged in my ear, and I stiffened.

"You mean the former lord, the Englishman, wants his title back?"

"Hell, no. He's just trying to collect the balance. This American, Nowicki, paid him only two hundred pounds for the documents and the survey, assumed the title, and began living it up. Charge accounts in the stores, restaurants, big social splurge—the whole bit. It's a perfectly legal transaction, except my client's screaming for his dough."

"This bird—the new Lord Burwash—does he have any assets?"

"Not a dime, but he sure sounds legit. You'd never know he was an upholsterer from Queens Boulevard, and his wife a dietitian."

"Well, if you ask me, you haven't a prayer," the first commented. "Your man's been had, Morty."

"That's what I told him," his colleague agreed. " 'Look, Your Lordship,' I said. 'Take my advice. Change your name to Nowicki, move to Jamaica, and go in the upholstery business. It's your only chance to break even.' But you know those English. He looked at me like I was talking a foreign language. They live in another world."

Paint Me a Pinion Immortal, Limner Dear

The first time I met Bertram Spitalny was in a life class at the Art Students League in the autumn of 1928. I joined it in the strange delusion that my stature as a comic artist would somehow be enhanced if I sketched the undraped female figure, and since the two scrawny typists I knew screamed the house down when I asked them to disrobe, I had to look elsewhere. The evening group I enrolled in was conducted by a distinguished teacher named Bridgman, most of whose precepts were lost on me except for his sonorous dictum, "Ladies and gentlemen, the breast is a cage." Whatever its anatomical significance, I took this to mean that matrimony was a trap. Bridgman was the exponent of a system he called "dynamic symmetry" that I was far too obtuse to understand, and our sessions were a curious half trance in which I gaped at the model nonplussed or strove to capture her curves with sticks of charcoal that crumbled maddeningly between my fingers.

Spitalny, whose easel adjoined mine, was a commercial artist specializing in posters—a pale, wraithlike chap with an explosion of hair like a Zulu's bursting from his head. He was a feverish and, I saw at once, accomplished draftsman, and he went out of his way to encourage and assist me. As the realization sank home that I was

not destined to be another Ingres or Delacroix, however, my en-
thusiasm waned, I skipped a class or two, and ultimately abandoned the course. Living in the Village, as we did, Spitalny and
I would run into each other now and then, chiefly in a barbershop,
where he must have gone to read the magazines, for his hair never
showed evidence of contact with scissors. He was assiduous in his
attempts to make me resume at the League, but I exuded such
inertia that he finally gave up. His own career in poster work, I
gathered, was flourishing; film companies sought him out with regularity to portray five thousand Apaches ambushing a wagon train,
five thousand Crusaders besieging Acre, five thousand Fuzzy-
Wuzzies storming a Sudanese fort, and similar panoramas. "I'm a
pretty good crowd man," he admitted modestly. "I get a kick out
of people milling around."

They were milling in earnest when next I saw him, about four
years later, and under grievous circumstances. A fat, needle-nosed
dilettante of my acquaintance, a Yugoslav importer, was married to
a lady so sumptuously endowed that men clung to lampposts and
sobbed as she passed. At that time, before columnists had begun
listing female proportions, there were no accurate statistics to go
by, but all agreed that Luba Pneumatiç was a lollapaloosa, the
Eighth Wonder of the World. It seemed outrageous that such
treasure should be lavished on a single fat foreigner, and fancying
myself in the role of Robin Hood, I set out to make him share the
wealth. What with orchids, perfume, bonbons, and costly lunches,
I was reduced to virtual beggary by the time I learned that Madame was a trifler, cold as marble, and, furthermore, stupidly enamored of her husband. My last shred of illusion vanished at a
soirée she held for what she archly described as a few intimates.
The sight of one woman holding court for thirty-seven men sickened me, and as I flung out I barged into Spitalny, his arms heaped
with roses. We stared at each other aghast.

"You—you too?" he croaked. "But she gave me to understand . . ."

I gripped his shoulder wordlessly in the gesture beloved of fighter pilots in Warner-First National productions, and left. At intervals over the years I caught sight of him across concert halls or theater lobbies, and once in a mob greeting an incoming liner, but we never managed to speak. Then, a few days ago, in a dusty bookshop on Fourth Avenue, where every prospect sneezes and only Mann, the owner, is vile, our paths again crossed. Springing from its catacomb with a hoard of Kate Greenaway prints he had unearthed came Spitalny, hair as tumultuous as ever but powdered with silver. We exchanged the ritual falsities about each other's youthfulness and adjourned to a nearby coffeepot. Spitalny's métier nowadays, it emerged, was industrial design—a field he had found more rewarding than posters in a monetary, if not an aesthetic, sense. "You must see the studio I own on West Eleventh Street someday," he said animatedly. "Used to belong to Daniel Chester French, the sculptor. Eighty feet long, paneled in walnut, four huge skylights—it's fantastic. And the way I came to buy it— well, you've heard Hollywood stories, I know, but this one's a daisy."

The saga had begun one morning in the early forties, he recounted, with a pressing summons from a large advertising agency. The executive who interviewed him dispensed with nuances. Hailing my friend as the Toulouse-Lautrec of the screen world, he offered him a six-week engagement on the Coast at four thousand dollars a week, round-trip transportation, and all living expenses. The nature of the assignment, he told his stunned listener, was undisclosed, but he pledged that it did not involve homicide, theft, or bodily risk. As to the client, a promise of the utmost secrecy was vital, for Stephen Surreptici's horror of publicity was a byword. At the mention of the name, bells of purest gold rang in Spitalny's head. Surreptici was a legendary figure, a young billionaire industrialist whose fortune derived from machine patents, airlines, and oil wells, and who dabbled in movie-making on a spendthrift scale.

"Your salary starts now—this minute," the adman's honeyed voice went on. "Here's your flight ticket and hotel reservation. Check in there and sit tight—he'll contact you. Above all, remember—mum's the word."

The scene Spitalny found himself confronting forty-eight hours later from the fifth floor of the Hotel Oriflamme in downtown Hollywood was scarcely what he had envisioned. No glamorous personalities like Paul Henreid and Vera Hruba Ralston tripped past, no pert starlets in halters or directors wielding megaphones. He saw instead a bootblack stand, a bankrupt nightclub, and a health-food shop with a trickle of patrons overdue at the embalmer's. The possibilities inherent in the view were limited, and in the weekend that dragged by without word his reason teetered close to the brink. Eventually, at ten-thirty one evening, a taciturn chauffeur appeared and drove him to a motel in the outlying district of Sherman Oaks, in a room of which he was enjoined to wait. On the stroke of twelve a tall, unshaven individual in a slouch hat and upturned coat collar descended from an ancient Buick sedan. He did not bother to identify himself; like Garbo, he assumed, not incorrectly, that the world knew who he was. "Here's the problem," he said abruptly. "My new western, *Hot in the Saddle*, is ready for release, but the poster they've designed for me has a serious flaw." He extracted a thick wad of paper from his pocket and unfolded it. "See if you can spot it."

The lithograph Surreptici held up before Spitalny depicted two figures, a cowhand and a girl of dimensions shaming Luba Pneumatiç's, struggling in the doorway of a barn. If the theme of the composition created any doubt, it was dispelled by the concupiscent grin on the *vaquero's* face and the haymow in the background.

The artist scanned it, perplexed. "It's a good workmanlike job," he said. "What bothers you exactly?"

"The way he's clutching her wrist, man," Surreptici said with distaste. "There's no *oomph* in the goddam thing. It's tame, pussy-foot, timid—like they were in dancing school. I want a grip that'll radiate desire—the blinding urgency of a sex-hungry wanderer of the plains!"

The repair seemed trivial enough to one who in his time had portrayed five thousand naked Visigoths, and Spitalny agreed to undertake it. The next morning, in a fully equipped studio prepared for him in the Wilshire Medical Building, he fell to work. Anxious to extend himself for so princely a fee, he decided on a multiplicity of studies—the entire axis of impetuous hand encircling reluctant wrist, with almost microscopic variations. Over the ensuing month, therefore, he executed an impressive anatomical chart that showed forty separate renderings of the subject in painstaking detail. His solitude, save for the rustle of the weekly four-thousand-dollar check slipped under the door, was undisturbed. The job complete, he phoned Surreptici and was bidden to rendezvous, again at midnight, in a roadside diner near Laguna Beach. Perspiration began mantling his forehead as the producer examined each drawing minutely without any reaction. At length, the latter broke the silence. "A true professional never resents criticism," he said, voicing the maxim that ever precedes the swish of the headsman's ax, "so I won't pull my punches. None of these is right. They're good, mind you, but not quite on the nose. However," he continued on a more sanguine note, "I . . . think . . . I've got a solution. I have, by cracky. If you could combine the elements of— let me see—Numbers 19, 26, and 37 there, we'd have exactly the clutch I visualized."

Spitalny was momentarily downcast. However, he had met perfectionists before, and while this one was exceptional, he reflected, so was the *quid pro quo*. Accordingly he retired to his atelier and, after ten days of prodigious labor, evolved a grasp he felt would tickle the most lascivious fancy. He unveiled his handiwork, so to speak, at still another meeting place calculated to throw Nosy Parkers off the scent—the back room of a Mexican social club in San Clemente. From the way Surreptici's lips tightened as he surveyed the drawing, Spitalny knew the verdict was foreordained. "My friend, I hate to say this," Surreptici said. "It's too photographic—too real. All the rapture's drained out of it, the wild ecstasy, the tortuous yearning to commune with a voluptuous body symbolized in that grab. We'll have to start in again from scratch. Let me explain the psychology of these two stormy petrels to you."

His discourse on the libidinal drive lasted fifty minutes, ending with Spitalny's promise to sleep on it and formulate a fresh approach. Instead, he hastened to the bank after breakfast, drew out his earnings, and caught the next plane east. By coincidence, the studio of his dreams, which he had long hungered to possess, had just come on the market, and, in a whirlwind of joyous solvency, he consummated the purchase on the spot. He was immersed in redecorating it a fortnight later, his ordeal half forgotten, when the advertising genie who engaged him telephoned.

He was beside himself. "What the hell is this, walking off the job?" he barked. "Mr. Big's almost in tears—he's afraid you had a nervous breakdown. Was it the money? If so, he'll up the ante to five thousand, six—"

"No, no," Spitalny pleaded. "Look, I'm only a hack, but I know my limitations. I washed out, I *failed* him—do you understand? I was a flop."

"You're demented, Jack!" the other cried. "He thinks you're a genius—a modern Da Vinci. He's crazy for you. All he wants is two weeks of your time—three at most. Now, cut the cackle and start packing—there'll be a limo there in an hour to put you on the noon flight to L.A."

The idea was abhorrent, but, as Spitalny gazed around his

studio, there danced in his head visions of the sugarplums an added eight thousand dollars would buy—armor, tapestries, rich carpets— and his resistance buckled. At their reunion a couple of nights afterward, in an orange warehouse in Azusa, Surreptici welcomed him like a prodigal son. Avoiding any hint of reproach, he shoul- dered full blame for impinging his wishes on him. The artistic temperament, he declared, in a burst of metaphor, was porcelain- fragile, a shy wild flower that wilted at the merest breath. Hence- forth Spitalny's brush was to follow its own bent without let or hindrance. All he asked was that should some cataclysm erase Hollywood, obliterating everything but the masterpiece he fore- saw, it might be a Rosetta stone wherewith archeologists could de- cipher the sexual mores of the age.

Spitalny brooded over his chart of forty drawings for a day. He discarded five, and from the remainder evolved a dozen combina- tions at random, twisting the importunate fingers into tentacles resembling those of an octopus. He then procured from Surreptici a blowup of the film clip the poster was based on, and from it traced the ravisher's actual grip, which he treated, unlike the others, with unsparing realism. When he placed the sum total of his work before Surreptici for judgment, the latter betrayed enthu- siasm for the first time. "Aha!" he exclaimed, rubbing his hands. "We're getting close at last—very close. That is, except for this one, of course." He indicated the tracing. "That's just plain dis- torted, kid—nobody's got a mitt like that. As for the rest, you want my honest opinion? They tease me, but they don't send me—know what I mean? Now, if you could manage to blend together the components of—hmm—Number 4, Number 7, and Number 11— *Hey,* what's the matter?"

"Nothing . . . nothing," said Spitalny faintly, and slid to the floor.

The smoke of midday hamburgers coiled up about us like altar fires, and the cashier's scowl plainly indicated we were *de trop,* as my friend concluded his recital. "Well, that's it," he said. "It was weeks before I could pick up a pencil, and even now it bugs me when someone fondles a woman's wrist. You know that TV commercial 'Would you hold hands with a cactus?' I have to leave the room."

"So do I, and I never laid eyes on Surreptici," I said. "Which version did he finally use, by the way?"

"Oh, the one on the original poster, naturally. But then, to top it off, they cut the haymow sequence out of the movie. Go figure."

"Ah, well," I consoled him. "You've a lovely studio to show for it, haven't you?"

"Yes, but I can't work there, damn it," he said. "I just use it to impress clients. And also, Luba loves it. . . . You remember her, don't you—Luba Pneumatiç that was?"

I did, and I got out of there real fast. After all, flesh and blood can bear only so much anguish in one day.

Let a Snarl Be Your Umbrella

The series of discomfitures I underwent in London several weeks ago—all of them petty and seemingly unrelated—began, if memory serves, at a West End chemist's the morning after my arrival. A thin-lipped xenophobe, whose face attested descent from a long line of flounders, he wrinkled his nose in scorn as I enumerated the toiletries I sought.

"Astring-o-sol?" he repeated. "What's that—one of those Yankee tranquilizers you folk eat like groundnuts?"

Rather than engage in a lengthy causerie, I asked if he had some toothpaste, on the order of Crest, containing Fluoristan. He did not, he rejoiced to say; the British varieties he stocked were mercifully free of any such adulterant. "And as for the particular toothbrush you mentioned," he added, "my advice is the same I give all our colonials. Just massage your gums with a twig."

My *amour propre* had barely revived when, a day or two later, I happened into a luggage shop off St. James's. From the opulent array of valises, shooting sticks, and bootjacks, not to mention the languid Guards type behind the counter, it was abundantly clear that the clientele was restricted to the wellborn. The customer ahead of me—also an American—was in a visible flap about the price of a cigarette case. "Thirty-six guineas?" she was protesting. "That's over a hundred dollars!"

"Quite," agreed the salesman, plucking the case from her hands. "May I suggest you root around Cheapside for something more commensurate with your purse? Good morning, Madam." He ebbed toward me. "You wished . . . ?"

"I'm thinking of a book box for my daughter," I said. "You know, those contraptions where the front and sides flop down—"

His eyes rolled upward in martyrdom. Spare him my explanations, he begged; even the most benighted must be aware that Crosspatch's had supplied book boxes to every royal house since the Plantagenets. Naturally, one couldn't hazard a guess at the cost of special-order items, but if inquiries were put forward, details might be forthcoming in a few weeks. After a pause unbroken save for the sound of my breathing, I indicated that a five-cent shopping bag would fulfill the purpose gloriously, and withdrew. The salesman bore my departure with the stoicism of a true Guardsman.

At an ironmonger's in the Brompton Road next day, a third attempt—this time to buy a flamethrower to eradicate the weeds from our garden path—also ended in stalemate. Despite a meticulous description of the mechanism as advertised in *The Countryman*, the shopkeeper betrayed not a glimmer of comprehension. Worse yet, he adopted the soothing manner used with dotards and the fractious, and propelled me firmly out the door. Pondering my rebuffs on the way back to the hotel, I began to see that they were all part of a pattern. Something was afoot, although what I couldn't for the life of me figure out.

The answer came from a wholly unexpected source. The following Monday I was returning by rail from a weekend near Towcester, in Northamptonshire. Sharing my carriage was a plump, bowler-hatted gentleman immersed in the contents of his dispatch case. Neither of us had progressed beyond platitudes when a sudden gust scattered his correspondence. As I bent to help retrieve it, my eye was caught by the letterhead on the top sheet.

" 'Creative Humiliation Associates, Ltd.,' " I said, mystified. "What in the world is that?"

"Oh, just a company I manage," he replied offhandedly. "Educational sort of thing. Equips all types of folk—clerks and shop assistants, hall porters, garage attendants, whomever—to protect themselves."

"Against what?"

"Why, customers, of course," he said, clearly surprised at the question. "Never heard of us? Ah yes, you're an American. Well, we teach 'em the dynamics: woolgathering, disdain, the snub direct and implied, *Schadenfreude*, the mechanics of sniggering, simple and compound exacerbation—the lot."

I ventured the opinion that I had met some of his graduates, and asked if by chance the institute ever permitted visitors. Mr. Huxtable fairly exuded cordiality. He would be delighted to receive me —to demonstrate a few tricks that, he added slyly, my countrymen might very well emulate. We parted at Waterloo with an appointment for the next day and his pledge that a stimulating experience awaited me.

Drumtochtie House, in Cockspur Street, was a rabbit warren harboring every imaginable kind of enterprise—Indian shipping agencies, experts in porcelain repair, costumiers, and societies for the propagation of birching. The decayed gentlewoman behind the desk in Huxtable's anteroom exhibited momentary misgivings, but the sight of his card dispelled them. With an injunction that class was in session, she waved me through an inner door.

The two dozen individuals listening to Mr. Huxtable were widely divergent types—several Jermyn Street fops, four or five persons in City attire, a few sharp-faced characters from the East End, and some pustular Mods with luxuriant hairdos. I tiptoed to a rear seat, and in short order managed to pick up the thread of the discourse.

"Now, the same rules apply to the news agents and tobacconists among you," Huxtable was saying. "Remember, no matter how mealymouthed he is, the chap who's invaded your shop has one purpose only—to muss up your stock and disrupt your routine. He's your adversary, and as such must be dealt with summarily. The involuntary step backward, the perplexed frown, the fingertips drumming on the counter, and the sudden conviction that you face a lunatic at large—these are your ingredients, and how skillfully you mix them will determine how soon you rid yourself of this pest. . . . Is all that clear? Very well, then, let's press on to the shirtmakers and hosiers." The Jermyn Street contingent sat up expectantly. "You fellows, like the bespoke tailors, are in an ideal position. You see all the client's pitiful inadequacies—the sunken chest, the skinny shanks—and it behooves you to make the most of them. Have you evolved any useful techniques?"

"Well, I titter behind my hand," said a Beau Brummell in a resplendent foulard shirt. "For those slow to embarrass, I shake my head as if to say, 'Gorblimey, what a mess.' When they flush up nice and rosy, you know you've brought 'em to heel."

"A toff with a fat neck is always surefire," put in a colleague of his. "You simply pretend the tape measure's too short."

Huxtable nodded. "Good show," he conceded, "but both those methods hardly scratch the surface. Now, over in Savile Row they've developed a really wizard ploy. Should the fitter discover someone with exceptionally long arms, he'll murmur the word 'chimpanzee' to his assistant. Not loud, mind you—just so the customer overhears. Then there's the distorting mirror, which I assure you takes the mickey out of the most inflated ego. Yes, you accessory men must face it—you've got to move with the times."

"Would you amplify one point you made earlier, sir?" a youth whose hair swirled to his waist requested. "You cautioned us specifically against the guffaw."

"Indeed, and I should have explained," said Huxtable. "The scornful smile, gentlemen, has twice the potency of the loud, derisive bray—just as the rapier, in expert hands, is far deadlier than the saber. There is no more beautiful sight than a customer taunted to the verge of apoplexy by a series of covert sneers, and he who learns to goad with delicacy and style can reap rich rewards in merchandising. All right," he said briskly. "So much for that. Suppose we hear from the footwear people."

A benign old party in a morning coat arose, identifying himself as Joskin, the Dover Street bootmaker. "We've our own special problems in the custom trade," he explained. "The man who buys ready-made shoes more often than not has a hole in his sock—an excellent pretext for the staff to giggle or ignore him till he flounces out. However, since we cater only to the gentry, whose socks are flawless, there's no expeditious way to humiliate them."

Huxtable's brows contracted in thought. "Can't you surreptitiously rip their hose with your nail whilst measuring the last?"

"By George, it never occurred to me," Joskin confessed. "Huxtable, that suggestion pays for the cost of this course twice over."

"Thank you," the head replied graciously. "As a matter of fact, you open up a fruitful line of inquiry. I don't wish to flatter the shoe clerks here to the exclusion of the rest, but you've always pioneered at infuriating the client. Now, it's obvious a man's at his most vulnerable when he's shoeless, and that's the time to strike at his dignity. What refinements come to mind?"

"Call him to the phone, so he has to hop around on one foot," a voice proposed.

"How about shouting 'Fire!'?" another chimed in. "Wouldn't he feel a bloody ass if he bolted out onto the curb with his garters flying?"

"Splendid," Huxtable said. "Work on those—sharpen and expand them. Remember, I'm here purely as a catalyst, to activate your thinking and evolve new modes of mortification." He paused for a sip of water, then addressed a youth in the front row. "Well, Molesworth, how are you faring with the ladies at—what's that department store of yours?"

"Bondage's," said the young man. "Coming along nicely, sir. When the fatties ask for a size twelve, I give 'em a playful little push and advise 'em to see a tentmaker in the Woolwich Road. Any of the other snobs you shoot down in flames by just recommending the budget shop on the sixth floor."

Huxtable consulted his notes and pocketed them. "Fine, that disposes of everyone today except you hairdressers," he said. "Our next session will confine itself to ways to render yourselves more odious. Meanwhile continue the treatment outlined hitherto— namely, tease and lacquer every lock, stock, and follicle on the patron's head and then predict her imminent baldness. Good afternoon and God bless."

As the room emptied, Huxtable came forward and greeted me amicably. I conveyed my appreciation of the privilege he had so generously extended. On the contrary, he rejoined, he hoped I would not regard today's class as typical; his roster embraced a variety of other people—tax auditors, ushers, and bus drivers—adept at browbeating the public but anxious to develop their proficiency. "And I'll whisper a tiny secret in your ear," he confided, assuring himself nobody was within earshot. "My associates and I are planning a course that'd be the exact opposite of this one—for customers. We'd show 'em how to thwart these bastards—to be just as noxious as they are. I say, look here," he exclaimed. "What's your opinion? Would there be any future for this kind of thing in the States?"

OK., I thought, you asked for it. "No, sirree," I said emphatically, "and don't think you're going to foist it on us. Remember something, Limey—we gave you a warm breakfast in 1776, a hot lunch in 1812, and we'll give you a sizzling supper any time you're ready. Put that in your pipe and smoke it."

I looked back at the man just before I slammed the door. Whether he was smoking or not I can't say, but one thing I'll promise you—he sure was burning.

The Skin You Love to Watch

Call me an Anglophile, scourge me with rods, heap coals of fire on my head—I yield to nobody in my respect for the British. Theirs is the language we speak (after a fashion), theirs our predominant culture, religion and dress. Granted the French cook better, the Italians woo with more zest, the Swedish are shapelier; when it comes to civility, decorum and good manners, the English lead the world. . . . OK, is my viewpoint sufficiently clear? You appreciate just how I feel? Good—because I want to retract everything I've said. It's balderdash. I'm so ashamed of it, in fact, that I may never be able to show my face again in public.

My disillusion dates from a report recently published in the Paris *Herald Tribune*, of a British TV documentary dealing with nudism. "Male and female anatomy was shown in full frontal frankness in the film screened over the color network, BBC-2," it stated. ". . . The nudists, who prefer to be called naturists, were seen romping around in summer camps, and some of them later crammed onto a settee to be interviewed by a fully clothed girl reporter." Many of the rompers could have used a pair to advantage, seemingly, for their middle-aged flab evoked a storm of protest from the viewers and TV critics. Wrote one of the latter, "A huge acreage of the human form was revealed, but most of the bodies on display would have persuaded me to take vows of celibacy." Another deemed the spectacle both silly and sad, and at a subsequent studio discussion with the nudists, a psychiatrist gave them the coup de grâce, declaring, "This is death to sex." In short, it was a tiptop demonstration of the law of diminishing returns—the more you see, the less the impact.

Now, this is no outburst of moral indignation at the BBC's transference of nudity from the bathtub to the home screen; thanks to courageous pioneers like Kenneth Tynan, the language of the livery stable has been made available to the humblest, and every schoolboy polled there in a nationwide schoolboy poll knew more about sex than his family obstetrician. What spooks me, on the contrary, is the network's inept showmanship, its total disregard for the juicy potential of skin as entertainment. A *documentary*, for God's sake, on a topic like that—it's as if the discoverer of the Cullinan diamond had elected to use it as a paperweight. Here is a gem infinitely more precious, with a thousand facets waiting to be polished by the craftsman's hand. Never once did anybody think to explore its romantic overtones, the excitement and catharsis it could generate. Still, one mustn't be downcast. Even if the British have proved unequal to the task, it behooves us to see that nudity gets a fair shake, as it were, over here, and out of sheer altruism for the good of the medium, I'd like to indicate how the wide-awake TV producer can exploit it in gripping yet artistic fashion.

Mindful that good theater springs ever from real life, let's use as a pattern for a possible teleplay an incident that occurred in Gainesville, Florida, a while back. The news account, emanating from United Press International, was headlined "Coed Found Guilty of Nudity" and read, "Coed Pamela Brewer, who posed nude for a men's magazine, was found guilty Sunday of violating University of Florida rules. A disciplinary committee composed of nine professors and two students found Miss Brewer, 18, guilty of 'indiscriminate conduct and inappropriate conduct.' She had posed lying nude on a bear rug." In that dry, prosaic dispatch, I contend, are the elements of a story as powerful as Nathaniel Hawthorne's *The Scarlet Letter*—a heroine accused of flouting the moral code, an outraged Establishment, a hue-and-cry for penance, and ultimate vindication. All one needs to transmute it into absorbing TV fare is a sharp pencil and a pair of asbestos gloves.

We open, accordingly, on the campus of Nossiter College, a small Ohio institution, where students congregate in the leafy walks discussing in hushed voices the plight of Crystal Gondorf. Everyone, without exception, is flummoxed; how could this demure but *zoftick* freshman, with a brain rivaling Spinoza's encased in the body of a Lollobrigida, have consented to pose in her birthday suit for *Leer* magazine? Not since Gaby Deslys took a milk bath in 1916 in the pages of Hearst's *American Weekly* has there been such brazen disdain for convention, affirm Nossiter's graybeard professors. The photograph in question has been examined under magnifying equipment by a panel composed of faculty members Hinch, Pericolosi, Cresap, Nachtigall, Louttit, Forkins, Pepper and Lustgarten, as well as by two nearsighted but unbiased students, Mitnick and Voles, and its authenticity verified beyond doubt. Under the circumstances President Butterfoss has no recourse but expulsion, and he has given Crystal twenty-four hours to establish her innocence or quit Nossiter's ivied walls forever.

"Oh, Zeke!" sobs the hapless Crystal to her fiancé, Zeke Dadirrian, captain of the football team, in a nearby coffee shop. "I never did it, I tell you! The whole thing is like some horrid phantasm spawned by Franz Kafka, author of *The Trial, The Castle*—"

"Yes, yes," Zeke interrupts. "This is no time to flaunt your literary knowledge. Of course you're guiltless, but how to prove it in the few hours we have left?" His minuscule brow furrows in concentration. "Wait! There is someone who can help us—Marty Craig, Chicago's top private eye, who has just built a fishing retreat on sparkling Prune Lake."

Love to Watch

"Oh, Zeke!" Crystal's eyes open wide in relief. "Do you think he could be persuaded, albeit reluctantly, to espouse our cause, unearth whatever scant clues he may discern, and construct a hypothesis enabling him to solve so puzzling an affair?"

"No," Zeke returns moodily, "and one reason why is because you won't take the mush out of your mouth. You're a wonderful girl, Crystal, but you talk like a sausage."

There are now two directions in which the story can progress. The first is that the lovers remain in the coffee shop sulking, which, while restful, does not perceptibly advance the action. The other course is that President Butterfoss, on the brink of senile dementia, stirs out of his lethargy, and in the interests of fair play, convenes the panel to re-examine the offending photograph. During the session a participant comments on the necklace worn by Crystal, speculating that a malicious hand might have pasted a snapshot of the coed's head onto the figure of some stripteuse like Hinda Wasau or Sherry Britten. A vigorous inquiry is launched: Crystal is summoned to have her dimensions checked with calipers, and presently the culprit is unmasked—Babs Crouthammel, a classmate who had hoped to supplant her in Zeke's affections. The nude's actual identify is never disclosed, which adds a bittersweet touch, and should a final fillip be needed, President Butterfoss could drop dead from hypertension. He is not an ingratiating figure, on the whole, and the viewers will be glad to be rid of him.

The kernel of an even more piquant situation, and one fraught with melodrama, is contained in a similar news item carried by the Chicago *Sun-Times,* to wit: "Baltimore (AP)—With more than a hundred men in frantic pursuit, a nude girl dashed across the College Park campus of the University of Maryland Monday night. The nude darted out of the shadows about 11 P.M. and raced across an open space in front of Cumberland Hall, a men's dormitory. Men poured out of the dorm and gave chase, but the girl reached a waiting car that whisked her away. The only casualty was a male student who injured his ankle when he fell down a stairway. Nobody knew the reason for the girl's dash."

In TV production, as in cookery, a cardinal rule obtains: good ingredients should never be wasted. The coffee shop frequented by Zeke and Crystal is an ideal locale for the accidental meeting of the duo involved in our second program. Visualize, therefore, a tempestuous, rain-swept vista in Baltimore as a cab draws up to its exterior and deposits handsome Ricky Gaylord, international society jewel thief. Moments thence, another cab appears bearing glamorous Diana Grenfell, who plies the same profession—and from that moment you practically have the audience eating out of your hand. What in the world has brought two international society jewel thieves, deadly rivals on five continents, to this improbable place unbeknownst to each other? The encounter explodes into crisp, crackling dialogue.

"You?" sputters Ricky in stupefaction. "But—but I thought you were on the Riviera!"

"And you in Salzburg!" she says, thunderstruck. "See here, Ricky Gaylord, if you try to cross me up—"

Well, as we all know, society jewel thieves have their own code of honor, and the reason for their presence soon becomes apparent. Both are intent on the same prize, the fabulous Galitzine rubies that Harry Galitzine, a sophomore at Maryland U., has just fallen heir to. The stones, of which only fifteen remain of the original tiara worn by Empress Alexandra of Russia, are each the size of a hen's egg, and, until Harry can decided their future, repose in a paper bag in his quarters. Ricky and Diana, discovering they are in love, evolve an ingenious scheme to purloin the treasure. In a phone call to the janitor of Cumberland Hall they learn that the room above Galitzine's is empty, and adopting the combined techniques of *Rififi* and *Topkapi*, they plan to bore through the floor, lower Ricky upside down, and abstract the bag with his teeth.

Their design comes to naught, however, with the disclosure by the janitor (whose tongue, by the by, appears to wag pretty freely) that Galitzine never leaves his room, but sits staring fixedly at the bag of rubies.

"It's hopeless, Diana," vouchsafes Ricky, pacing the floor. "If the chap only sent out for food, we could render him *hors de combat* with a sleeping tablet, but he eschews all nourishment. He isn't human, I tell you—"

"You think not?" An enigmatic smile illumines Diana's lips. "Eliminating hunger, darling, there's still another drive that motivates we mortals, *n'est-ce pas?*"

"Great Scott!" bursts forth Ricky. "You mean, create a diversion wherein a naked girl races across the campus, causing the dormitory's occupants to erupt and give us access to the swag?"

"That's more cumbersome than what I had in mind, frankly, but it'll do," Diana admits. "The problem, though, is whom can we inveigle to strip off their vestments? Oh, well, I suppose I might as well be the one. OK—help me unzip my dress."

"Wait a minute," Ricky protests. "We're still in the coffee shop, and it's nowhere near nightfall. It strikes me you're in an awful hurry to get your clothes off."

Diana nods sheepishly. "I'm sorry, precious. You must think me an awful goose."

"Silly," he says indulgently. "Here, leave me kiss your dear little snub nose ere we address ourselves to solving the multitudinous bugs inherent in our plan."

Which are legion, plainly, as the two soon ascertain. How to alert the more than a hundred residents of Cumberland Hall that an unclad female will sprint across the campus that evening? With time too short to mount a whispering campaign, a notice has to be posted on the college bulletin board. To assure visibility, moreover, the floodlights normally used only at the Prom must be activated—

an obstacle overcome by bribing the janitor. At length, however, all is in readiness. The getaway car is stationed on Vesey Street, its motor idling, as the minutes slowly tick away to 11 P.M. (No chauffeur exists to pilot the machine, regrettably, but the pair cannot afford a confederate.) Inside the dormitory, tension has risen to an almost unbearable pitch as the collegians pretend to be immersed in their calculus, civics, etc., but furtively consult watches. Suddenly the sonorous peal of bells sounding the hour is heard, and Ricky and Diana, crouched in the shrubbery, spring into action. Like some breathtaking nymph fired into life by the imagination of Bernard Geis or the Grove Press, our heroine bounds over the quad; simultaneously the horde of frenzied males within emerges baying in hot pursuit. And up the staircase, tense and phantom-swift, glides Ricky past the rooms of Galitzine's neighbors, Rex Tentz and Simon Fantom-Swift; he throws open the door, and there confronts as strange a sight, God wot, as his eyes have ever beheld. For here on the table is an empty paper bag, pinned to it a mocking note that reads. "Better luck next time, *mon vieux*. Boris." Yes—despite their well-laid plans, Ricky and Diana have been outwitted by the greatest jewel thief of them all, Boris La Flange, who had been masquerading under their nose as—you guessed it—the janitor.

Now, admittedly there are threads here and there in both stories that need interweaving, what are technically called "loose ends" in TV parlance. Furthermore, I wish to make it clear that nobody is wedded to the plots outlined; it may, for example, prove more feasible to switch the scene of the foregoing to a girl's college and have Ricky run naked across the greensward, or conversely, show Diana, fully dressed, fleeing from a hundred nude scholars. These are details, ephemera to be mulled over by production-wise executives. The one factor that cannot be gainsaid—and if they gainsay it, they are blind little fools—is that nudity, treated with taste and

Love to Watch

intelligence, can be stellar home entertainment. It always has been, and so long as it doesn't frighten the horses, in Mrs. Patrick Campbell's immortal phrase, let us return it to the people to whom it rightfully belongs. But for heaven's sake, fellows, lay off those documentaries.

Out of This Nettle, Danger . . .

That nameless, one-ton angular abstract sculpture recently in-stalled in the Hall of Justice now has a name, "Serious Hazard." That's what the National Safety Council's San Francisco chapter, safety consultants to The City, has called it in letters to City officials. . . .

The edges of one protruding metallic arm are "razor sharp." Anyone falling against this protuberance "is in danger of suffering serious injury," said Iver C. Larson, executive vice-president of the Safety Council's San Francisco chapter. . . . Larson viewed it not for its art form. He and his office aid, Miss Eva Metzger, are old hands at Hall of Justice safety. Through their efforts several years ago, when there was a rash of policemen falling out of new-type swivel chairs, they had new bases installed on the chairs, ending the humpty-dumpty falls.—San Francisco Examiner

From the Battery northward to Madison Square, Manhattan lay muffled in mist and eerily silent save for the hoarse cacophony of foghorns from the bay and the encircling rivers. In Wall Street's financial district, usually agog with feverish activity, only a few gray wraiths moved gingerly, lest they be clobbered by taxis inching through the murk. Charismé Ismay breathed a sigh of relief as she hurried into the Usurers' National Trust Building and stripped the kerchief from her honey-colored hair. If she vouchsafed no answer to the cheery salutation "Fine weather for ducks, Miss Ismay" from Sam, the fatherly old Hebrew at the newsstand, and from Mike, the fatherly old Hibernian in the elevator, both knew her too well to take umbrage. Nobody could be more ebullient as a rule than Charismé, acknowledged even by her own sex to be the prettiest and most popular girl in the building, but on this morning she was abstracted, sensing that some emergency must have caused so early a summons from her employer.

" 'Lo, beautiful," quipped Carrots, the red-headed, irrepressible office boy, as she entered. "Say, when are you and I ankling toward the altar?"

"Just as soon as you get your longies, shrimp," she riposted, doffing her coat and sailing into the inner sanctum. Despite the hallowed interchange, the youth's doglike devotion had touched her, and she threw him a smile that left him radiant all morning.

The man who stood ruminating at the window inside was no longer young; indeed, his ruggedly handsome head was flecked with silver, albeit the keen, hawklike visage bespoke vibrant energy and purpose. A tireless watchdog of the public weal, Ambrose Chanel had sponsored innumerable reforms heretofore deemed visionary—the hourly collection of banana skins to safeguard pedestrians, the adulteration of glue with horseradish to curb juvenile sniffing, the substitution of plastic paper clips for steel as weapons in the schoolroom. A man of iron self-control, one would have judged; withal, at the sound of Charismé's greeting, a shadow of pain darkened his face. Ever since the day he had chosen this wide-eyed Skidmore graduate from among a score of others as his assistant he had loved her to distraction, with every fiber of his being. But he was doomed to silence, chained to a woman who had not kept pace with him—the outcome of a college escapade. He had endured torment that might well have broken a weaker man. As he turned to face the girl now, though, his voice was steady, and only the knuckles strained white in his brown, sensitive hands hinted at the turmoil within.

"Greetings, my dear." Chanel's was the cool, impersonal gaze of a patron of a high-class fish market. "Sorry to drag you out in such beastly weather, but we've some problems. Not insurmountable, I hope."

"I brought along my alpenstock and crampons, just in case," she twinkled, quick to catch his allusion. "Well, Chief, what's the first glacier?"

"Hmm, rather a tricky one. You've heard of Proximity Dimity?"

"The billion-dollar lingerie cartel? Of course—they've just put up that new skyscraper on Park Avenue, with the Henry Moore sculpture in front."

"Good girl. Well, about seven last evening, the copy chief of Engels, Freeboard, Wildonger & Pfaff, an ad agency in the building, stumbled as he came out and caught his head in an aperture of the statue. Seems he'd had a few prior to joining a client at the Biltmore bar. Anyhow, he passed out and lay trapped there for over an hour."

"Didn't people notice anything unusual?"

"No, they thought it part of the composition. After he awoke and began screaming, someone called the rescue squad, which finally extricated him by coating his head with Vaseline. It's a freak accident, I'll grant you—a man with a head that small mightn't come along for years—but we can't afford another like it. The Old Man's got the wind up."

"What old man?"

"Search me—some gaffer in Bryant Park," Chanel said impatiently. "The point is, how do we cope?"

"Couldn't the hole be plugged? Cement, or, better yet, a temporary material, like asbestos?"

"We'd have a lawsuit on our hands, princess. Sculptors are a touchy lot."

"Wait a sec." Charismé chewed thoughtfully on a nail. "You know those little round flaps they install sometimes to let cats go in and out?"

Chanel beamed at her. "Wizard!" he approved. "That does it to perfection. By jingo, Carrie," he blurted out, momentarily deaf to the import of his words, "I don't know what I'd do without you." Then, as their eyes met, he mastered his embarrassment. "Righto, the next item. This is industrial rather than cultural, I suspect. One of our fieldworkers reports that the personnel of two dairy restaurants on Second Avenue handling sour cream have been stricken with snow blindness."

"But it's their own fault. We recommended that they wear dark glasses, like skiers."

"They claim they can't tell the difference between the blintzes— the cheese, the cherry, and the blueberry. No, the cream's to blame —we've got to evolve some way of reducing the dazzle."

Lost in reflection, Charismé stared at the ceiling, and the swelling curve of her throat sent another quiver of pain across Ambrose's darkly handsome features. How unlike she was to her whose objurgation and endless beefs he had borne in penance for a youthful folly. A sudden wild impulse to declare his love surged beneath his polished exterior, but he fought it down. When his assistant spoke at last, her question startled him.

"Have you ever examined a white-on-white shirt, Ambrose?"

"My dear girl! What in the world—?"

"It's a matter of optics, really. You see, the makers insinuate a tiny, hardly noticeable pattern into the weave, as a contrast to relieve the eye. That's what the sour cream undoubtedly needs—a sprinkling of poppy or caraway seeds—coconut, even. Anything that would break up the shimmer."

Her superior emitted a low, astonished whistle. Incredible that a mere child from Skidmore, unversed in science, should have solved in a flash of insight a riddle that had perplexed the keenest minds on Second Avenue. Of course, it remained to be seen how the minds would react to coconut on their blintzes, but that could only be determined by trial and error. Uncoiling his lean, six-foot length from behind the desk, Chanel stood gazing down at his protégée in unfeigned admiration. "You're miraculous," he said, and went on abruptly, "Look, I hate to burden you unduly, but an even more vexing problem's arisen, and, frankly, it's a beast. You recall reading about the policemen who like to sleep on duty? Well, it appears that while 'cooping,' as they call it, they tend to fall out of their prowl cars."

"You mean, the doors won't stay closed?"

"Precisely, and there seems to be no way to anchor them. The poor chaps are being concussed right and left, not to mention having their uniforms hopelessly besmirched."

"Can't the seats be tilted back farther?"

"That's been tried. The blood rushes to their heads, causing dyspnea and befuddlement."

"I don't suppose a car without doors would be practical," Charismé pondered, frowning. "The law's minions have to emerge quickly in case of an emergency."

"Oh, all sorts of expedients have been suggested—pneumatic suits and Lord knows what," Chanel returned gloomily. "I'm afraid we're up against a stone wall unless one of us gets an inspiration—Hello!" he broke off. "The sun's come out. Now see here— I've been a nasty, selfish ogre to enslave you this way. Take the rest of the day off. Go to an art gallery, have your hair done—"

"Don't you like it the way it is?" Charismé's nether lip, luscious as a ripe fruit, sagged forlornly.

Chanel's heart constricted in his breast. How he longed to draw her to him and extoll its shining beauty. But stern honor forbade. "This is an order," he said gruffly. "Be off with you, Miss—do you hear? Scat!"

As Charismé walked slowly homeward along Third Avenue later

in the day, her thoughts strayed back to his remark. She paused to examine her new coiffure in a reflecting shopwindow and wondered if he would notice it. Womanwise, she had long known of the creature who stood between them, and, while too generous to hate her, had striven to make the office, at least, a refuge from domestic agony. So absorbed in contemplation was she at the moment, in fact, that she barely heard the warning shout, "Watch it, lady!" from a demolition she was about to pass, and jumped back in the nick of time. Three workmen were loading debris into a truck from an overhead chute. As she waited for the dust to subside, some sixth sense impelled her eyes upward. One of the men had begun to lash down the rubbish with a tarpaulin, the corners of which his mate was knotting to the chassis. Charismé watched him spellbound.

"You there, Mister!" she called out. "I say—Tony!" The workman, whose olive skin and gleaming teeth indeed proclaimed him a native of sunny Italy, raised inquiring eyebrows. "Why are you tying those ropes there?"

"To keepa theesa tarp froma flying off, Signora," the fellow explained. "You no do that, she rolla in de gutter (*rigagnoletto nelle vie*)."

"Oh, thank you *enormemente!*" Charismé told him joyfully, and sped off, leaving a very perplexed Neapolitan to scratch his head in wonder at the *bellissima's* intent. All the way to the nearest call box her heart thumped in elation, and it seemed an eternity before she heard Chanel's deep response on the wire.

"Ambrose?" The excitement she struggled to contain quickened his own pulse on the instant. "Remember that inspiration you said we both needed? Well, I've had it!"

One week afterward, Charismé, her face aglow, sat in her superior's office, listening to him read a citation from the police commissioner which those who knew that ordinarily reserved individual would have deemed nothing less than ecstatic. Never in his years on the force, he asserted, had he been so indebted to a single person as he was to Miss Ismay; her proposal that his men secure their car doors with string while cooping had achieved spectacular results. In a five-day test not one concussion or besmirched uniform had been reported, and the precaution had been made obligatory procedure henceforward.

Ambrose paused, and she fancied a strange tenderness in his voice as he resumed. "I haven't read you the postscript, though. He deputizes me—well, the old duffer empowers me to express his gratitude with a kiss."

A fiery blush mantled Charismé's cheek, and she arose hastily. "Please, Ambrose," she began. But before she could escape he had blocked her path and was holding her in his powerfully muscled arms—a new Ambrose, gone the shadow of pain that had seared his countenance over and over.

"Oh, my very dear, listen to me. There's much more than that I have to tell you. I'm free at last. The connubial specter that's been bugging us—it's gone, vanished."

Unable to credit her ears, she heard his voice pour out in an impassioned gush. His wife, madly jealous and scorning all the rules of safety he had worked to disseminate, had waxed their kitchen floor to glassy smoothness, and, in mounting a chair to fetch a rolling pin wherewith to strike him, had somersaulted and cracked her noggin like an eggshell. "Well, there you are," finished Ambrose resignedly. "We warn them, we yacket away night and day, we spend the public funds to emphasize the jeopardy facing them, but they never learn, do they?"

No, thought Charismé, snuggling closer in his embrace, and yet out of their travail had come a shared experience, a way of communicating that would enable the two of them to go on. And that, in this world of hazard and rapid technological change, was something.

My Life in Scotland Yard

Outside of King Faisal's harem, the council chamber of the Politburo and Secretary Rusk's cerebellum, there are few places in the world harder to penetrate than the Black Museum of Scotland Yard. This fabled storehouse of felony, reputed to be the tastiest ragout of murder, forgery, burglary and sexual katzenjammer on earth, had long been a legend to a boy reared on Hearst's *American Weekly*, the exploits of Raffles, and the forty-odd volumes of *Notable British Trials*. Some five years ago in London I whimpered so plaintively of my longing to visit it that official hearts melted and I was given an escorted tour. The experience was riveting, to say the least. That such infinite ways existed to dismember, hoodwink, mulct and ravish one's neighbor I never dreamed. I never dreamed at all, in fact, until after I saw the collection, and then, for a full week I slept with a night light and a bureau firmly wedged against the door.

My tour began in the slightly musty office of Mr. Protheroe, the departmental superintendent in charge of the crime section. A craggy, soft-spoken gentleman combining the best qualities of C. Aubrey Smith and Jean Gabin, he rumbled a greeting and studied me from under his tufted eyebrows.

"Hmm, extraordinary," he commented. "Look here—has anyone ever told you you're the exact spitting image of Dr. Hawley Harvey Crippen?"

It was piquant to learn that I resembled the classic poisoner who, in 1910, had expunged his wife and escaped to Canada with his mistress disguised as a boy, and I made a mental note to conceal the information from my credit bureau. The museum's guide, an affable retired inspector named Wemyss, then took me in hand— conquering, I felt, an impulse to take me by the collar—and conducted me down, along with two Australian police officials and their wives, into the subterranean gallery.

The raison d'être of the Black Museum being educational rather than morbid—it was established in 1879 to train the personnel of the Yard—the initial exhibits were largely historical in flavor. Of particular interest to me was a frieze of wax facial sculptures of criminals executed at Newgate, many of them evocative of movie magnates and agents I had hobnobbed with in Hollywood during the 1930s. Here also were the uniform worn by Sir Roger Casement, hanged for treason in 1916, and the death mask of the person understandably ranked by the authorities as the arch murderer of all time, Heinrich Himmler. The section following dealt with various instruments of violence taken from marauders—a full profusion of coshes, or blackjacks, knuckle-dusters suitable for all seasons, knives and edged tools in every cunning guise, and, of course, bicycle chains and like modern refinements. These progressed smoothly into the paraphernalia of housebreaking, a display of skeleton keys, jimmies, and saws for illegal entry calculated to make any second-story worker salivate with desire. Though ingenious to a degree, they nonetheless paled beside the handiwork of the forgers adjoining: the banknotes with which the Third Reich had hoped to flood Britain and wreck its economy, coinage large and small minted in home workshops, phony dog-racing tickets, spurious postal orders, fake unemployment stamps, and finally, a masterpiece of a one-pound note that some Teutonic genius had labored eighteen months to create. The poor dear, in idealistic German fashion, had apparently lost sight of how little it would buy. In the event, it bought him twelve years in quod.

"Now, then, friends," said our guide, leading us into the mayhem division, "better buckle your seat belts, because anyone with a weak stomach is in for heavy weather."

It was an accurate forecast, for the subject next under scrutiny was multiple murder, typified by such renowned ghouls as Nevil Heath, Christie and Haigh. The recital of their enormities, illustrated by closeup photographs, was so explicit that both ladies promptly caved in and fled, and my own vision developed a grainy herringbone pattern like a TV screen out of focus. I rather wanted to lie down, but the stone floor underfoot was yawing from side to side and I couldn't find it.

"I say, mate," I whispered to one of the Australians, a beefy chap. "Would you mind carrying me piggyback the rest of the way?"

"Fend for yourself, Jack," he said thickly. "I've problems of my own." It was only then I noticed that he had sunk down on one knee and was struggling to arise, his face a ghastly aquamarine. Luckily, before Wemyss had to apply mouth-to-mouth breathing, the three of us recovered sufficient aplomb to press on to the rear of the museum, where the memorabilia of sexual offenses were grouped.

Broadly speaking—and the goodies on view compelled Wemyss to speak that way—the section would come as no surprise to anyone familiar with Krafft-Ebing, the gamier publications of Lyle Stuart, or the catalogue of the Sex Shop in Kobe, Japan. There was the standard weaponry of flagellation—birch rods, whips and knouts—souvenirs of sadomasochism, like cinch belts embossed with nails, and such stylish transvestite impedimenta as opera pumps with nine-inch diavolo heels. The dark corners of exhibitionism and self-gratification were also illumined for rookie policemen of tender upbringing. Apologizing for my innocence, I asked our guide if ownership or use of these artifacts was a legal transgression. His reply was admirable—one that I thought our native Comstocks might profitably ponder.

"We're not guardians of public morals, guv," he said. "The behavior of people in private is their own affair. It's when they advertise this bilge for sale, though—when they photograph and traffic in it—that they come within our purview."

The cumulative effect of the tour, heightened by a claustrophobia that dogs me like the common cold, must have shown in my face when I regained Mr. Protheroe's office. He paternally inquired whether I felt at all queasy.

"*Pouf*," I retorted with an airy gesture that overturned an inkstand onto his correspondence. "T-tell me, Inspector, how long have you been in Scotland Yard?"

"Well, I began as a constable on point duty at nineteen and I'm seventy-four now. A lightning calculation should provide the answer."

"In those fifty-five years, sir," I said, making it, "I take it you've seen every form of human infamy and degradation. Have you arrived at any conclusion about mankind in general?"

He ruminated a moment. "Not really," he said. "Except for one thing. I can't be sure, but I've reason to believe that brown-eyed men are very often bigamous."

While the memory of the Black Museum could hardly be said to excite nostalgia, I occasionally toyed with the thought of revisiting it on successive trips to England, but no feasible excuse presented itself. Quite recently, however, a curious mishap pitchforked me into a second tour. Hastily changing for dinner one evening at my

London hotel, I discovered I had neglected to insert the celluloid tabs we fops use to stiffen a shirt collar. Rather than remove the garment, as even a three-year-old fop would have done, I attempted a suicidal maneuver. I fumbled open the collar, jammed the two celluloid points upward into their slots, and inevitably punctured my jowls. The lovely I dined with later at Tiberio's (a Miss Haldeman-Julius related to the book people) assured me that the garniture of court plaster I wore was smashing.

"Gracious, you may be starting a vogue for white adhesive beards," she said, helpless with laughter. I knew that romance had curdled for that evening, and frigidly released her hand. "Still, I do wish you'd have those blowholes attended to, pet. Here's my doctor's address in Wimpole Street."

Dr. Steptoe, who treated my lesions next day, proved to be a friendly, knowledgeable sort. We chatted about professional matters—I was able to be of some help to him, having had six months of premedical training at college—and found he belonged to a medico-legal society whose members were permitted access to Scotland Yard at intervals. The upshot was that on a dark November morning a week later I joined a small group of distinguished practitioners in the reception room of the Yard's new premises in Broadway. They all wore badges inscribed with their names, but Steptoe, my sponsor, was nowhere in evidence. After a few moments he rushed in, a bit disheveled.

"Listen, old boy," he said in a hurried undertone. "I've an emergency case—can't go through with you, but take this."

He whipped out his badge and affixed it firmly to my lapel. "There—that'll identify you. Cheerio."

He had barely cleared off when Mr. Wemyss, the same functionary who had ushered me around earlier, materialized. He shook hands with each of the others in turn, but betrayed distinct perplexity on seeing me.

"Ah—haven't we met before, Dr. Steptoe?" he asked. "You're a dead ringer for someone I've seen—I'll stake my wig on it."

"Possibly Hawley Harvey Crippen," I said ingratiatingly. "I'm told there's a marked resemblance."

"Ha-ha—good show," he said, participating in the general chuckle. "No, it's somebody else—kind of a rat-faced bloke. Fact is, chaps, we've got to be on a constant alert here. All sorts of weird boffins try to sneak into the Yard on false pretenses, and if we ever catch them—"

The guttural sound he emitted, reminiscent of a crunch, engendered goose pimples, and I took care to straggle behind the party as we proceeded through the museum. The new quarters were a decided improvement over the chill catacombs of yore. With ingrained British respect for tradition, the creamier items had been retained and convenient niches provided everywhere for the horror-stricken to faint away in. It shortly became evident, however, that we medical men were privileged to inspect curios ordinarily hidden from the laity. Opening a drawer that exuded a strong odor of formaldehyde, Wemyss extracted a bonelike sliver about five inches long.

"Now, here's an interesting case," he observed. "Several years ago a pig farmer in Hants chanced to notice his wife was missing. He'd seen her a month or so before around the potting shed, but he was a dour, uncommunicative cove, and as the hired man was also missing, he assumed the pair might have sloped off together. At length he reported the disappearance to the local constabulary, who dug up the stableyard and found this. What do you make of it?"

"The fourth lower rib of a malnourished female approximately thirty-six years of age," asserted one of my colleagues, and handed me the specimen. "You agree, Dr. Steptoe?"

I rubbed it on my sleeve, surveyed it closely, and returned it. "I most emphatically do not," I said. "If you will examine the underside with a pocket lens, you will perceive stamped in the surface the legend 'Peal & Co.' It's a plastic shoehorn."

"Blast!" fumed Wemyss. "We hanged the wrong man. Ah, well," he resumed philosophically, "you can't make an omelet without breaking eggs. Let's move on to the toxicology cabinet there." The showcase to which he directed us held a selection of vegetable and mineral poisons used by divers malefactors for pleasure and profit. "I daresay you've run across many of these in your practice, gentlemen. Would you care to identify them?"

A bald-headed individual with a black spade beard and glittering eyes—whose name, oddly enough, happened to be Henri Landru—spoke up. "Prussic acid, strychnine, henbane, upas and nightshade," he said, ticking them off. "But zat last white powder—*nom d'un cochon*, eet baffles me."

"Permit me," I said. I took out a pinch and sniffed it. "Ah, quite. It's arsenic, unquestionably. It has the unmistakable odor of peach pits any reader of detective fiction would recognize at once."

Wemyss, still smarting under my reproof about the shoehorn, hooted triumphantly. "Well, that shows what you know," he taunted. "It *is* peach pits, ground up and placed there to confound just such weisenheimers as you. I guess that's telling him, eh, fellows?"

I submitted gracefully to the chaffing that ensued, but the opportunity to reinstate myself soon arose. Wemyss was recapitulating the details of a bizarre case that had rocked the academic community at Cambridge several years before.

"You undoubtedly followed it in the press," he said. "Lord Broomhead, a Scottish nobleman and the heir to vast estates, was a wild young cub whose excesses were the talk of the university. What with wenching and drinking, he'd acquired a pretty unsavory reputation, and most decent young women shunned his company. Well, he started forcing his attentions on a publican's daughter who was engaged to Eric Yeast, a chemistry student.

Yeast warned him to stay away from his fiancée, the two had words, and soon afterward Broomhead's body was fished out of a bog."

He opened a bin and produced a leathery object, completely spherical and roughly a foot in diameter.

"The exhibit you see here, subsequently discovered under Yeast's bed, was first believed by the coroner to be a fossilized matzo ball, but was later established as Broomhead's liver, which the chemist had skillfully preserved with kosher salt and tannic acid. Despite this damaging evidence, the Crown was unable to secure a conviction, and the affair remains a mystery to this day."

The sphere was passed from hand to hand, and my colleagues without exception confirmed the official report. Both the enlargement and the pebbled surface were characteristics they had observed in the hepatic organs of other topers. Notwithstanding, I felt strangely dissatisfied.

"A wild surmise, Mr. Wemyss," I said. "Did Eric Yeast ever engage in athletics of any sort?"

"Why, yes," he returned slowly. "I seem to recall he was an enthusiastic footballer. A forward on his college team, in fact."

"Indeed," I said. "Well, I'm afraid the law is guilty of a striking anatomical booboo. This is a Spalding regulation rugby, and if further corroboration is necessary, here is the neck of a rubber bladder protruding through these laces."

"Great Scott, so there is," Wemyss exclaimed, dumfounded. "I remember now that the postmortem disclosed Broomhead's liver to be intact. Dr. Steptoe, you've solved a riddle that has puzzled some of the keenest minds in the department. How in the world did you arrive at it?"

I smiled indulgently. "The answer is simple, as Holmes was wont to observe to Inspectors Lestrade and Gregson of your organization," I replied. "You *see*, but you do not observe. Well, my dear sir, thank you for a most rewarding morning, and with your permission, I must transfer my energies to numerous callers crowding my consulting room."

I left behind, I may say at the risk of seeming immodest, half a dozen persons so transfixed with admiration that they had turned to stone, and they may very likely be standing there yet. Should you ever get into the Black Museum—one chance in a million, and mine are even less—you'll find them on the right-hand side in the sportswear section, next to the leather accessories and whips. If you don't see what you want, just ask the floorwalker. That's one establishment that has everything, as sure as my name is Dr. Stephen Steptoe. Forgive me—I meant Hawley Harvey Crippen.

Too Many Undies Spoil the Crix

My little gray home on West Forty-fifth Street, all six depressing floors of it, looked as tawdry as ever when the cab rolled up in front, but from halfway across the sidewalk a new appendage caught my eye. Bulging out of the fake-marble trim around the entrance was a stylish bronze plaque that read "Jampolski Arms" in low-relief script. Guzek, the super, had just finished buffing it with a chamois and was squinting at the result, a cigar stub clamped in his teeth.

"Say, what gives?" I asked. "Don't tell me the building changed hands while I was in Boston."

Guzek shrugged. "The owner's idea," he said. "He felt the joint needed more class."

"But who's Jampolski?" I said. "*His* name's Sigmund Rhomboid."

"It's his common-law wife," he said. "He picked it on account of she's got these lovely white arms."

The thought of the spongecake beneath Gotham's callous exterior, without a troubadour like Nick Kenny or Odd McIntyre around any longer to extoll it, brought a momentary lump to my throat, but I choked it back and went into the foyer. The usual accumulation of trash mail welcomed me—mournful appeals from atomic spies for a new trial, threats from Internal Revenue—along with the standard weekly bleat from Roxanne. Los Angeles was a cultural desert, our divorce had left her with migraine and permanent insomnia, and enclosed was a bill I had overlooked from I. Magnin's. To top everything off, the cleaning woman had neglected to dust my flat, owing, she explained in a note written in Linear B, to her brother's sudden demise in Richmond. Poor thing —that made the twelfth relative she had buried since Christmas. If her necrology was accurate, it surpassed anything outside Defoe's *The Journal of the Plague Year.*

I was hardly out of the shower before Ned Bluestone called. His voice was in the key of C, so anxiety-ridden that my receiver shook. Why hadn't I phoned him after the first Boston performance, wired him, contacted him on arrival? What kind of a press agent was it who disappeared for days on end? In all his experience as a producer—

With a sharp cry I cut short the familiar narrative of how he had risen from booking Bluestone's Merry Maids on the Poli circuit to Broadway eminence.

"What's wrong? What happened there?" he demanded.

"It's Mrs. Jampolski," I said breathlessly. "She just ran down the fire escape stark naked, followed by a man with goat's feet. I'll dig you later."

By the time I reached the office Bluestone had worked off some of his adrenalin on subordinates, an agent or two, and a few overseas calls, but he still twitched uncontrollably, and, with his greenish complexion, he could have doubled for a grasshopper in a Karel Čapek fantasy. "Well, spill it, can't you?" he snapped. "What's the verdict? Have we got a show?"

"Ned," I said, "now that you're *bar mitzvah*, the gold watch you wear symbolizes a man's responsibilities. Gird yourself—it's a bomb."

"You didn't buy it," he said, with a true showman's instinct.

"I'll spell it out," I said. "There are some soporifics, like *The Sound of Music*, that lull the theatergoer. *Let's Skip Dinner* goes beyond that—it maddens. I don't want to alarm you, but the Broadway première of this play will be another Night of the Long Knives. They'll eviscerate you—hunt you down with dogs."

To my surprise he nodded somberly. "I knew it the minute I read the script. I hated it, but when that Mrs. Ample Hindquarters and her society jeweler, Sterling Flatware, offered to put up the scratch, I lost my judgment. Maybe if we sent for Abe Burrows—"

"Not a prayer," I said. "Believe me, no digitalis in his satchel or anybody else's can save this one. Close it, I beseech you."

"What, and sacrifice the parties I lined up?" He recoiled from the unclean thought. "Don't be an ignatz. We still got an out, and it's a blockbuster—a bold stroke of genius." He fumbled a clipping out of his desk. "Read that."

Headlined "Not So Tough," the item had been culled from a column of theater miscellany in the *News* under the byline of James Davis. It ran, "The Broadway critics who leave overcoats behind and spend intermissions outside the theater in comfort while others shiver aren't as rugged as they seem. One critic's valet told us they *all* wear two or three sets of underwear under their pants and jacket."

"Well, I've dealt with some devious minds in my time, but yours is the original Hampton Maze," I said perplexedly. "What's the point?"

"Schlemiel! Idiot! Don't you get it?" Bluestone crowed. "We bribe the respective valets to forget the extra underwear a few days before we open, and the critics all come down with colds and flu. So we draw the second-string reviewers, which they're good-natured, kindly exponents of live and let live, not like these other vultures."

Spoil the Crix

"Ned, it pains me to say this," I said. "You've swum away from the float. The strain of this production—"

"I figured it from every angle, and it can't miss," he said, his juggernaut careering over me. "The *Farmer's Almanac* predicts sub-zero temperatures the rest of the month. The shows preceding us, I'll get the managers to seat the critics near the doors, in a good strong draft. If necessary, we plant someone behind to sneeze on them. I guarantee the whole kit and caboodle's in bed with fever opening night."

Inured to show-biz hysteroids by long association, I realized the futility of argument. "Well, the whole thing sounds wacky to me," I said. "How the hell can Umlaut, on the *Times*, and Jack Chopnick, of the *News*, afford valets on their salaries?"

"Precisely!" said Bluestone joyously. "That's why they're vulnerable. Their manservants probably work for peanuts, and if you slip 'em a fin or so to overlook the extra union suits, why, it's pennies from heaven. Now, here's the names my girl wheedled out by pretending to be a *Time* researcher. Get busy, and walk on eggshells, for Crisake. This could be dynamite if it leaked."

Had Eric Ambler and Graham Greene linked arms with E. Phillips Oppenheim, they would have been stumped to invent the machinations I engaged in the following week. Under the guise of Sigmund Jampolski, proprietor of the Fragrant Hand Laundry, I called on the retainers in question—all of them English, as it developed—and earnestly solicited the household business. The prestige of handling such distinguished wash, I explained, was so great that I was prepared to do it for nothing—in fact, I offered them a bonus of twenty dollars apiece for the privilege. The alacrity they responded with convinced me that I could safely proceed to the second, and more delicate, stage of my plan. I invited each in turn, beginning with Yelverton, Umlaut's man, to have a drink. Our first encounter was purely social; I rhapsodized about Britain, feigned deep interest in their careers and problems, and did my utmost to cultivate rapport. At our next meeting I casually led the conversation around to their employers. I ventured that anyone who wore two of three suits of underwear, as the *News* had disclosed, must be a bit of a hypochondriac.

Yelverton's reaction, typical of the rest, was heartwarming. "A *bit?*" he echoed. "Why, Mr. Umlaut's absolutely bonkers on the subject of his health! Ah, Jampolski, nobody knows what I endure —the poultices, the croup kettles, the endless complaints about his aches and pains. Sheer imagination, of course."

"Arising from insecurity and his humble birth, doubtless," I said. "This may seem odd coming from a laundryman, Yelverton, but I majored in psychology at Loyola U., and there's only one way to cope with people like that. They must be deprived of their crutch—in this case, excess underwear. Why not restrict him to a single suit some evening?"

"Good Lord, I wouldn't dare," he said, taken aback. "What if he caught a chill on the liver?"

"Balderdash," I said forcefully. "The sudden knowledge that he was liberated from his neurosis would make him eternally grateful —he'd idolize you."

"We-ll-l-l, maybe." He looked dubious. "No valet is a hero to his man, you know."

"Unless he earns it," I said. "Tell you what, Yelverton. I'm so certain my theory's sound that I'll back it up with hard cash. Would a hundred dollars tempt you to try it?"

His face registered such bewilderment, tinged with suspicion, that I decided not to press him; I wanted the poison to circulate in his veins. Shortly afterward he phoned me with a counterproposal, which he found some hesitation in wording. A lady friend of his— his fiancée, really—had taken a fancy to a small diamond brooch in Lambert's priced at four hundred and thirty-five dollars. Did I regard it as a wise investment? You know more about psychology than I do, you muzzler, I thought, and asked him for time to consider.

When I called Bluestone to OK the expenditure, he screamed bloody murder. "What are we running—a soup kitchen?" he cried. "Offer him a cheap Swiss watch or something! My cousin in the jewelry center can get me a rakeoff."

"I'm having the same headache with Copestone, the bird who works for Wasservogel, on the *Post*," I said. "He's holding out for a vicuña coat. And Rowntree, who looks after Zemel, on *Women's Wear*, gave me a song and dance about a sports car."

In the tirade that ensued I gathered Bluestone was about to call the DA's office and lodge charges of extortion, but when I succeeded in interjecting the word "boomerang," he subsided. I was empowered to go to two hundred dollars; anything more would be downright vampirism and deductible from my own stipend. As for the task of persuading the valets to synchronize their mischief on the same night, Bluestone took a magnanimous line. "Now, let's not try to butcher the whole gang," he counseled. "I don't want every single critic in bed with pneumonia—just enough so's we get a fair shake from the small fry. Immobilize the key people, but remember, don't offend anybody."

In the end, and after a prodigal outlay of flattery, liquor, and the minimum of cash, I managed to win over Yelverton, Copestone, and Clunes—the last, Chopnick's batman on the *News*. The role of Jampolski, meanwhile, was proving arduous; I was at my wit's end directing a corps of messengers to collect and deliver the critics' laundry. They were a carping lot, these gentlemen of the press, as quick to pounce on flaws in my work—the wrinkled cuff, the missing button—as those in the plays they appraised. Nevertheless, the fuse I had laid was ignited on schedule. The thermometer had dropped, my trio of cat's-paws had cut back on their employers' insulation, and *Let's Skip Dinner* was closing in Boston preparatory to the Broadway première when fate hurled a thunderbolt. Irving Cubbins, our male lead, inadvertently set fire to his toupee while smoking in bed at the Hotel Touraine, sufficiently fricasseeing his scalp so that another zombie had to be flown in from the Coast. To allow the replacement time to get up in the part, Bluestone switched the production into Philadelphia for a week. The next morning he phoned me from the box office in a state bordering on delirium. The show had drawn rave notices, the most ecstatic in memory, and the ticket line was impeding traffic as far west as Valley Forge. All previous plans, consequently, were scrubbed; New York was to be a glittering first night, covered by strictly topflight critics capable of assaying a theatrical gem.

It was infanticide to puncture his balloon, but I had to tell him the truth. "The damage is done, Ned," I said. "It's too late. Umlaut's at Lenox Hill with laryngitis, Wasservogel was carried out of the Alvin last night with his eyes streaming, and Chopnick has either quinsy or whooping cough—his physician won't say."

"They can have cholera for all I care!" he bellowed. "You get those three to their chairs Tuesday night even if you have to use a stretcher. Tell the nurse to feed 'em orange juice, vitamins—call Michael DeBakey in Texas for a free opinion!"

"You have but to command, *mon général*," I said dutifully, and hung up. I cleaned out my desk, took a cab to "21," and had a four-hour lunch with the prettiest girl I knew—a doll reminiscent of Aileen Pringle—at the end of which I somewhat expunged Bluestone's indignities by signing his name to a ninety-dollar check.

Let's Skip Dinner, sadly, didn't quite justify its producer's forecast as the hit of the century. The invective that greeted it in New York, in fact, would have dumfounded even a connoisseur like Hugh Kingsmill. The second-string critics attended, clad in only one suit of underclothes, and voted it the most aptly initialed hallucinogen of the year, the deadliest blight to befall entertainment since *The Ladder*. Bluestone instantly vanished into television, where he was soon entrusted with the guidance of an entire network. When, six months later, I applied through an intermediary for a job in its press department, he turned to stone. "Don't mention that bastard's name to me," he groaned. "He was associated with one of my worst disasters."

Lock Lips—Monkeyshines in the Bridgework

I can pinpoint it unerringly—it was the last week in June when I became conscious of a faint but unmistakable emphasis on dentistry in the press, almost as if someone were giving me a sly nudge. Nothing explicit, to be sure—just a line here and a paragraph there that, along with an incisor that wobbled when I bit into piecrust, honed my sensitivity to the subject. The first hint, a mere throwaway in a Broadway gossip column of the *News*, concerned a well-known thrush: "Lois Hunt, who sings with Earl Wrightson, is a licensed Pennsylvania dentist." The item might have packed more journalistic punch, I felt, had it portrayed her as unlicensed, but, as a resident of the state and longtime admirer of the lady, I glowed at the diversity of her achievements. Shortly afterward another and more obvious dental innuendo caught my eye—an orthodontic coup in the Midwest reported by the *Times*. "False 'talking' teeth have been developed," it stated, "to tell a University of Michigan dental researcher what it feels like to chew. . . . This is the first time single teeth capable of radioing information have been made. The teeth are designed to disclose the forces that act on them when they chew. . . . The talking teeth resemble ordinary false teeth used in bridgework. Each tooth is packed with six miniature radio transistors, twenty-eight electronic components, two rechargeable batteries, and an antenna."

Psychosomatic or not, by Thursday of that week the slightest pressure on my incisor caused it to sway like a Lombardy poplar, and, bowing to the inevitable, I phoned my dentist in the county seat for an appointment. Dr. Crunch, his receptionist divulged, had flown to Malaya to seek gutta-percha for fillings, but he had left as locum tenens a Dr. Fangl, who would see me forthwith. As it happened, I had some policies to discuss in Doylestown with Bodley Risk, my insurance man at Gollancz-Durnheim, Inc. ("Our Motto: Gol-Durn Your Problems"), and after the fine print had been spelled out to my consternation, I went along to Crunch's office. A jet-haired Juno with smoldering eyes, in a surgical tunic that accentuated a notable physique, welcomed me into the inner cubicle and, enveloping me in the scent of Mitsouko secured a plastic bib around my neck. Supposing the vision to be a new nurse, I asked when Dr. Fangl would materialize.

"Oh, forgive me," she said, in a husky contralto that awoke memories of Kay Francis, Elinor Glyn, and tiger-skin couches. "I'm Bianca Fangl—I thought perhaps you recognized me. I sang with Lloyd Pettibone."

"Not *the* Bianca Fangl?" I asked incredulous. "The one that does all those operettas and record albums?" Her lashes fluttered acknowledgment of my homage. "I've never seen you in the—ah—flesh, but I've enjoyed you for years. Your renditions that is," I corrected hastily.

Her smile revealed three hitherto invisible dimples. "Why, how sweet of you," she murmured. And how perceptive of her to notice my sweetness, I thought with thumping heart. "Yes, Lloyd and I just closed at the Whisper Lounge in Detroit, and I always sandwich in a few weeks' dental practice during layoffs. All this bending and stretching"—she illustrated—"it's good for the figure, I think."

"Wizard," I concurred. "Your colleague—is he a part-time dentist too?"

"No, Lloyd's in a slate quarry up in Lehigh County," she replied. "He drills those shingles they use on roofs." The similarity of avocation reminded her of professional duties, and she reached briskly for a dental mirror. "Now, what seems to be the trouble?"

The problem was crystal clear, the solution even more so. The errant tooth would have to be replaced with an artificial one cabled to its neighbors. The principle, as Dr. Fangl expounded it in terms comprehensible to a layman, was the same as that used in stabilizing a snow fence or the spiles of a wharf. I retreated into a network of evasion: whatever shakiness she had observed was pure nervous reflex, I was psychologically unprepared for any drastic measures, and, furthermore, my underwriters disclaimed all responsibility should I conk out under anesthesia. Dr. Fangl pooh-poohed my qualms. The changeover could be effected painlessly in an hour, thanks to technological advances. I was in superb physical condition, she said, with an admiring squeeze of my biceps—virile enough for a man twice my age. Goose that I was, I knew I was succumbing to feminine witchery, but some indefinable fear—perhaps that if I remained obdurate she might try to kiss me into submission—eroded my will, and I weakly gave in.

The actuality, happily, was less rigorous than I anticipated. True, there were moments when Bianca's *embonpoint* heaved with exertion and my fortitude was threatened, but forty minutes later I was able to view the new incisor, anchored firmly in place, in a hand mirror. As she smoothed my wayward toupee and I relaxed, she favored me with a few selections from her repertoire that skillfully implemented the Novocain—"Cherry Pink and Apple Blossom White," "Three Little Fishies," and "How Much Is That Doggie in the Window?" Then, as I rose to leave, she issued a word of warning.

"This restoration I've done is something new," she said. "It's very complex and terribly sensitive to its environment."

"You mean it hates being where it is?" I asked, affronted.

"Goodness, no," she said quickly. "You've got a lovely mouth, I assure you." The impulse to swap tributes was alluring, but I mastered it. "The idea is, you must be awfully careful of the things you chew. We've got ways of finding out."

"Who—you and that Lloyd Pettibone?" I asked, with a surge of jealousy.

"Never mind, foolish boy," she said. "Just stay away from pretzels, hard rolls, apples, and such, and don't crack any nuts with it. Now, run along, and remember, Big Sister's watching you."

So vivid was the impact Bianca had made on me, and so earnest her injunction, that I took pains to screen every morsel I ate the following week. On Sunday morning, however, there occurred the first of a chain of incidents that shook me profoundly. Deep in Suzy Knickerbocker's log of the activities of Stavros Niarchos, the Alfred Strelsins, and Contessa Pecci-Blunt, I was munching half a bagel larded with Novy and cream cheese when the phone rang. The rich contralto purr over the wire belonged to only one dentist on earth, and behind it I could hear the sound of water splashing on a tiled surface.

"It's Bianca—Doctor Fangl," she was saying urgently. "I just stepped out of the shower to get your message." Whether it was the bagel or the image of my caller in her birthday suit that constricted my speech, I replied thickly that nothing was amiss, I hadn't called. "I *know* that," she said, impatient. "I got a flash from your jaw. You misbehaved—you're eating a bagel."

"I—I just had a couple of bites," I stammered. "It wasn't toasted, honest. . . . Look, hadn't you better slip into a fleecy robe or something? You're liable to cach cold."

"Now, don't shilly-shally." Her tone became that of a schoolmistress. "I cautioned you to avoid stress on that tooth, and I expect cooperation. Soft buns, corn bread, Danish, or scones, but that's it—do you hear? You're lucky you've got a guardian angel in your head to look after you."

My own interpretation, requiring no dental diploma, was that I was harboring a spy, and though I yielded with a show of grace, my appetite began to dwindle appreciably. After a fortnight of yogurt, semolina, junket, and similar pap, I was so undernourished I burst into tears over trifles and even turned faint during commercials for dog food. The breaking point came one evening as I was passing a Fanny Farmer shop in the Port Authority Bus Terminal. Dizzied by the heavy aroma of chocolate, I ran in, bought half a pound of fondants and marzipan, and then, swept away, added a piece of butterscotch to nibble while my purchase was being wrapped. I had barely swallowed it before a saleswoman emerged from the stockroom with word of an imperative toll call from a Dr. Fangl in Pennsylvania.

Dumfounded at the extent of her surveillance, and hot with resentment, I sprang to the phone. "See here, Doctor, what is this?" I demanded. "Can't a person raise his sugar curve without you poking your nose in? I'm entitled to *some* privacy!"

"And so am I," she retorted, with equal heat. "Where do you think I was when I got that alert just now? For your information, I was in a porch hammock with a very attractive gentleman of my acquaintance."

I apologized for interrupting her tête-à-tête, observing rather waspishly that Lloyd Pettibone's dialogue was clearly more fascinating than any I could offer.

"None of your affair who it is," she said, and I realized in an access of misery that some Doylestown square had checkmated us both. "The issue now is that you deliberately and willfully ignored my orders. You're playing with fire, gnawing on a confection like that. What do you suppose I put in there—an emery wheel?"

"I can't help it," I whimpered, striving to excite her compassion, if nothing else. "I'm run-down, famished. I need an incentive to go on living—the feeling that someone like you cares—"

"But I do, Sidney," she assured me, with sudden warmth. "Most dental sessions are humdrum, but ours was—well, different. And besides, I'm constantly in touch with you, as you know. Now, we'll overlook this slip for once, but hereafter, anytime you're worried about some goody—be it apples, caramel, licorice, whatever—promise to check with me beforehand. Cross your heart."

Well, I acceded out of *force majeure*, and, I suppose, the same quenchless hope that impelled Hillary to vanquish Everest. Nothing untoward happened until I was confronted with an ear of corn several weeks later at a dinner party. My host, a novice in the country, flaunting his first produce, was hungry for approbation; it was unthinkable to plead I must have clearance from my dentist, and I plunged ahead. The humiliation that followed was insupportable, beyond description. Even though Bianca's jeremiad was not audible to the company, my own reaction was, since the phone was but a few yards distant from them. Unable to endure her scorn, I gave her the full weight of my tongue. I impugned her dental skill, branded her a heartless flirt, and, distractedly reaching for the ultimate insult, accused her of singing off key. The rest of the evening was a nightmare. The other guests, many of whom were in wine, were quick to seize on and embroider my outburst, and I was subjected to raillery so merciless that I sickened. In the circumstances, there was only one anodyne. I poured myself a thimbleful of brandy, and at two o'clock was conveyed home in the rear of a neighbor's jeep spread out like a starfish.

It was the measure of a deeply generous nature that when Bianca entered her office the next morning and beheld me in the chair, haggard with remorse, not a word of censure did she utter. Instead, and with a sad gentleness that shamed me afresh, she subjected her handiwork to a painstaking scrutiny to insure it was intact. Then, signifying I was dismissed, she turned away—the better, I suspected, to hide the moisture dimming her great, lustrous orbs. Some gesture of penitence, some avowal of my regard other than the check I would mail her in a few months, was obligatory, and I forced myself to make it.

"This . . . this is the end, I suppose," I said, sighing. She nodded, but made no reply. "Bianca, I know I've been a beast. Still, it wasn't all my fault, believe me. It's your tooth that came between us—this little white sneak, blabbing everything I did. Oh, I realize I'm not the only pebble on the beach—you must have scads of other patients with talking dentures to worry about—but let me say one thing. You're straight, and clean, and fine, and you deserve a man who can fulfill the best in you."

"Oh, my very dear." Suddenly she was all radiance again, my slight forgiven. "You're trumps, too, so I'll tell you a secret. Lloyd Pettibone and I are washed up. I've found a new partner here in Doylestown with a glorious voice—the fellow who runs the meat counter at Hutzler's Market. We've been rehearsing nights in my hammock, and we open a week from Tuesday at the Megrim Room in Newark. Guess who I want at a ringside table that night to sing to?"

Well, I was there, and I can testify she killed the people. Her partner was OK—if you go for that sort of schmalz, which I personally don't—but I think I deserve some credit also. I ate chow mein with soft noodles during her act so that my tooth wouldn't distract her, and, to judge from the melting looks she threw me, she got the message, all right. Your singing dentists like Bianca Fangl aren't made in a day. One has to keep on trying.

And, in the Center Ring, That Stupendous Death-Defying Daredevil . . .

How many people are there, I wonder, who still sparkle up at the memory of a film called *Variety* they saw a while back—forty years ago, to be exact. The question is purely rhetorical, the answer self-evident; I recall the whole thing as vividly as if I'd seen it yesterday. U.F.A. made it, and the three principals were Emil Jannings, Lya de Putti (honest Injun, that was her real name), and Warwick Ward. The plot itself was no bargain—the ruination of a stellar trapeze act because of a casual frolic of Miss de Putti's with Mr. Ward in the Fruit of the Loom—but the aerial feats the trio performed were breathtaking, and for the best of reasons: Alfredo Codona, the wizard of the flying rings, and his partners doubled for the actors. I saw the picture four times, reacting so volcanically to Codona's forward triple somersault that I almost rent the chair in front of me to matchwood. Yes, *Variety* had a potent effect on me, both then and subsequently. It induced a lifelong adoration of circus fliers, it generated a journey overseas, and in the end it led to profound disillusion. But let me set down the circumstances in some rough sequence.

225

At that precise moment in the fall of 1927 I was in a state of acute indecision regarding my future. I'd recently read *The Moon and Sixpence,* and, like every young tinderbox of my generation, I closely identified myself with Charles Strickland, its protagonist. The idea of spurning civilization and withdrawing to Tahiti to paint was pretty alluring. On the other hand, I felt a definite kinship with those immensely debonair figures of Michael Arlen's in *The Green Hat;* maybe I ought to plunge into the social whirl of London, engage a flat in Half Moon Street, and drain the cup of debauchery to its lees. *Variety,* in an indefinable way, resolved my dilemma. Its climactic scenes had been shot in Berlin's celebrated cabaret the Wintergarten. It suddenly came over me that my existence would acquire new purpose, a real meaning, if I could visit the actual locale of the movie and behold life duplicating art. A fortnight later I was steaming eastward aboard the *S.S. Leviathan,* which was conveniently steaming in the same direction.

I hung around Paris only long enough to sip a *fine à l'eau* at the Dôme in the hope that somebody would mistake me for a habitué of Montparnasse (I was also strongly influenced by *The Sun Also Rises*) and caught the night express to Berlin. The occupants of my compartment were everything E. Phillips Oppenheim and I envisioned. There were a couple of secret agents trying to pass themselves off as Swiss businessmen, an aristocratic old Italian *contessa,* a pair of Scandinavian lovebirds, an English spinster with a reticule full of Tauchnitz novels, and a small, talkative party in a whipcord suit who introduced himself to me as a Polish engineer. His baggage, consisting of eleven cardboard suitcases of graduated sizes, filled the racks to overflowing and occasioned audible resentment from his neighbors. Soon after we crossed the German frontier the engineer burrowed into his luggage, produced a gigantic sausage and a loaf of pumpernickel, and fashioned a hillock of sandwiches. Distributing these among the company, he then conjured up half a dozen collapsible metal cups, filled them with cognac, and proposed a toast to international amity. By the time we rolled into Berlin everyone in the carriage was expansive, even the spies, and a state of utter bonhomie prevailed.

Thanks to the concierge at the Adlon, I secured a table in the loges of the Wintergarten at several times its cost and, fortified by a flagon of Rhenish, prepared to succumb to the witchery of my surroundings. It soon became apparent that something was radically wrong. The entertainment was fourth-rate vaudeville—sleazy animal acts, maladroit acrobats who floundered in and out of trampolines, and monologists whose patter, luckily, was incomprehensible to me. Panic-stricken, I summoned the headwaiter and tried to elicit from him, by flapping my arms, what time the aerialists came on. Eventually I was given to understand that there had been none on the bill for several years, nor were any scheduled in the foreseeable future. Enraged at my folly in embarking on a wild-goose chase (*eine wilde Gänsejagd*), I was about to leave when a snarl of trumpets ushered in the star attraction of the evening—an American dance orchestra. One of the saxophonists, a bulbous chap in the front row, was strangely familiar, and midway through a somewhat less than uproarious rendition of "Down by the Winegar Woiks" I recognized him as Tubby Funkhouser, a college classmate I had rigorously avoided as a drip. Notwithstanding, I instantly sought him out backstage, and we fell on each other's necks like castaways reunited. The rest of the evening is a blur, but I remember the two of us in some grisly *Nachtlokal* in the Kurfürstendamm buying wine for three elderly harpies straight out of George Grosz's inkwell and ultimately being toted through the Adlon's lobby with my feet dragging.

Fruitless though my quest had been, I never swerved a hair thereafter in my devotion to aerialists—and Codona above all—but about a year ago I lost my heart to another superb gymnast, a lady named Violette LaFong, with the Ringling Circus. Miss LaFong was an equilibrist whose specialty was working on the high trapeze under the most hazardous conditions. Using no net and defying the law of gravity, she swung hither and yon as effortlessly as a gibbon, catching herself by heels or chin as the audience moaned in anguish. The finale of her turn was so spectacular that one had to steel oneself to watch. Maneuvering herself by degrees into a headstand on the trapeze bar, she tossed a length of rope to an assistant forty feet below. The lackey then began slowly agitating the rope so that the trapeze described an ellipse. Its course grew longer and wider, Miss LaFong's perch ever more perilous, until the spectators whimpered for mercy. When she finally granted it and, ceasing her gyrations, slid gracefully to terra firma, the applause was orgiastic.

The day after I saw her I rang up a Russian friend of mine, a scenic designer and painter many of whose canvases have dealt with aspects of the circus. "You know all kinds of gifted people, Alexei," I began. "There's a trapeze artist over at the Garden, a woman—"

"By the name of Violette LaFong," he finished. "I'm in love with her too. Forget it, my boy. This lady is not for groundlings like you and me."

"Look, I'm not talking about love or marriage," I said. "I merely want to kneel before her and pay homage. Can you arrange it?"

"Falling off a log," he said. Alexei prides himself on his grasp of the vernacular. "She's a Russian, like everybody in the circus, and all us Russians know each other. You saw Massimiliano Truzzi, the juggler? A Russian. Unus the Great—the one that stands on his finger? Another Russian. I can name you fifty—"

I cut short his roll call of Muscovites under the big top, and we fixed a rendezvous for the next day. From the welcome shown Alexei by tumblers, clowns, and roustabouts as we made our way through the labyrinth beneath the Garden, it was plain he had not exaggerated. The tiny kimono-clad figure that opened the door of

That Stupendous Death-Defying Daredevil . . .

Miss LaFong's dressing room was quite different from what I had expected. Her broad shoulders, disproportionate to her height, gave her a peculiarly foreshortened appearance, and her face, while comely and reminiscent of Olga Baclanova's, was haggard from strain. Alexei introduced me in a spate of Russian I interpreted to mean that I was an ardent admirer, for she squeezed my hand gratefully.

"Ah, gentlemen, you are too kind," she said. "Here, seat yourselves wherever you can find. Throw that valise in the corner. . . . So, you really enjoyed me?"

"I can't tell you," I said. "I wouldn't believe anyone could do that headstand you finish with."

"Nobody can, my friend," she said. "Who wants to practice four years like I did before I showed it? Alexei, you remember Dolores Montoya, that big brunette? She tried in Stockholm, but she fell, poor thing."

"Discipline," said Alexei. "This is what separates the sheep from the goats. The whole secret of the artist is discipline."

"Also force of habit, tovarich," she said. "You do something long enough, I don't care what, it becomes second nature. Which it's a lucky thing, because if I stopped to ask what am I doing up there, it's goodbye Violette LaFong."

"I hope it's not an impertinent question," I said, "but what *does* a person think about when she's whirling around upside down on a trapeze?"

"Well, I personally am worrying about my financial problems," she confessed. "Money, money the whole time. How much it costs to clean my costumes, the tips I hand out in hotels, the prices I have to pay for my props. Ropes, for instance. How much do you think they charge for that long rope my assistant pulls? Make a guess."

"Eighteen cents a foot?" Alexei asked.

"Ha-ha!" Violette barked. "Foolish man—you see what you know? It used to cost thirty cents a foot. Now it's sixty-five! Who can afford it?"

"But your life depends on it," I objected.

"Pah! A piece of clothesline would give the same effect," she said. "The worst of all is that assistant—a real *durak*. Ninety-five dollars a week for posing in a red tunic, and he's drunk half the time. No, I tell you, when I add up my expenses and taxes up there, I get heartburn. It's all I can do to keep my balance, I'm so angry." She arose and extended her hand. "Well, boys, you must excuse me. I have to dress for the grand spec."

As Alexei and I emerged into the workaday battle of Eighth Avenue he stole a sidelong glance at me. "Why the letdown nose?" he inquired.

"Oh, nothing. . . . Another illusion gone, I guess."

"Yes, it don't pay to get too close to genius," he said. "One time in Paris I went through fire and water to meet Picasso. What do you think he talked about? How much his camel's-hair brushes cost him. Watch *out!*" He jerked me out of the path of an oncoming limousine, and then, as it raced on, stood staring after it, transfixed. "Listen," he said, his voice trembling. "You know who was in that car? Sophia Loren!"

"So what?" I said.

"My God, man!" he exploded. "Are you made of stone? This is not simply a woman—this is all women rolled into one. I'd go through fire and water to meet her—just to breathe the same air. A person like this could change your whole life, give you a new perspective . . ."

10:30, and All Quiet
on West 45th Street

*Insurance to Stop Actor "Drying Up" . . . Mr. Norman
Vaughan, compere and comedian, has insured himself against
forgetting his lines when he opens in Boeing-Boeing at the
Royal Court Theatre, Liverpool, on May 22. His £75 policy
will give him £5000 cover. . . . Mr. Arthur Harrison, head of
J. A. Harrison (Brokers) Ltd., Birmingham, who have extensive business dealings with stage personalities and entertain-
ers, told* The Times *that this was their first insurance of an
actor against fluffing his lines. . . .*

*By the terms of the policy Mr. Vaughan binds himself to
strict conditions:*

*No alcohol to be consumed for three days and three nights
before the opening;*

In bed by 11 P.M;

*No strenuous sports or any strenuous activity, particularly
the night before, or on the day of the show. . . .*

*The underwriters and Mr. Arthur Harrison reserve the right
to telephone Mr. Vaughan any time up to five hours before
the show begins and ask him to repeat any part of the script
at random.*—The Times, London.

Max Wishbone, president of the DAR (Dynamic Artists' Representatives, Inc.), shouldered open the door of the coffee shop adjoining the Hotel Brismont and scanned the interior for his client. He saw Milton Locksmith, eyes swollen and face contorted with misery, hunched in a booth at the rear. The dazzling neon overhead, reflected off the profusion of Formica and aquamarine plastic about him, so heightened his normal Broadway pallor that the agent was taken aback. "Holy crow, man," he exclaimed, "are you all right? Those nuts in your cheeks—you look like Phil Harris after a rainstorm."

Locksmith glared at him. "I'm a wreck, if you want to know," he said malevolently. "I never slept a wink all night. I was pacing the floor, chewing my nails, phoning people that have been dead ten years—and it's all your fault, you muzzler. You and your goddam insurance policy."

"Now, wait a minute, Locks—be reasonable," Wishbone implored. "We did it for your own good, baby—to protect you— didn't we? I mean, this great part which it's a windfall every performer dreams of, and if you blow on opening night—"

"Listen, Wishbone," the actor said, trembling with suppressed outrage. "Are you implying I can't retain my lines?"

"Who's implying? I only meant that none of us are getting any younger—"

"Well, quit talking like a dramatic coach," Locksmith snapped. "I've been in forty-one productions here in eighteen years, not counting stock with Jessie Bonstelle and nine seasons with the Chattanooga Mummers. I followed Walter Pidgeon in *The Happiest Millionaire*, I replaced Don Ameche in four different roles, and John Hodiak refused to go on unless I was costarred with him." He stabbed his forefinger into the other's chest. "Name me one occasion—one single instance—when I failed to pick up a cue!"

"Sweetheart, would I handle you if you were a stiff?" expostulated Wishbone. "In my office, you're up there with Olivier and the other greats. But you artists working at white heat—you're spendthrift, you don't husband your genius. Nobody can rehearse like fourteen hours and then galvinate around the clubs with some beetle till dawn. That's where this policy safeguards you against brain fag, don't you see? Mark my words—just lay off the sauce, grab some shut-eye, and you'll slay 'em Thursday night in Wilmington. You'll cop a Tony award!"

"Well, the role *does* have possibilities," admitted Locksmith. "It's kind of a challenge, a Greek shipping magnate." He deliberated. "I was wondering should I wear a monocle."

"A monocle by all means," the agent concurred. "And a white piping on the vest, like Onassis and all those cats. You got any good big speeches?"

"No, but I fatten 'em up wherever I can," Locksmith said. "The author practically had a stroke at the run-through yesterday."

"Ach, *playwrights*," said Wishbone. "We'd be better off without 'em. Well, now, Milt," he continued, briskly consulting his watch, "better cut along to rehearsal. No booze again today, mind you, and in bed by eleven sharp—promise?"

Locksmith nodded cheerlessly. "I'm all tensed up like the rope in that TV commercial," he complained. "Maybe I'd relax if I bowled a few frames or rode around Central Park on a bike."

"With your ticker?" Wishbone was aghast. "You're liable to wind up with a tag on your feet, for Chrisake. The only exercise you ever had was Indan hand wrestling with some other lush at P.J.'s. Look, Milton, the policy specifically reads '*no strenuous activity* for a period—' "

"OK, OK," said Locksmith. "I'll borrow a couple of goofballs from the ingénue. She eats them like peanuts."

"You're making a mistake gastricwise," Wishbone cautioned. "Why not have a nice whitefish sandwich before retiring, and a bottle of Dr. Brown's? You'll wake up a new man, I guarantee."

With a sigh, Locksmith acquiesced, and the two parted. Late that evening Locksmith tottered onto the sidewalk outside the Belasco, giddy with exhaustion. The director, anxious to quicken the pace of the play, had excised three entire scenes, transposing the rest in such fashion that the cast was thoroughly muddled. Actors collided in midstage, lovers' meetings were aborted by mysterious phone calls, and at one point the string of pearls on which the dénouement turned had to be retrieved from a nearby delicatessen, whose messenger had mistaken it for a gratuity. To compound everyone's inquietude, the producer had just issued an unnerving last-minute ukase. The show was so far above expectations, its success so assured, that an out-of-town booking and previews were superfluous. The scenery, therefore, was being rushed to completion, the critics had been alerted, and *She Stoops to Yonkers* would open cold two nights hence. As the company listened, a thin imperceptible dew broke out on their temples—the phenomenon long known to Equity members as flop sweat.

The handwriting on the wall was all too clear to Locksmith as he crept slowly toward the Luxor Baths. It was disastrous enough to be involved in another turkey, but this time, thanks to Wishbone's misplaced zeal, any form of nepenthe was strictly off limits. Whatever happened, he must catch a few hours' sleep and drill his lines until he was letter-perfect. He must shake off the vision of ice-cold Martinis, of boisterous high jinks at the Lambs. As he paused by a taproom on Sixth Avenue to envy the happy throng within, he abruptly became aware of someone nearby watching him. The face was unfamiliar, yet Locksmith was positive he had seen the man recently—around the hotel, at the theater? He crossed the street and, abreast of the baths, cast a swift glance behind him. The man stood twenty yards off, still eying him fixedly. An hour and a half later, when Locksmith regained the Brismont, he saw the stranger idling before a coin shop next door. Locksmith made straight for him.

"See here, fellow," he said. "What's the pitch? Are you following me?"

"That's right," the man returned calmly. "It's eleven-thirty—you should have been in bed a half hour ago."

"Who the hell are you, telling me when to hit the hay?"

"Your underwriter, that's who." He thrust a card at Locksmith. "De Witt Federbush, of the Transglobal Casualty Corporation. There'll be ten thousand smackers riding on you when that curtain goes up, my friend, so you better not be punchy. Get upstairs and work on your part. We'll be listening—we got taps all over the joint. Nighty-night."

In the ensuing twelve hours Locksmith managed by prodigious labor to master his sides, but the effort took its toll and his withdrawal symptoms were formidable. At rehearsal next day, during a scene that required him to skip downstage and crouch behind an easy chair, he overshot and barreled into the pit, which was providentially shrouded with a tarpaulin. Subsequently a fit of the trembles overtook him while he was trying to catch a beanbag tossed by the juvenile, and the piece of business had to be dropped. It was on the morning of the première, though, that his afflictions redoubled. He was gulping a cup of coffee at Whelan's in Duffy Square when the pharmacist approached and, certifying his name, conducted him to a phone booth.

"This is Irene Nemesis, in the Transglobal office," said a female voice. "I have the script of *She Stoops* in front of me. Kindly repeat the dialogue where you seize command of the houseboat."

"They took *out* the houseboat," protested Locksmith. "It's a duckblind now. The heavy hides the necklace in a haversack—"

"We're not interested in the plot," she broke in irritably. "Just your twelve lines, please, word for word. I've only a small spool of tape."

Somehow, and with crippling exertion, Locksmith complied, and reeled out of the drugstore. Two successive catechisms—one at his barber's, the other as he was struggling into pencil-striped pants at Brooks Costume—dispersed any doubt of his guardians' tenacity. Throughout the dress rehearsal, a traditional Gethsemane, Locksmith fancied he heard the scratch of recording equipment; eyes peered at him from the darkened boxes, spies hovered in the wings, and his head throbbed bestially from the tyranny of concentration. Nor did it palliate his misery to have Wishbone slither up to him afterward with a list of the nuances he had missed. To the electrified surprise of bystanders, Locksmith jammed the agent's hat down over his ears, frog-marched him up the aisle, and flung him into the lobby. The outburst brought him the first serenity he had felt in a week.

Midway through the second act that evening it became apparent to all on both sides of the footlights that a record was being set. Never within living memory had a play aroused such a mixture of confusion, ennui, and rancor in an audience. At times there was a low, prolonged growling among the patrons, which threatened to swell into violence and then subsided as drowsiness gripped the house. Even the ushers abandoned all pretense and slept unashamedly at their posts. As the cast, meanwhile, entangled itself ever deeper in flypaper, the one person displaying any semblance of aplomb was Locksmith. Line after line rippled from his lips; if he paused a hairbreadth, it was only to race on with fresh energy. He was easy, suave, self-assured—until the third-act climax, wherein he was called on to renounce his vast maritime empire to protect a woman's reputation.

"Take them!" he declaimed hoarsely. "Take everything—my fleet, my estates, my racing stables, my art collection, my sculptures by Praxiteles . . . Praxiteles . . ."

In that horrid moment, as he blacked out, Locksmith realized that the rest of the speech had forever flown. An immense panic seized him; he knew that, given one more Praxiteles, the audience would pick up the chant and the stage manager would ring down the curtain. Only one expedient, time-honored but dependable, was left. He strode to the apron, loosened his collar, and, drawing a deep breath, inclined his head nobly upward. "I see Barsad, and Cly, Defarge, the Vengeance, the Jurymen, the Judge, long ranks of the new oppressors," he began. The audience saw nothing of the sort, but they knew the voice of Sydney Carton at the foot of the scaffold, and they listened, rapt. "I see the lives for which I lay down my life. . . . I see her with a child upon her bosom, who bears my name. . . . I see him winning it so well that my name is made illustrious there by the light of his. . . . It is a far, far better thing that I do than I have ever done; it is a far, far better rest that I go to than I have ever known."

The roar of approbation, the frenzy of applause still echoed in Locksmith's ears the midday following as he sat in the Brismont coffee shop, nursing the worst hangover of his life. Opposite him, and all rosy forgiveness, Max Wishbone excitedly read forth the critical hosannas. Let bells peal out their gladsome tidings—a great artist had risen superior to his material, Thespis stood vindicated, the Fabulous Invalid was hale again.

"And look at these offers!" he exulted, scrabbling through a mound of telegrams. "Merrick wants you for Escoffier in *The Joy of Cooking*, Grove Press for their musical of *Waiting for Godot*— you're loaded! Not to mention what you're legally entitled to from the insurance company!"

"Let's skip that dough, Max," said Locksmith restively. "They might start yelling fraud. As it is, the author's screaming that I threw his script out the window."

"Yeah, who needs it?" Wishbone shrugged disdain. "You're on Easy Street. Just get in there tonight, even if the show *is* folding, and repeat that same terrific performance."

Locksmith hesitated, the pallor of his cheek suddenly grown pink with embarrassment. "Max," he said sheepishly, "I—I hate to tell you, but I don't think I can remember the lines."

Plus Ça Change

Of all the hamlets strung along the watery eastern border of Pennsylvania none, I daresay, offers less sustenance to the eye or spirit than Wormsville. From whatever quarter of the compass one approaches it, one is seized by an almost palpable miasma, an ineradicable conviction of doom. The main street, a somber parade of groceries, lunchrooms, and package stores, straggles a scant two blocks from a taproom at one end of town to an alehouse at the other, and the inhabitants, as a rule, follow suit. Most of them, while ambulatory, are too spent to engage in physical labor, and, in any case, Wormsville's economy—a chicken hatchery and a weaving mill—is so flaccid that it absorbs only a handful of the townsfolk. The remainder either circulate about mournfully chronicling their operations, past and impending, or congregate in the taverns to discuss their eligibility for relief. The prospect of attaining it in Wormsville, save in the narrowest material sense, is nil.

I was all the more startled, therefore, to detect a slight but unmistakable aura of change in the place on returning to it recently from a sojourn abroad. In three decades of residence nearby I had come to accept Wormsville's stagnation as inevitable and progressive, and what I saw electrified me. A new five-and-ten-cent store, with a façade of mustard-yellow asphalt shingles that dizzied the vision, had blossomed out of the erstwhile barber shop. Next to it was a gay little boutique of chromework and plate glass housing a cut-rate dry cleaner, and, cheek by jowl, a matching jewel box curtained in asbestos, occupied by a dance instructor. It seemed a dubious augury that the three should be closed in midmorning—bankrupt a month after their inception, I discovered later—but they certainly spruced up the thoroughfare. The wave of renovation, it developed on further scrutiny, had also engulfed Brimmer's stationery store, in the adjoining block. The entrance had been refurbished in knotty pine, a display of green plastic tableware had been substituted for the sun-baked caramels in the window, and a gaudy nut-roasting machine, its enamel pans heaped with cashews, had been installed near the cash register. Mr. Brimmer, apart from a new set of dentures, appeared unchanged; peering through the door, I could see him still propped up against a showcase like one of Madame Tussaud's waxworks, staring into infinity and brooding over his pancreas.

The major alteration wrought in my absence, though, greeted me when I reached my objective, the Wormsville National Bank. A morose little dungeon with a brown sandstone front, the bank had crouched for years between the town pharmacy and an extravagant Victorian dwelling, all gingerbread, stained glass, and castellated turrets. The tenants of the latter, a series of osteopaths and chiropractors, had been successively disbarred for malpractice, and a gaggle of Third Avenue decorators had plundered the house of its curlicues. On its former site I now beheld a drive-in area contiguous to the bank, presumably enabling depositors to transact their affairs at the wheel. A stark cement-block wing, resembling a bomb shelter, debouched into it; visible within, a hairless young man was tallying long strips of lollipops kept as *douceurs* for clients' children. To lend an air of consequence to the parent structure, there had also been added an antebellum portico of fake brickwork supported by four gigantic columns. The effect, if not quite as impressive, was strikingly reminiscent of a West Coast tourist attraction I remembered from the thirties—Eddie Cantor's mansion in Beverly Hills. Resolved to kick aside any aged servitors who might accost me knuckling their polls, I strode up to it, shouldered open the fourteen-foot door, and stepped into the vestibule.

The contrast between the showy exterior and the havoc inside was, to put it mildly, formidable. All that remained of the bank as I had last known it was the vault; the rest—the tellers' cages, the bookkeeping section, the executive cubicles—had been demolished, leaving an echoing rectangular void littered with rubble. Off in a corner, an enclosure improvised from several sawhorses displayed a sign identifying it as the manager's temporary office. The official behind the desk, a plump, tallowy party with eyes of flint and a permanent frown stenciled on his forehead, bore no resemblance to the fatherly old gentleman who had humored my overdrafts in the past. As he shifted his gaze from the caller he was engaged with, I felt a current of Arctic air pass between us.

"Yes—what's the difficulty?" he demanded, with the clear implication that, whatever it was, it was insuperable.

"Why—er—nothing, actually," I said, feigning the type of insouciance spies exhibit near fortifications. "I—I merely wanted your advice about a financial matter, so to speak."

"Involving a loan?" he asked suspiciously.

I gave him a coy blend of smirk and shrug to signify that even if it did, the amount at stake was paltry.

He nodded toward an adjacent chair. "Be right with you," he said, and turned back to resume his colloquy. "Now, then, Schwabacher, what were you saying about those ball-points?"

"Just this, Mr. Cheesewright," said the other, leaning forward earnestly. "Nadir Novelty's been supplying banks and business houses across the nation with giveaways for building customer confidence since 1959, but we've never had such sensational results with an item. I tell you, depositors go wild about it, and no wonder. Think of it—a pen with a gauge that shows exactly how much they've got in their account!"

"Humph," said Cheesewright, openly skeptical. "Let's have a look at it."

"Coming up," said Schwabacher. He dug into the briefcase in his lap and extracted a pen with a serrated protuberance on its cap. "See this tiny celluloid dial with the numbers? Well, each time you add to or subtract from your checking account, you twist the dial to conform, giving you a handy, instantaneous report on where you stand."

"Yes, and everybody else in town," the manager grunted. "We may be a small community here, Schwabacher, but we're self-respecting. Take that man there," he said, jerking his thumb in my direction. "God knows whether he's solvent or not, but he'd like us to think so. Suppose he had a pen sticking out of his pocket showing a balance of only thirty-seven dollars?"

The figure was so close to my own estimate that I felt a sudden mantle of perspiration spring to my face. Fortunately both Cheesewright and the salesman were too absorbed to notice, and plunged into discussion of an alternative souvenir—a plastic thermometer, the gradations of which were measured in dollar signs. This the banker vetoed as equally unfeasible; whenever the temperature dropped, he declared, the recipient would be unpleasantly reminded of imminent penury and might visit his spleen on the donor. Confronted with such monolithic sales resistance, Schwabacher threw in the sponge. He uttered a sharp animadversion on the ingrained conservatism of rural financiers and their crabbed refusal to move with the times, and, zipping up his briefcase, flung out.

The interview had evidently had a salutary effect on Cheesewright's spirits, for when he swung around toward me his scowl had vanished. "That young man's a hustler," he commented. "He's got gumption, which is more than most of these spineless chumps you see hereabouts. I like to do business with a live wire, even if I don't buy anything."

Unable to grasp his logic but eager to ingratiate myself, I hastened to agree. "A person's got to be an awful good judge of character in your job, I bet," I said, with warm understanding. "Well, sir, I tell you the reason I dropped in. I had in mind to buy a television set, to replace one that was stolen, and I wondered if you—that is, the bank, or you acting in behalf of the bank, I mean, you being the manager, or, rather, the successor to the manager I used to know, Mr. Pindyke, and a lovely man he was, too—so I hoped, or, rather, wondered, whether the bank as a whole, and you as a whole, would be agreeable . . ." My throat constricted under his unwavering gaze, and I croaked wordlessly.

"You wish us to finance the set—that it?" asked Cheesewright, his eyebrows starting to beetle again. I nodded brightly, and there was an ominous pause. "What assurance do we have that you could meet the payments?"

"Well," I said, bridling, "after all, I'm hardly a stranger in these parts. I've been a depositor here twenty-five years—bought two cars through you people—"

"OK, no need to fly off the handle," he said, and opened the filing cabinet at his elbow. "We'll soon determine the truth of that." Half expecting him to produce a lie detector, I was somewhat relieved to see a manila folder emerge. "Your name?"

I told him, and by the time he had finished deliberating over the flimsy summarizing my history, I knew I was on a lee shore and breaking up fast. The expression on his face as he glanced up, nevertheless, was not quite as merciless as I anticipated. He seemed a trifle puzzled. "These automobiles you spoke of," he said. "You're aware, of course, that they were secondhand?" I blinked at him, vainly trying to comprehend the relevance of his question.

"What I'm getting at," he pursued, "is that in each case you chose to buy a secondhand car rather than a new one. Is that correct?"

"I—I guess I couldn't afford anything else at the time."

"Nonsense," said Cheesewright harshly. "It's got nothing to do with money—you're simply averse to improving your standard of living. Look at this transaction back in '53, for instance. Why did you purchase a used refrigerator?"

"They stole our other one," I faltered.

"That place of yours is certainly a robbers' den," he observed. "You ask me, I'd say you were a pretty poor risk for a new TV set. . . . It *was* a new one you wanted to buy, wasn't it?"

"Why—er—not exactly," I said, feeling my cheeks grow pink. "I mean, the party that had it took excellent care of it. The cabinet just gleams."

"There you are!" Cheesewright's tone was triumphant. "Precisely my point! You don't want the better things of life—you're content with the slapdash, the makeshift, the second-rate. Where's your pride, man?"

"Gee whillikers, you may be right," I confessed sheepishly. "My wife always says I settle for skimmed milk instead of cream."

"That woman knows you inside out," he asserted. "You got to expand your horizons, get a whole fresh approach. What about a nice little sailboat to skim up and down the Delaware, for example? Or a new pool for your guests to splash around in, come the dog days?"

"Say, that sounds nifty," I said. "Well, by George! I didn't realize you folks were prepared to loan money for luxuries like those."

"Who said we were?" asked Cheesewright, instantly glacial.

"But I understood you to say—"

"I don't know what you understood, Buster," he broke in. "I'll tell you this much, however. If you think we stay in business by financing secondhand TV sets for every passing hayseed, you're in the wrong pew. Furthermore, it's mighty lucky you came in when you did, or I'd have had to issue a summons for you." He held out the flimsy, stabbing his forefinger at a notation. "Here, look at this."

The entry was succinct and unequivocal. Far from possessing a balance of thirty-six dollars, I owed the bank a sum slightly in excess of four hundred and ninety. The account, it appeared, had lain dormant since 1941, accumulating a monthly service charge of two dollars, year in and year out, with grim regularity. Under the circumstances there was only one possible solution, which I adopted forthwith. I buried my face in my hands and burst into convulsive sobs. And then occurred one of those miracles that revive one's faith in humanity. Touched in some hidden wellspring of compassion, Cheesewright tore my flimsy to bits, buried *his* face in his hands, and also broke down. After our emotion had exhausted itself, he gently drew up a promissory note for the full amount, which I signed, and, conducting me to the portico, he bade me adieu. As for the TV set, I figure we'll do without for the time being. The minute I pay off the Wormsville National, I plan to take a good secondhand trip abroad.

Thunder Under the Kalahari

or, Aliquid Novi Ex Botswana?

The unthinkable has happened and Botswana, the former Bechuanaland, may well be destined to see its economy enriched by the discovery of a supply of truffles in the Kalahari Desert. . . . Truffles, so intimately and more or less exclusively associated with France and Italy, grow in the Kalahari Desert and are part of the diet of the Bushmen. These primitive little people, who include the raw meat of game felled by poisoned arrows as well as snakes among the delicacies they eat, can produce a bucket of truffles in a half an hour or so in season.—The Times, London*

Sir: . . . True as it is that the Bushmen have been eating them for years, the idea of systematically marketing the truffles is not new either. As long ago as 1912 two European adventurers applied to the British authorities for a truffle monopoly in the Kalahari area of Botswana. Their grandiose scheme of bottling or canning the Nabba or "Kalahari Potata" (sic) for a world market was however turned down.—Ibid.*

The circumstance that brought me to the Mushmouth Arms in Bexhill-on-Sea in a rainy week out of season was not at all fortuitous. In reading the short stories of Beerbohm, Maugham, Saki, W. W. Jacobs, and Stacy Aumonier, I had observed that many of them followed a classic, almost ritualistic pattern. The narrator, convalescent from a bout of flu, was immured in a dreary seaside resort, where some fellow guest, usually eccentric, saw fit to impart a remarkable tale. The only confidences arising from a fortnight's stay in London—from barbers, cabmen, and hall porters—were too humdrum for repetition, and, determined to enrich my trip by whatever means, I seized on the convention. I slogged about in wet shoes until I caught a small but serviceable laryngitis, installed myself in the most depressing hotel I could find on the southern coast, and within hours was delivered into the hands of the very person I had envisaged.

At lunchtime the sole occupants of the Mushmouth dining room besides Mr. Hesseltine, a spidery old party at the table next to mine, were two spinsters in knitted balaclavas and a lard-faced wraith in holy orders absorbed in his breviary. The instant I glimpsed my neighbor, I realized he was in a highly emotional state. His eyes, magnified by thick lenses, roved continually about him as if anticipating some unwelcome visitor, the cutlery rattled an obbligato on his plate as he chewed, and he started violently at the smallest untoward sound. One required no advanced degree in psychology—the man was the living embodiment of terror. Hardly had our desserts of fig-and-custard pudding arrived when he sprang up with a choked cry.

"Who's that? What's he doing?" he quavered, peering at the squat figure in white busying himself with a tray at the sideboard.

"Calm yourself, sir," I admonished him. "It's only a Pakistani busboy."

"So you say," he retorted cunningly. "How do I know that?"

I suggested asking him, and was proved right; the lad hailed from Karachi, and Hesseltine, whether from excessive relief or gratitude for what he interpreted as my concern, proposed I join him in a glass of port on the veranda. Under the influence of a second glass, he ventured a few cautious autobiographical details. A retired Foreign Office official, he had spent most of his half-century career in minor administrative posts out of England—the treaty ports of China, Kabul, Ljubljana, Beirut, Auckland, and so on. As a consequence of a long life abroad, he felt disoriented in his homeland, but, he said—and he gave his words a peculiar emphasis—a chap was much safer here. Suddenly an innocent remark of mine generated an abrupt, disquieting turn in the conversation.

"What about Africa?" I asked. "You weren't ever tempted by places like Kenya . . . the Sudan . . . Bechuanaland?"

He was on his feet again. "Why did you say that?" he demanded, quivering. "Nobody ever mentions that—that last place! You must have had a motive."

Stoutly as I disavowed one, he appeared unconvinced, and, with a suspicious glare, stamped off the veranda. By evening, however, he suffered a change of heart, cornering me in the solarium to ask indulgence for his gruffness and entreating me to dine with him. Throughout the brown Windsor soup and the halibut, Hesseltine's behavior was unexceptionable. He discoursed at length on the decline of the Empire, deplored the severance of the American colonies—which he blamed on the Hessians—and altogether conformed to the stereotype I nurtured of a retired British diplomat. And then, just as the waitress laid the main course between us and withdrew, every shred of his poise vanished with electrifying suddenness. I removed the bell, and Hesseltine's gaze shifted from the biscuit he was crumbling to the cold cuts within. Immediately he was back on his feet, eyeballs distended and features overspread by a deathly pallor.

"Look there!" He extended a shaking finger, his voice muted to a hoarse whisper. "Do you see it—between the salt beef and the salami?"

"Of course," I said, wondering what the deuce possessed him. "It's pâté—surely you're familiar with it. Those are truffles—"

The derisive laugh he essayed emerged as a croak. "They may be to you, sir," he said wildly. "To me they're a warning, and, believe me, those tiny devils will stick at nothing. They're fiends, I tell you—remorseless, horrible." He clenched his fist. "Ah, but I'll teach them," he said through his teeth. "They'll rue the day they trifled with Monk Hesseltine. . . ."

Well, I couldn't make head or tail of his ranting, and, frankly, I didn't much want to. I was getting pretty sick of Mr. Hesseltine and his assorted tremors, his half disclosures that led nowhere. I mean, thanks to Beerbohm, Maugham, et al, I'd marooned myself in an impossible situation, and what guarantee was there that this eccentric—a loathsome little roach, by any standard—would ever divulge his story? So, promptly after dinner, I packed my things, left a forwarding address in London, and cleared off. As I crossed the lounge I beheld Hesseltine in a corner, his head buried in a newspaper, and reflected how becoming it looked; someone should advise him to wear it that way permanently. He must have spied my departure through the swing doors, because he bolted to his feet once again—a reflex I also had had a bellyful of. It was the last I saw of him, and, as subsequent events proved, almost the last anyone did.

Three days later at Grommet's, my favorite West End hotel, I was breakfasting in the Edwardian atmosphere carefully preserved for Americans when word came that a lady wished to see me. To my undisguised gratification, she was a tall, ravishing brunette— no longer a girl, she must have been twenty-seven if a day—with wide-set violet eyes, a creamy complexion, and a figure that narrowly missed being voluptuous. At the sound of her name, I gave an involuntary start—a residue, doubtless, of my sojourn at Bexhill-on-Sea.

"Cosima Hesseltine?" I repeated. "Are you related to the man—"

She nodded gravely. "His niece," she said. "Uncle Monk wrote me that if anything happened to him I was to notify you. I'm afraid it has." She sighed in manifest perplexity. "He was murdered by a poisoned arrow night before last."

I stared at her, unable to credit my senses. "Poor old duffer, then there *was* some basis . . . I say, do they know who did it?"

"Not a single clue. It's like the other time, two years ago, when Daddy succumbed. That was a poisoned arrow too. Oh, I'm so alone." She swayed, and I daresay would have fallen had I not quickly caught her in an encircling arm.

"Here, child, suppose you have a cup of tea and tell me about it," I urged. "And remember, I'll need every detail, even those you deem unimportant, if we're to get to the bottom of this."

In actual fact, Cosima's knowledge of the prior case was all too scanty, since she had been botanizing in the Hebrides at the time, but she imparted several bits of information that seemed significant. For one, Jabez Hesseltine—actually her stepfather, and quite ancient—had wandered much in Africa in his youth, where his brother, Monk, was stationed. (So that explained the latter's cryptic fear of Bechuanaland, I thought exultantly.) Furthermore, Jabez had sustained *his* mortal wound during an archery contest at a charity bazaar in Shropshire, one participant in which had been a pint-sized African, who disappeared in the melee.

"A pure coincidence, possibly, and yet . . ." Striving to construct a hypothesis from what I knew, I had to confess myself baffled. There was, nonetheless, another element worth exploring, and I seized on it. "Miss Hesseltine, do you recall your stepfather's ever expressing aversion to any particular food? Try to remember— it may be vital."

"Let me think." She chewed her nether lip pensively, without, however, marring its lush ripeness. "He didn't fancy bangers and mash, or treacle tart, and he disliked potted shrimp—Wait a moment!" She giggled in recollection. "He utterly abhorred truffles! Flew into a passion if anyone even breathed the word."

"Capital!" I exclaimed. "I see a glimmer of light in the murk.

Now, a final query, and I hope you won't consider it officious in the light of our short acquaintance. What are your financial circumstances?"

Thoroughbred that she was, she never flinched at the question; rather, womanlike, she intuitively understood that her cause was mine henceforth, our paths intermingled. Her answer, though, only added fresh mystification. Twice a year following Jabez Hesseltine's demise she had received a draft for twenty thousand francs from a Monsieur Épinard, resident in Périgueux. ("The heart of the goose-liver country," I interjected, hanging on every word.) No explanation accompanied the money, and while Cosima was sorely troubled that its source might be felonious, she had reasoned, womanlike, that it was there to be spent, and spent it freely.

"D-do you think that was terrible of me?" she asked tremulously. "After all, a girl needs clothes—she can't go around naked. . . ."

I thought the time unpropitious to argue the point, and besides I wanted an hour's solitude to puzzle things out over a pound of the best shag. I therefore packed Cosima off to her flat in Haunch of Venison Yard with the injunction not to stir, and applied myself to the problem. What with the impact of my caller and the fumes of the tobacco, it was heavy weather evolving a rationale, but when the phone shrilled and a frightened voice came over the wire, I instinctively knew the situation was no longer static.

"On the bathmat!" Cosima was well-nigh breathless. "A wee little footprint, like a pygmy's! Oh, darling, it was ghastly! I was just getting into the tub, without a stitch on—"

"Yes, yes," I broke in, vexed at the implication that I could not visualize the scene. "It might have been the charwoman's, or a chimney sweep's. Have you checked?" She had, and neither could enlighten her. A sudden inspiration struck me. "Cosima—you noticed nothing else? A piece of bowstring, perhaps? An exotic, musky odor of any kind?"

"No, but I found a scrap of cloth, of the sort aborigines wear—"

Under the Kalahari

"Listen to me carefully, my dear," I said in a tone that brooked no dissent. "You are to join me in forty-five minutes at the West London Air Terminal in Cromwell Road, taking an overnight bag. Your life is in very great hazard, as is that of someone else, and pray that we arrive ahead of the nemesis stalking you both. And hurry, I implore you, if you value my love."

Five hours later the plane that had borne us over the placid, rolling expanse of south-central France touched down at the Périgueux airport, and by dusk the two of us, albeit travel-worn, were engaged in a feverish search for Polydore Épinard, Cosima's mysterious benefactor. No trace of his whereabouts could we elicit until our zigzag course led us to Mme. Embonpoint, *patronne* of the town's leading restaurant, Le Poulet en Empois (The Chicken in Starch).

"*Bien sûr,*" she said, smoothing her bombazine reminiscently. "A valued client and an old beau, Polydore—we used to attend dinner parties together and I always bestowed my favors on heem. He dwells in a mansion at Autrefois, three leagues distant. Singularly, you are ze second gentleman who inquires for heem zis *après-midi.* A small African type—*un homme primitif,* visibly—was here not ten minutes ago . . ."

The rest of her speech was lost on us, for we were already *en voiture* speeding toward Autrefois. Épinard's villa, set in a walled enclosure barred by massive gates, looked an impenetrable fortress; not a light showed in its grim façade, nor did our repeated halloos evoke any response. Providentially, an overhanging branch offered access to the grounds, and seconds afterward we were crouched outside a ground-floor window, the catch of which had been left unfastened by some oversight. With a reassuring squeeze to bolster Cosima's courage, I flung open the sash, parted the heavy curtains, and stepped inside. In the same instant a portly, bewhiskered gentleman whose purple nose exactly matched his dressing gown sprang from an easy chair and caught up a poker.

"Who are you, sir?" he demanded angrily. "By what right do you invade the residence of Polydore Épinard, head of the Syndicat Facultatif des Exportateurs de Truffes [Discretionary Council of Truffle Shippers] in this unprincipled manner?"

"Explanations are superfluous at the moment, Monsieur, other than to introduce Mademoiselle Hesseltine, a person with whom I believe you are not unacquainted," I rapped out. A look of utter stupefaction, tinged with guilt, blanched his countenance. "For the rest, I can assure you that if you wish to see tomorrow's sunrise you will obey my instructions to the letter. Have you by some chance a portrait bust of yourself?"

"As it happens, *oui*," he vouchsafed, pointing to a nearby bookshelf. "A lifelike head presented by grateful colleagues in recognition—"

"Spare the particulars, friend. We are not compiling a biography," I interrupted. "Pose the sculpture here next to the window, and let us drape over it your smoking cap and gown for added verisimilitude. . . . There," I said briskly. "I think the shadow on that pane will lure the game we want. And now, into the shrubbery with the three of us to await developments."

They were not long in coming. Scarcely a quarter of an hour had elapsed before a dwarfish figure, clad in a loincloth and armed with a bow, stole onto the moonlit lawn. He had taken aim at Épinard's silhouette and was about to loose his frightful missile when, at a concerted signal, his intended victim and I threw ourselves on him. How a mere homuncule could have displayed such amazing strength was beyond me, but his struggle was unavailing, and soon, trussed up like a fowl, he was en route to Périgueux in the custody of two gendarmes, a very chopfallen Bushman indeed, to answer for his misdeeds.

"A little more cognac, *mes amis*? Do, I beg of you—it has no equal in the district." We were in Épinard's study, numb with fatigue but absorbed in his history of a bizarre cabal hatched in Africa five decades earlier. "Well, as I was saying, Jabez Hesseltine and a fellow adventurer named Hoopoe, prospecting in the Kalahari in 1912, stumbled on the truffle deposits used by the Bushmen. Playing on the credulity of the savages, they promised their chief a substantial share of the millions they foresaw, assuring him in honeyed words (*paroles de miel*) that they could secure a monopoly through Monk, then commercial attaché in the British Consulate. The quartet swore a blood oath to honor the agreement—"

"Whereupon the Hesseltines betrayed their confederates," I finished. "They sought you out and so panicked you at the impending threat to French truffle culture that you paid them a staggering bribe to abandon the enterprise."

"I confess it," Épinard admitted sheepishly, "though how on earth you arrived at it I cannot imagine."

I said that, given certain postulates, the conclusion was inescapable.

"As was Bushman vengeance," he corroborated. "They expunged innocent Hoopoe in their fury, then the Hesseltines, and had it not been for you and your fair adjutrix I might have been a *canard mort* this minute. Shall I ever be able to repay you?"

"Well, those semiannual drafts to Cosima will help, if I read aright the promise in her eyes," I said. A blush rivaling that of a peony confirmed her readiness to have Épinard spend the rest of his life taking care of us both. "*Alors, Monsieur*, it has been a momentous day, but now our *chemins* must diverge. *Adieu.*"

And so we left one adventure and began a second, my Cosima and I, two victims of another archer—the blind bowboy, sometimes yclept Dan Cupid. But I guess the gods—Beerbohm, Maugham, and Saki—willed otherwise. I was seated in the hairdresser's at Grommet's next morning when this eccentric—a manicurist . . .